FOAL

The Autonomous Revolution

OTHER BOOKS BY THE AUTHORS

The Virtual Corporation
(HarperCollins, 978-0877306570)

The Autonomous Revolution

Reclaiming the Future We've Sold to Machines

BY William H. Davidow

AND Michael S. Malone

Berrett–Koehler Publishers, Inc.

Berrett-Koehler Publishers, Inc.
1333 Broadway, Suite 1000
Oakland, CA 94612-1921
Tel: (510) 817-2277
Fax: (510) 817-2278
www.bkconnection.com

Ordering Information

QUANTITY SALES. Special discounts are available on quantity purchases by corporations, associations, and others. For details, contact the "Special Sales Department" at the Berrett-Koehler address above.

INDIVIDUAL SALES. Berrett-Koehler publications are available through most bookstores. They can also be ordered directly from Berrett-Koehler: Tel: (800) 929-2929; Fax: (802) 864-7626; www.bkconnection.com.

ORDERS FOR COLLEGE TEXTBOOK / COURSE ADOPTION USE. Please contact Berrett-Koehler: Tel: (800) 929-2929; Fax: (802) 864-7626.

Distributed to the U.S. trade and internationally by Penguin Random House Publisher Services.

Berrett-Koehler and the BK logo are registered trademarks of Berrett-Koehler Publishers, Inc.

Printed in Canada

Berrett-Koehler books are printed on long-lasting acid-free paper. When it is available, we choose paper that has been manufactured by environmentally responsible processes. These may include using trees grown in sustainable forests, incorporating recycled paper, minimizing chlorine in bleaching, or recycling the energy produced at the paper mill.

Cataloging-in-Publication Data is available at the Library of Congress.
LCCN: 2019035137
ISBN: 978-1-5230-8761-7

First Edition

26 25 24 23 22 21 20   10 9 8 7 6 5 4 3 2 1

Produced by Wilsted & Taylor Publishing Services
Copy editor: Nancy Evans, Wilsted & Taylor
Text designer: Michael Starkman, Wilsted & Taylor
Jacket designer: Alvaro Villanueva, Bookish Design

If we are to be judged
by the wonderful things we create,
I am a great man because my wife, Sonja,
and I have created a loving, happy, and
accomplished family with excellent values
whose members have gone on
to create more wonderful things.
This book is dedicated to them.

William Davidow

For my two sons,
who will see both sides of history.
And four wonderful women—
my wife Carol, sister Edie,
Leslie Lopez, and the late Linda DiNucci—
for getting me through the tough patch.

Michael Malone

Contents

Foreword

David M. Kennedy

TO STUDY THE HISTORY OF HUMAN LIFE and human societies is to study change. If there were no change, our understanding of any given moment in time would yield the key to understanding all moments in time. History as a method of inquiry would then resemble science, whose central quest is to elucidate the constants of the physical world that constitute the "laws" of nature. History, like science, would then have predictive value—although making predictions about humanity's future in a world without change would be a decidedly no-sweat matter of "same ol', same ol'," hardly requiring powerful analytical chops.

But history knows no such laws, and historians no such sinecure. The objects of historical analysis, by their very nature, are in a state of ceaseless flux. Historians have long found this characteristic of their subject matter both fascinating and frustrating.

More than 2,500 years ago, the pre-Socratic philosopher Heraclitus (a melancholic man living in the then-Persian city of Ephesus, whose figure in the foreground of Raphael's famous Vatican fresco, *The School of Athens,* is customarily thought to be modeled on Michelangelo) insisted that remorseless change was the very essence of the universe, confounding all efforts fully and finally to comprehend it. "No man," he summarily said, "ever steps into the same

river twice." That's certainly the pithiest and probably the profound-
est statement ever made about the mystery of time.

Since the dawn of the Industrial Revolution more than two centuries ago, many observers have asserted that the river of time has
been palpably accelerating its flow rate, posing ever-greater challenges to our capacities for comprehension—not to mention our
ability to peer into the future. The great American historian Henry
Adams memorably inscribed that thought into the American canon
in his 1918 autobiography, *The Education of Henry Adams*. Few if
any students of history then or later have brought to their labors
more impressive analytic gifts than Adams's. Yet, standing in the
Gallery of Machines at Paris's Great Exposition in 1900, contemplating the enormous physical and social transformations unleashed by
modern industrial technologies, even Adams was gobsmacked. He
found himself, he reflected, with "his historical neck broken by the
sudden irruption of forces totally new."[1]

William Davidow and Michael Malone now take their place in
the venerable tradition of such students of change as Heraclitus and
Henry Adams—though their historical necks remain unbroken
as they focus their formidable explanatory acumen on the myriad
changes that are today transforming the terms of life for billions of
people in every corner of planet Earth. Notably, they have migrated
a familiar scientific term—*phase change*—into the domain of historical analysis, with intriguing effect.

Even casual students of the physical world will recognize that
phase change describes transformations in form without changes in
chemical composition. Water's presence in different states—liquid,
solid, and gaseous—is a well-known example. So, too, Davidow and
Malone argue, *homo sapiens* does now and will continue to inhabit
societies with governments, schools, churches, markets, media, and
an array of other institutions. But while human nature may remain
a constant, the *forms* of each of those creations that have served
humanity's needs for individual aspiration and collective existence,

as well as the patterns of their interaction and interdependence, are transmogrifying at an astonishing and arguably unprecedented rate.

The sources, drivers, vectors—and challenges—of those many alterations in form are the subjects of this timely and incisive book. Its central argument is that we are living through a massively consequential phase change in which the cumulative impacts of several structural transformations—technological, political, economic, behavioral, and even attitudinal—are maturing and converging into a tsunami of unexampled challenges and opportunities. We are on the cusp of an era that will bring new ways of doing business, new ways of working, new ways of governing, communicating, recreating, and new ways of *living*. All will demand new rules, new norms, new structures and infrastructures, new tools, and new thinking.

In a work studded with arresting insights, few are more unsettling than the following, offered in the context of the authors' discussion of artificial intelligence, and the "Autonomous Revolution" that is utterly upending the world of work, and therefore education and even human memory:

> The Autonomous Revolution will embed functional intelligence in autonomous machines. In practice, this means that the systematic development of human knowledge through education and work experience will have less value than it did in the past. Humans may continue to expand their knowledge and skills by accessing databases on the Internet, interfacing directly with the IoT (Internet of Things), or eventually having devices implanted in their bodies that will enhance their physical and mental abilities. But the real repositories of practical knowledge will shift to autonomous devices, which will learn much more quickly than people can. In situation after situation, automatons will substitute for humans.

That sobering perspective recalls a story, perhaps apocryphal but nonetheless instructional, about a conversation sometime in the 1950s between Henry Ford II, the CEO of Ford Motor Company, and Walter Reuther, the head of the United Automobile Workers union. Gesturing at an array of early-generation robots working on the assembly-line floor, Ford smugly declared that not one of those machines would ever go on strike, nor would they ever pay dues to Reuther's union. "Maybe so," Reuther allegedly replied, "but not one of those machines will ever buy an automobile, either."

Reuther's riposte anticipates Davidow and Malone's depiction of a future in which hyper-disruptive innovations such as artificial intelligence and distributed 3-D printing will have solved the ancient problem of how to make things, even while raising an urgent new problem of who will buy those things, and what they will offer for them in exchange. This is but one example of the countless visions of the future that readers will encounter in *The Autonomous Revolution.*

———

While historians have long been preoccupied with change, they have been especially so since the eighteenth-century Enlightenment—not surprisingly, since they have lived in an environment where time itself seems to have been dramatically sped up by the engines of the great revolutions—political and industrial—with which the eighteenth century came to a climax. But many, probably most, of those historians (Henry Adams conspicuously excepted) have also often made an unexamined elision between the observation that change has occurred and the judgment that improvement has resulted. The conception of time most common among modern historians has been teleological, informed by a sense of advancement toward a future all but guaranteed to be both materially and morally superior to the past. That's the considerably weighty meaning infused into the idea of "progress" that so many Americans have long found so congenial, so "natural," in fact.

That kind of congenital optimism pervaded the Western project for more than two centuries, nowhere more so than in America. The conception of history as progress, in short, has simply been part of a larger and ubiquitous cultural attitude that has many components: belief in the power of reason to secure and even amplify the beneficent influence of science and technology; confidence in the logic of democracy to pacify relations among citizens and among nations; an expectation that the march of time will lead to upgraded standards of living, increased human dominion over nature, even to mastery over the constraints of biology, including victory over disease and possibly even over the ultimate mysteries of birth and death.

Those comforting notions are less easily entertained today. Indeed, a countervailing narrative has taken root in our culture, exemplified by the popularity of science fiction. Writers like Ray Bradbury, Philip K. Dick, and Margaret Atwood, and filmmakers like Stanley Kubrick, James Cameron, and Ridley Scott almost invariably conjure a future where technology has gone berserk and life looks mighty scary and mightily morally objectionable compared to the placid present.

The Autonomous Revolution may at points read like science fiction, but its authors engage their subject not as fantasists but as historians. They write in the vein of another philosopher of history, G. F. W. Hegel. Writing in 1820, in the springtime of the Industrial Revolution, Hegel declared that "the owl of Minerva takes flight only as the shades of night are gathering." In plain language, Hegel meant that even the wisest among us can only begin to comprehend the character of an era as it is fading away, giving way to another, which will remain inscrutable until it, too, cedes its place in history to a successor.

We are at such a passage now. For all our understanding of the dynamics that have characterized the last two centuries, we still peer at the future through a glass darkly—though the kind of informed understanding of the past, both distant and immediate, that

The Autonomous Revolution offers can surely help us see a bit more clearly into the world that is aborning.

Heraclitus is also known as "The Weeping Philosopher," because he apparently suffered from chronic melancholia. It's permissible to believe, in turn, that his melancholia stemmed from his inability ever to fix time long enough to see the world as clearly as he wished.

Despite the frequently unnerving data that it presents, there's no weeping but plenty of wisdom in *The Autonomous Revolution*. It's a wisdom nurtured by a deeply considered sense of history. It indulges in neither the easy optimism of the school of "progress" nor the bleak pessimism of so much science fiction. It recognizes the inevitability of change, but resolutely refuses to roll over in its path. Above all, it summons all of us to recognize the shape and scale of the changes already gathering such impressive force. It urges us not to succumb to the future, but to shape it. "One thing is certain," the authors conclude, "if we choose to treat phase change as business as usual, we will become its victims."

The Autonomous Revolution

DIGITAL LEVIATHAN

IT IS HARD NOT TO SENSE that something vast and unsettling is emerging from beneath modern life. Even here in Silicon Valley, where we have become accustomed to continuous change, this time it somehow seems different—a change so sweeping and complete as to be unlike anything we have ever before experienced.

But it isn't just here that this change is becoming apparent; the harbingers are everywhere. Institutions upon which we have rested our faith, some of them for centuries, now seem to be deeply troubled, with no obvious remedy short of dissolution and replacement. Education, government, law, religion, marriage, work, the economy, science . . . all seem, in the two decades since the turn of the millennium, to have become increasingly dysfunctional and under siege. Indeed, when we were pondering the subtitle for this book we considered "Why nothing seems to work anymore." We can't help thinking that, even in those intervals when times are good, when the economy is up and unemployment down, that this is merely a brief respite, before the underlying reality reasserts itself.

One might argue that this is simply progress, that mature institutions are always becoming obsolete and being replaced. No doubt that is, at least, a part of what is happening. But you would have to look deeply into human history to find another era when almost *every* institution faces an existential challenge. It is almost beyond imagination.

That fact, in itself, may be why we feel this sense of disquiet. No one alive today has experienced such a widespread transformation.

But there have been times in history when civilizations have experienced widespread transformations. Authors experiencing them are typically bewildered at how times have changed, but show very little understanding of what has happened. Meanwhile, the authors of the next generation exhibit such a fundamentally different reality in their sense of time, reality, and their own selves that it is as if the entire natural world has been created anew. Roll forward another generation, and it is as if there has been a collective amnesia, and the writers and diarists have no insights into their grandparents' lives, much less how they saw the world. Even the basic rules for how people live and interact seem to have been completely rewritten. In the end, sometimes the only clues to what happened can be found in literature and myth, in the rise of new religions, and deeply buried in unreliable statistical tables.

We speak all the time of social, cultural, and scientific "revolutions." Our history books are organized around these pivot points—the Christian era, the Renaissance, the Enlightenment, the Age of Exploration, the electronics age—but as profoundly influential as they were in human history they don't reach the level of transformation about which we are speaking—that is, of true points of inflection during which essentially *everything* changes, when humanity seems to have stepped through a doorway from one world to the next.

Pundits emerge at inflection points. They frequently propose simplistic solutions to complex problems or, because of their narrow focus, fail to understand the implications and impact of their technologies. Facebook is a case in point.

In reflecting on these predictions, we have often thought of the words of Nicholas Butler: "An expert is one who knows more and more about less and less until he knows absolutely everything about nothing"[1] and nothing about everything else (our addition). As we go forward to confront the challenges facing us, it is extremely important to listen to divergent opinions, pay attention to those who analyze the situation from different perspectives, and view with caution the pronouncements of those who know everything about technology and understand almost nothing about its social consequences.

As you will read in the following pages, we believe that in the surviving memory of humankind, this has happened only twice—and, tellingly, both transitions, especially the first, left us all but incapable of entering into the minds and the worldviews of those who lived before.

What we *do* know is that the historical inflections didn't come as a bolt from the blue. There were clues beforehand: important changes (new inventions, cultural crises, natural disasters, and other events) that combined to set off a chain reaction that, figuratively, left nothing but debris of the old world.

A quarter of a century ago, the two of us saw a comparable set of events that portended a similar turning point—but at that time it was only in the business world and the potential impact was orders of magnitude smaller. What we saw was that information technology and computers were intersecting in such a way that they were transforming how enterprises would be organized, how they would manufacture goods and provide service, and how they would interact with their customers.

The result was our book *The Virtual Corporation*. Our title entered the language to describe the new horizontally organized, "edgeless," adaptive companies that enlisted their customers in everything from product design to service . . . in other words, the very type of enterprises that define today's economy.

We were right in our prediction—it was indeed a paradigm shift—but wrong in our calendar. We expected that virtual corporations would take a decade or more to become ubiquitous. But a hidden force was about to burst on the scene that would propel this revolution faster than we envisioned: the World Wide Web.

The genesis of this book was similar. Having been present at the birth of social networking, massive multiplayer games, autonomous vehicles, modern artificial intelligence, and all of the other defining new technologies of the twenty-first century, we have watched with growing dismay, even horror, at how many of these developments have morphed into increasingly malevolent threats to human privacy and liberty. Living in Silicon Valley, we watched firsthand, with growing trepidation, the effects of the modern networked, digital—virtual—world on its most passionate users. Like millions of other people, we found ourselves increasingly dismayed and frightened at how the world we once knew seemed to be going off the rails right before our eyes.

The difference was that we had been here before—albeit it in an infinitely smaller way—with the virtualization revolution of industry. And that experience propelled us into a conversation the like of which we hadn't had in twenty-five years.

We had both read the many media articles and prognosticators' proclamations that we were now passing through a "third (or fourth) Industrial Revolution," but we knew that classification was inadequate—even dangerous, because it might convince the world to seek solutions in variations of the old rules when, in fact, all the rules were about to change. We pursued our research not just in tech or commerce, but in history, sociology, psychology, economics, and the arts—every place that was signaling impending radical change—looking for early clues to the nature of what was to come; all in the knowledge (as with the virtual revolution) that when the change did occur it would likely be shockingly, terrifyingly quick.

We also knew that these same technologies, when used properly, could take us one step closer to Utopia. They were creating a world of abundance, driving large unmeasured increases in human productivity, greatly improved products and services (many of which had been costly in the past but would be free in the future), more energy-efficient ways of living, and miraculous cures for disease. And we also knew that if our leaders confronted these challenges aggressively, as others had in the past, most of us would be beneficiaries rather than victims.

The result is this book. We make no claim to being able to characterize with any accuracy or detail what the future will look like on the other side of the pending historic inflection—by definition, no one can. But we we have identified early indicators that will help us react quickly and more successfully to the transformation that lies ahead.

Inevitably, most of these indicators are warning signs; this book is filled with them. Why wouldn't they be, when everything is about to turn upside down? Yet, if we are to thrive in this pending new world, we should be welcoming every warning we can get. If we don't despair, facing reality can only make us better prepared.

Despite these warnings, and our analysis of the growing dysfunctionality of modern life in the pages that follow, we hope that the reader will come away from this book with a sense of optimism. We should never forget that human beings are extraordinary creatures—brave, endlessly creative, adaptive, and born survivors. Over the course of the last million years, we have gotten through much worse.

But the biggest reason to be optimistic is that, with the two epic sociocultural transformations humans have experienced in recorded history, each time we emerged on the other side with longer lives, superior health, more education, and greater overall wealth than we had ever known before. There is no reason to think that this time will be any different.

But first we have to get there, intact. History suggests that won't be easy. We owe it to our descendants to get it right. We hope this book will start the conversation about strategies to do so.

CHAPTER ONE

THE AUTONOMOUS REVOLUTION
A Third Social Revolution

FOR THE THIRD TIME IN HISTORY, society is undergoing a social phase change. We are well on our way to creating the Autonomous Revolution.

Its two predecessors, the Agricultural and the Industrial Revolutions, have taught us what to expect. Our institutions will assume new forms and operate using different tools and according to new rules; our sense of time, space, and self will be irrevocably altered. Our memories of what came before the new epoch will be skewed, and the few revenants from the past that do survive it will have limited applicability in the future. But at least for a time, our gut instinct will be to continue to apply the old rules, values, and beliefs, in a losing battle with the inevitable.

The societal phase changes of the past enabled us to gain control over the natural world, create civilizations, and live comfortable and meaningful lives. But those achievements came at the cost of great human suffering. Though we forged societies with common goals, beliefs, and values, the tools that we used to do it included wars, revolutions, crusades, jihads, and genocides. Empires rose and fell. New empires are emerging today—in many ways bigger and more powerful than the great empires of the past. But they are arising in a territory we never anticipated—the virtual realm—and in the forms of corporations such as Facebook, Google, and Amazon.

Society is already feeling some of the early effects of the Autonomous Revolution. The ice-hard stability of the good job is being replaced by the indeterminate "gig." Countless other jobs have been shipped overseas or automated out of existence, devastating the middle class. Mind-altering processes are being used to reengineer our children's brains. Our Brave New Social Networking world looks less open and connected every day—and more and more like the dystopian surveillance states of George Orwell and Aldous Huxley.

If we want to turn the forces of the Autonomous Revolution to our advantage, we need to see them as they are, and not through the lenses of our old rules, values, and beliefs. Only then can we develop the reasoned approaches that will allow us to mitigate their less desirable side effects and benefit from the great advances they make possible.

If we aggressively and intelligently manage those changes, we will live in a world of abundance. We will build stronger communities and families and have better and more efficient government. Human productivity will increase. Civilization will become more energy-efficient and our environment cleaner. Health care will be tailored to meet our individual needs and life expectancy will increase. The quality of products and services will improve, and they will be individualized to satisfy our personal tastes.

But achieving those benefits will require us to manage the challenges of the impending, massive, change in a rational fashion. At the very least, we will need great leadership to get us through.

This book is not about what will happen. Much of that is as yet unknowable. Rather, it is about how to manage the inevitable, and the place to begin is by understanding societal phase change.

We have been living with societal phase changes for ten thousand years. Despite that, it is the contention of this book that we have never really understood them. As a result, much of our historic adaptation has been characterized by violence rather than reason.

It doesn't have to be that way.

CHANGING FORM

Let's look at the process more closely. The term *phase change*, like *quantum shift*, *paradigm*, and *virtual*, comes from the world of science and technology, in this case, the world of physics. The phenomenon is something we experience frequently in everyday life.

Anyone who has put water in a freezer has witnessed it. Collections of water molecules that are warmer than 32 degrees F exist in liquid form. Below that critical temperature they become ice and sometimes form beautiful crystals like snowflakes. When water changes to ice, it undergoes a phase change.

When water changes phase, it changes its form. And the rules governing the behavior of ice bear no resemblance to the rules governing water. That's why physicists and engineers use the rules of fluid dynamics when dealing with water and those of solid mechanics when dealing with ice.

The tools we use to deal with water are pumps and pipes. But pumps won't pump ice, and ice breaks pipes. In water's solid phase, we use snow shovels, plows, and icebreakers. What is crucial to appreciate is that our understanding of water gives us no clues about how to deal with ice.

Human social systems go through structural transformations that are similar to phase changes in physical systems. Since we are talking about social systems and not molecules, the analogy is inexact, but when enough structural transformations accumulate in a human society, its institutions change form, obey different rules, and require different tools to manage them.

In the physical world, phase changes are distinct and frequently happen in relatively short periods of time (there are also many examples of extremely long phase changes, such as in geology, when sedimentary rock changes into metamorphic rock). Phase change in human society is a relatively slow process, measured in human lifetimes, and it tends to be cumulative—a set of minor structural transformations combine to create more significant ones, which then add up in their turn. These structural transformations occur in the realms of technology, science, medicine, ideas, politics, economics, religion, and more.

Minor structural transformations are narrowly focused, affecting specific areas of human endeavor, and they happen quickly. You have probably experienced dozens of them in the course of your life. Look at the world around you—and then try to remember the world of your childhood. If you are in your fifties, the differences are remarkable. Think of the media you grew up with and the media you use today. When you were younger you watched broadcast television and listened to vinyl records; you read printed newspapers, magazines, and books, and the movies were something you went to. If you watch television today, you probably receive it over cable or through the Internet; your record collection is on your smartphone; the news is curated for you and sent to you via your social network; and when you need an encyclopedic reference, you search Wikipedia. Movies are streamed to your home by Netflix, Amazon Prime, or any of a host of competing online services.

In the past, written information and recorded music were inscribed on physical objects—printed-and-bound pages, grooved and later digitized discs. Today they reside in invisible bits and bytes. The physical infrastructures that support the media have changed as well. Screens, smartphones, and fiber optic cables have replaced newsstands, delivery trucks, and printing presses. Media business models are different. You no longer have to purchase an entire album of music; you can buy your favorite song. In the past, broadcast television was free and you paid for your local newspaper. Today, you subscribe to online video services but can read hundreds of newspapers, from every corner of the world, on your screens for free.

Major structural transformations occur when minor structural transformations accumulate and interact, impacting broad segments of the economy and society. Since they are a result of agglomeration, they happen relatively slowly.

Right now, any number of minor structural transformations are happening in the financial industry. For example, consumers can use Apple Pay and Google Pay to make payments at retail establishments, substituting their smartphones for their credit cards. Once the payments are entered, they are processed over the old credit card networks. In China, smartphones are being used as a platform for peer-to-peer payment systems. Using applications such as WeChat, smartphone customers made $5.5 trillion in payments without the need to run the transactions through a credit card network.[1] Facebook's recent announcement about forming a virtual currency consortium, Libra, is an example of the type of development we should anticipate in the future—a harbinger of a world where credit and debit cards may become obsolete and currencies are ruled by commercial enterprises.[2]

The first experiments with online banking date all the way back to 1981. In 1996, NetBank, the first truly successful Internet bank, was founded. In the early 2000s, automated portfolio management software began to be widely used by financial advisers. Today, robo-advisers that manage investment portfolios for consumers are available from companies such as Betterment and Wealthfront for a fraction of the cost of human advisers.[3] Scores of other financial applications (Fintech) are available, and countless more are in the development pipeline.

When peer-to-peer payment systems are integrated with peer-to-peer lending systems, Internet-only banks, and robo-advisers, the future of credit cards, retail banks, and financial advisers as we know them will be challenged. When much of the financial services industry has been absorbed into virtual space and is operated by automatons, a major structural transformation will have occurred.

A similar story could be written about the media industry. Minor structural transformations affecting print, recording, broadcasting, and publishing are combining to create a major structural transformation in the media space.

Social phase changes occur when major structural transformations combine and interact over extended periods of time, changing institutions and norms so completely that an entirely new form of society emerges. The Agricultural Revolution gave birth to cities and civilization; the Industrial Revolution sealed humanity's dominance over the natural world. The transformations they induced were complete and all-encompassing.

Each societal phase change ushered in new infrastructures, new forms of society, commerce, governance, and belief systems. What emerged as a result of each of these transformations was almost a new human species, one that depended on technology for its survival and that would be unable to survive if it traveled back in time.

The Autonomous Revolution is being driven by a fundamental change in our relationship with machines—in particular, with intelligent machines.

The truth is that the advent of our Autonomous Revolution is already affecting every aspect of our lives—even introducing new forms of space and time. The automatons that we are creating are already acting as if they are a new collection of species that, under the direction of their controller masters, have begun to challenge the primacy of *homo sapiens*. If we cannot yet discern the details of the individual streets and buildings of this new world, we can already see, emerging from the mists on the horizon, its spires. And that may be all the warning we get.

Look around you. Everything is transforming before our eyes. The nature of work is changing. The good job is going away. New business structures are displacing old ones. The Internet of Things promises to serve our every need, and in the process become the platform for a massive new economy—a surveillance economy where our every action is monitored. Computers are peering into our brains to learn our thoughts, understand our emotions, and influence and direct our behavior.

Lives are moving from a physical space that has no purpose and that we have shaped to meet our needs . . . to a virtual space that increasingly attempts to shape our actions to meet the needs of its controllers. New value systems are emerging—and in the process, new definitions of freedom, liberty, and free speech are emerging in their train.

Our perceptions of fairness are changing as well. Automatons threaten to create millions of "ZEVs"—people of Zero Economic Value—individuals you would not hire even if they worked for free. In other words, the prospect of a world with millions of purposeless people has become a real possibility. The Protestant work ethic, on which our society and economy were built, is now in danger of setting unrealistic standards for evaluating human worth.

The Autonomous Revolution has already upended much of what we once took for granted. What mattered in the past (giant command-and-control corporations employing tens of thousands of people; huge factories filled with machinery; books; automobiles; television broadcasts that routinely captured as much as half or more of the universe of possible viewers) is becoming much less important.

We are struggling to deal with the new forms, tools, rules, and norms. Memorization is a lost skill. Declining numbers of us believe in objective journalism. IQ is no longer regarded as a true measure of intelligence. We don't think of robots as employees yet, merely as very smart machines, ancillaries to our own labors. But the wages we pay robots already determines the value of human labor.

The economy is starting to obey different rules. Rises in productivity no longer power economic expansion. The costs of necessities, like health care and housing, are rising, while the value of middle-class work is falling—trapping tens of millions of people in a downward cycle of purchasing power. Income inequality is rocketing to historic highs.

Suddenly commercial enterprises, not repressive governments, are what pose the direst threats to our individual freedoms and privacy. Their scrutiny and surveillance follow us everywhere. They search not only our files but also our minds. They restrain our choices by placing us in algorithmic prisons without the benefit of an open trial or the right to confront our accusers—or even to know who they are. The Star Chamber that was once presided over by gray-haired men in a palace has changed venues: it now resides in corporate headquarters filled with kids in black t-shirts.

As we move larger and larger portions of our lives into virtual space, commercial enterprises not only make choices for us but also increasingly program our behavior, from the number of steps we take each day to the amount of time we are allowed to play a game before we are forced to take a break.

Businesses that once had physical form are being reduced to applications that we execute on smart devices we carry in our pockets and wear on our wrists. Some rules are changing, and many others are being written from scratch. The past is no longer a reliable guide to the future; our experience and acquired wisdom are as likely to betray us as guide us. It is as though we must learn everything anew.

Perhaps most disquieting of all is that the Autonomous Revolution will be characterized most of all by the speed of its change. It is coming astonishingly *fast*. Whereas the Agricultural Revolution transpired over millennia and the Industrial Revolution over centuries, this current transformation will be measured in decades.

When reflecting on the litany above, it is easy to become pessimistic about the future. But answers exist for many of these problems. In what follows, we propose what we believe would be some effective solutions, and are certain that many other valid approaches exist. We must also remember that the technologies creating many of these problems can also be used to solve them.

For example, automation causes the value of work done by many to decline. As a result, it puts pressure on incomes. But that automation also currently reduces the cost of many services, has the potential to make much of education free, and has consistently reduced basic health care costs. And, even as we fear the advent of the surveillance state, aggressive actions are already being taken in Europe to better protect individual privacy. Later in the book, we propose a more radical approach that we believe would effectively solve the problem as well.

We must keep in mind that the technologies of the Autonomous Revolution are creating a world of abundance. That means that most likely we will have on hand the resources required to face our problems.

That said, we also know from past experience that the failure to address the challenges created by phase change during the Agricultural and Industrial Revolutions led to wars and vast amounts of human tragedy. We don't believe that this is inevitable with phase change; but, that said, we must struggle with all our might to not let it happen again.

With so much at stake, one of the messages of this book is that the time to take action is *now*.

SUBSTITUTING ONE FOR ANOTHER

The major forces that drive phase change are what we call substitutional equivalences: when we replace one fundamental way of dealing with the world with another that is radically different, but that performs a similar (if not identical) function.

For example, during the Agricultural Revolution, a new form of food production substituted for an older one—the cultivation of grain for hunting and gathering. Indirectly, in the form of feed for the domesticated animals that became our main sources of protein, and directly, in the form of bread and beer, one source of calories replaced another.

In the Industrial Revolution, mechanical power was substituted for muscle power. Factories replaced piecework and cottage industries, and their workers were paid wages instead of sharing directly in the results of their production. A market system of suppliers, manufacturers, distributors, retailers—and ultimately cash-paying consumers—replaced tradespeople bartering their goods in marketplaces. These equivalences spawned more. For example, civilizations that developed during the Agricultural Revolution invented writing, which in many cases substituted for verbal communication—a very important equivalence that happened as a result of the fundamental equivalence created by agriculture.

Unlike the Agricultural and Industrial Revolutions, which were primarily driven by just one equivalence, the Autonomous Revolution will be driven by three: information, intelligence, and spatial equivalences.

1. *Information Equivalence.* Information equivalence is what allows us to substitute virtual processes for physical ones. Much of what goes on in our lives and businesses is information transfer and processing in disguise. We go to a retail store to find out what is available and at what price. We engage in business travel to exchange information with customers. Those functions can be moved to virtual space and, when they are, the existing processes change form, operate by different rules, and use computation as their basic tool. The retail store becomes an online store, the customer trip becomes a video conference, and the office building that served as a customer support operation becomes a voice recognition and speech synthesis system hooked to a database and an artificial intelligence system that generates responses.

2. *Intelligence Equivalence.* Just as the Industrial Revolution replaced muscle power with mechanical power, the Autonomous Revolution will use artificial intelligence and artificial senses of touch, vision, sound, smell, and taste to replace and vastly enhance human minds. The Industrial Revolution was a 250-year campaign to increase workers' economic productivity via mass production and their intellectual abilities via public education. The Autonomous Revolution will embed functional intelligence in autonomous machines. In practice, this means that the systematic development of human knowledge through education and work experience will have less value than it did in the past. Humans may continue to expand their knowledge and skills by accessing databases on the Internet, interfacing directly with the IoT (Internet of Things), or eventually having devices implanted in their bodies that will enhance their physical and mental abilities. But the real repositories of practical knowledge will shift to autonomous devices, which will learn much more quickly than people can. In situation after situation, automatons will substitute for humans.

3. *Spatial Equivalence.* Activities we used to do in physical space are being transferred to virtual space. Relationships that used to be carried out over coffee are continued over social networks. When crime, terror, and war all move to virtual space, the troops become automatons that do not bleed. Private citizens and military groups alike have access to intercontinental cyber-missiles carrying nuclear cyber-bombs. Crypto-currencies like BitCoin and the Ether may displace the coins and bills that are issued by nations. Games that used to be played on boards or on ballfields get moved to virtual space with participants from all over the world. Virtual teams play MMORPGs

(massively multiplayer online role-playing games), slaying monsters and dragons. Unlike activities in physical space, many cyber-actions are almost infinitely scalable and come with close to zero incremental costs. Now for the biggest challenge of all: not just games but business, currencies, crime, terror, and war are moving to a world that has virtually no governance. For many of these activities, the rules really are different, because there are no rules.

None of these equivalences existed to an important level fifty years ago. Now, it is hard to find a corner of the developed world—and of most of the developing world—that isn't affected.

The goal of this book is to provide readers with an understanding of the processes that are creating the Autonomous Revolution, its implications, and the types of things we can do to benefit from them. One thing is certain: if we choose to treat phase change as business as usual, we will become its victims.

Each of these three phase changes has occurred with increasing speed. The Agricultural Revolution transpired over the course of twelve thousand years, as civilization emerged from its tribal roots and nation-states and empires came into being. The Industrial Revolution transpired over two centuries, changing the form of society and its economic, political, and cultural institutions. For example, the urban share of the population of the United States was just 6.1 percent in 1800; it is more than 80 percent today.[4] The Industrial Revolution created jobs in urban environments for those who were no longer needed to work on the farm. Economic entities—corporations such as General Motors, Standard Oil, and U.S. Steel—achieved the scale and power of nations in just a matter of decades.

There is no sure way to measure rates of societal change. Some important changes, especially in the areas of business and the media, are occurring in months in today's virtual environments—a rate of change that is one hundred times faster than in the Industrial

Revolution. But to argue whether rates of change are one hundred times faster than in the past, or just fifty or ten times faster, is to miss the point. The Autonomous Revolution has already started, and we won't have much time to adapt to the new social, economic, and governance forms that it is unleashing, not to mention its new values.

In what follows we will delve into the history of phase change, paying especial attention to the role of substitutional equivalences as they create new norms. While these equivalences may seem minor, the changes in the rules that they precipitate can be enormously important. When political blogs and "citizen journalism" first began to proliferate on the Internet less than twenty years ago, they seemed, if anything, to be a boon for democracy. Had we understood how radically the rules were changing, we might have recognized the darker implications of "fake news" much sooner. So too, we might have foreseen the dangers of a fully uncensored Web (child pornography, terrorism, etc.) on the one hand, and the politically biased censorship of social network content by the employees of their parent corporations on the other.

In subsequent chapters, we will explore how phase change is rewriting the rules of business while driving what we call non-monetizable productivity, the bipolar economy, and the destruction of millions of jobs. Then, we will look at how phase change is impacting our government, our notions of privacy, liberty, and freedom, and the way that society is likely to function in virtual space. In each of these sections, we will suggest how to deal with the challenges that these substitutions present.

In the process, we will suggest some new regulations and laws that are likely to be extremely controversial. Some of our prognostications may be uncomfortable or unbelievable to many. Some of them, we freely confess, trouble us. But we have followed our speculations to their logical conclusions, wherever they may lie. We also know that we do not have a monopoly on good ideas. Human ingenuity has always been our greatest survival skill. Over time, as we better understand these unfolding changes, no doubt numerous creative and effective solutions will emerge. We suspect that many modern Malthusians will be pleasantly surprised.

Historically, social phase change has provided fertile ground for utopian movements. At the birth of the Agricultural Revolution humanity began to formalize its laws and religions and to develop the incipient marketplaces that gave rise to trade, money, and banking. The Industrial Revolution gave rise to republican democracy, modern capitalism, Communism, Fascism, and Romanticism.

And what of the Autonomous Revolution?

The poet Ezra Pound wrote about humanity's inexhaustible hope that a "palpable Elysium" is waiting just around the next corner. It is easy to imagine how technology could usher in a golden age, yet it is also easy to imagine how things could go horribly wrong. Tellingly, Pound thought he had found his Elysium in Mussolini's Italy.

Dealing with the phase change of the Autonomous Revolution is the great challenge of our age. Human beings are infinitely resourceful, and, if we will use them in a thoughtful and responsible way, our new intelligent tools will give us the power to create a better world. It can be a world with a universally high standard of living, longer life spans, robots that will free us from drudgery, safer communities, and access to a fascinating and exciting virtual universe.

All of these things are tantalizingly within reach; some are here already. They may not be enough to create Utopia, but they can bring us a lot closer to it than we are today. Surprisingly, a primitive form of that ideal world once existed in Silicon Valley.

The Ohlone tribe lived largely unmolested for thousands of years in what is now the southern San Francisco Bay Area. Then as now, the geography was gentle and the weather kind. But unlike today, when Valleyites are famous for their long work hours, intensity, and ambition, the Ohlone lived a life of comparative leisure. Anthropologists estimate that they only worked about ten hours per week, the women gathering the acorns that lay everywhere on the ground, the men occasionally hunting the abundant animal life, or spearing fish and harvesting shellfish from the Bay. The rest of their time was spent in relaxation.

It is not impossible that the average citizen of the Autonomous Revolution will have much in common with the Ohlone. Fifteen hours a week may be all that they have to work to maintain a comfortable standard of living, with the rest of their time dedicated to the pursuit of leisure.

Of course, there were some downsides to the Ohlone lifestyle: occasional plagues and droughts, and, thanks to the bits of gravel that got into their mortars when they were crushing acorns, most of the tribespeople's teeth were ground down to their gums by early adulthood. Still, it was a rather idyllic existence. But it ended—we even know the exact time and date that societal phase change reared its ugly head: at 7 o'clock on the morning of January 12, 1777. That's when Father Junipero Serra's expedition held morning prayers for the first time at the original site of what would become Mission Santa Clara de Asis.

From that moment forward, the Ohlone's world operated on a clock. Though they had missed the Agricultural Revolution, the Industrial Revolution ran over them like an avalanche. The Ohlone adopted a new diet and were exposed to a host of new diseases. They were drawn into jobs in the new tanneries and in the white men's cities and towns. By 1852 their population had shrunk from 300,000 to just 1,000.[5]

But if the Ohlone were blindsided by the Industrial Revolution, we have seen the Autonomous Revolution coming for some time— it is of our own making, after all. And we can learn from history.

It is our fondest wish that, unlike the Ohlone, we can avoid much of the pain, and can have our paradise and our social phase change, too. We hope this book will help make that possible.

CHAPTER TWO

A BRIEF HISTORY OF SOCIAL PHASE CHANGES

Why This Time Things Are Different

HUMAN PROGRESS is the product of a host of structural transformations that have culminated in a few big societal phase changes. Once set into motion, those societal phase changes are continual and overlapping. The Agricultural Revolution has been going on for twelve thousand years, the Industrial Revolution for more than two hundred. The Autonomous Revolution has only just begun.

This chapter will take a closer look at the dynamics of societal phase change, focusing especially on the onset of the Agricultural Revolution, the Renaissance, and three different epochs of the Industrial Revolution.

It is a mistake to assume that structural transformations are synonymous with technological change. While some structural transformations do have a technological component, many others don't. From the bubonic plague to the impact of Darwin's theory of evolution, the historical record is replete with structural transformations that were not technologically driven. Though the internal combustion engine is almost certainly one of the big culprits in the climate change we are experiencing today, climate shifts have been causing massive structural transformations since before the first histories were written. Desertification played a role in the collapse of the Harappan Civilization in the Indus Valley around 1300 BCE, and environmental degradation has been one of the biggest drivers of mass migrations.[1] Paleoclimatologist Douglas Kennett has theorized that drought led to the decline of Mayan civilization.[2]

Christianity, Islam, democracy, Communism, the Enlightenment, free-market capitalism, and the scientific method are all examples of structural transformations that were driven by ideas and beliefs. That said, there is no shortage of evidence that technology is a great driver of new thought systems and vice versa. While the Protestant Reformation sprang from the minds of men such as Martin Luther and John Calvin, it was catalyzed by the generalized use of printing, which made it possible for vernacular Bibles and tracts to be widely disseminated. The current rise of populism is a reaction to the technology-enabled substitutional equivalences that are driving the Autonomous Revolution.

Still, the main focus of this book is on transformations that are driven by the rise of general-purpose technologies. In our definition, *general-purpose technologies* are ones that have broad effects on the economic and institutional structures of society. Among history's most important are agriculture, writing and numbers, printing, electricity, mechanical power, and many forms of information technology.

A significant lag often occurs between the introduction of a technology and the changes associated with it. Our modern views are somewhat skewed because so many recent discoveries and inventions have been adopted very quickly. For example, the Model T Ford debuted in 1908; by 1927, when it was discontinued, more than 15 million were on the road. The interval between the first demonstrations of semiconductors at Bell Labs in the 1940s and the global adoption of microprocessors was less than forty years, a blink in human history. But much more typical is the lapse of more than a century that divides the invention of the Babbage Difference Engine and the introduction of ENIAC, the first modern electronic computer, or the almost thousand-year interval between the Chinese invention of block printing and Gutenberg's printing press.[3] Although ingenious and even profound, it wasn't until much later iterations of these inventions were disseminated that they became revolutionary, rule-changing, and structurally transformative.

PAST PATTERNS

One is always tempted to declare the most recent wave of new technologies, from atomic power and genomic medicine to powered flight and artificial intelligence, as the most important ever experienced by humankind. But an objective observer would also stand in awe of the technologies that gave rise to and propelled the Agricultural Revolution.

The structural transformations that led to the Agricultural Revolution began to accumulate in the Levant around 10,000 BCE, when people first began planting cereals and legumes, and spread throughout the Fertile Crescent over the next two thousand years. Agriculture was also discovered independently in other parts of the world—in China in 6000 BCE, in South America between 7000 and 8000 BCE, in sub-Saharan Africa around 5000 BCE, and so on.

Early farmers struggled to generate surpluses. The trade-off for settling down on the land and enjoying a more comfortable life was periodic famines. Over time, numerous discoveries and inventions increased agricultural productivity, making famines rarer and more survivable. Sheep, goats, cattle, and pigs were domesticated between 9000 and 7000 BCE. Farmers began using irrigation around 6000 BCE.[4] Tools increased agricultural productivity as well. The first farmers used digging sticks and simple hoes. With the domestication of draft animals around 4000 BCE, farmers in Mesopotamia now had the muscle power to drag simple scratch plows through their fields.[5]

By about 4000 BCE, the transition point for a societal phase change had been passed in Mesopotamia. Agricultural productivity was generating sufficient surpluses to support significant urban populations.[6] By 2900 BCE, Uruk was a walled city of about 2.3 square miles with a population of sixty thousand, making it the largest city in the world.[7]

With the development of cities, civilization emerged. Divisions of labor spurred even more productivity as people specialized in specific products and services. Harvests were stored in central facilities, which created a need for record keeping. By 4000 BCE, Sumerians were using clay tokens to keep track of inventory.[8] Over the course of a few thousand years, number systems emerged. Sumerians also developed cuneiform, the first form of writing.[9] People began to record their history. *The Epic of Gilgamesh*, the first record of a real-life individual and, as it is often called, "the world's oldest story," was inscribed on clay tablets around 2000 BCE, some seven hundred years after its eponymous hero had reigned over Uruk.[10]

Those cities were dependent for food and fuel on the farmers and woodcutters who lived in their surrounding regions, and so they both protected and controlled them. City-states emerged, which eventually grew into vast empires, such as those of Greece, Rome, and Persia, which built huge militaries and expanded by conquest. Trade routes crossed whole continents. By 900 BCE, the Phoenicians had established themselves as a great trading power throughout the whole Mediterranean region and as far afield as Britain in the north and India in the southeast.[11]

A continual stream of inventions powered the ongoing revolution. Though the medieval era witnessed much technological backsliding, the principles of crop rotation were discovered during this time. The heavy plow was invented as well, and improved versions of the harness made it possible for draft animals to pull them.[12]

The Second Agricultural Revolution coincided roughly with the beginning of the Industrial Revolution, around the 1700s. It was powered by new crops like corn and potatoes from the New World; new forms of organization, such as large single-owner holdings; mechanical equipment that replaced muscle power; and, later, railroads, which transported harvests.[13] The so-called green revolution that began in the middle of the twentieth century (also called the Third Agricultural Revolution) used genetic science, pesticides, and new methods of cultivation to vastly increase yields. The productivity improvements have been staggering. In the 1800s, agricultural labor made up 83 percent of the American domestic workforce.[14] Today, its share is about 1.5 percent.[15]

To summarize, the Agricultural Revolution changed the rules, tools, and institutions that govern every part of people's lives. When humans first began to plant foods they settled in villages, a new form of social organization. As these grew into cities, city-states, and ultimately empires, kings, administrative bureaucracies, and eventually representative governments replaced tribal chieftains.[16] Humanity adopted a whole new set of tools, from domesticated animals and plows to brick-making and architecture, writing, arithmetic, military strategy, banking, and the use of money.

It is difficult to compare the social phase changes of the Agricultural Revolution to those we are experiencing in the Autonomous Revolution today, but it is worth a try.

Because communications were slow and long-distance travel extremely difficult, the spread of the Agricultural Revolution was achingly slow by modern standards. Information about a new process or technology employed in another land might take decades to arrive, and if a catastrophe occurred—a plague or a natural disaster, a disruptive change in governments—it might just be local news and virtually unknown elsewhere.

Today, by comparison, the news, if not the adoption, of a structural transformation can spread around the world almost instantaneously. The good news is that the benefits of the change are felt immediately. The bad news is that there is no cushion for the shock. The structural transformations we are experiencing today will be fully felt within decades or even years. The time we have to adapt is compressed by at least a factor of 100.

Since a large portion of the prehistoric and ancient world was engaged in the production of food, the Agricultural Revolution directly touched a very large share of the population. But a lot of the social phase change effects were indirect. The specialization that increased productivity affected only a small share of the population—people who lived in settlements with populations in excess of five thousand. Until 1500 CE, this described only about 10 percent of the world's population.[17]

This is very much not the case today.

TRUE PHASE CHANGE

The period between ancient times and the Renaissance was more heavily influenced by idea- and belief-driven structural transformations than by general-purpose technologies. This is not to say that many important inventions weren't developed during those years, but only to note that their effects did not create social phase changes. New forms did not emerge; the old rules continued to work pretty well. The future was nowhere near as discontinuous as it had been in the earlier epochs of the Agricultural Revolution, or as it is today.

With the exception of cartography, Greek technology does not appear to have had many effects that rose to the level of a societal phase change. Instead, it was Greek ideas that created phase change, among them, the concept of democracy, many of the principles that gave birth to science, and the philosophical fields of metaphysics and ethics. The Romans made a number of important inventions that greatly improved civic infrastructure—arches, sewers, aqueducts, roads, and concrete.[18] As a direct result of these inventions, larger cities became possible. Ancient Rome's population ballooned to around 1 million. But the city embodied the same form and was governed in roughly the same fashion as it grew.

As noted earlier, important inventions were developed during medieval times, in agriculture and elsewhere. The crossbow and gunpowder upended military technology, but wars were still wars.

The mechanical clock made it much easier to coordinate activities and changed work patterns. But the nature of work did not fundamentally change. Not until the Industrial Revolution were people paid for going to work rather than selling their production directly.

Two belief systems that emerged during this epoch, Christianity and Islam, were part of widespread social phase change. They transformed the way large portions of the world were governed. The new tools they used to control behavior were ideas of redemption and eternal life as opposed to force.

Printing was the first major general-purpose technology to emerge after the invention of agriculture, and it powered the first modern communications revolution. The printing press and movable type, invented by Johannes Gutenberg around 1440,[19] made mass communication possible, democratizing the spread of information.

Until Gutenberg, the Catholic Church had produced a large proportion of books. Monasteries had scriptoriums where large numbers of monks copied texts. Because books were so difficult and costly to produce, the church was able to exert high levels of control over thought and ideas. In the early 1400s, authorities ordered two hundred manuscripts of heretical writings burned. Since most scribes worked for the church, some of those seditious works were lost forever.[20]

Printing changed the dynamics of book production. Print runs were quite small initially—on the order of a few hundred books—but even that was more than a single scribe could produce in a lifetime. It has been estimated that the printing press was more productive than a scribe by a factor of more than 100,[21] an increase of productivity that is frequently associated with societal phase change. Many of the productivity improvements that occurred during the Industrial Revolution also reached these levels.

Thanks to the printing press, in 1517 Martin Luther was able to widely disseminate the Ninety-Five Theses that launched the

Protestant Reformation—a very important structural transformation. The spread of printing was, of course, slow by today's standards; it took nearly sixty years for it to reach most of Western Europe.[22] Over time, printing enabled the birth of civilization's first mass media. The first printed newspapers were published in Europe in the early 1600s and almost one hundred years later in the United States.[23]

One of the most significant structural transformations that newspapers caused was a weakening of the power of the church. Before printing, people learned about the news at church. Monthly, weekly, and daily newspapers attenuated the church's influence, opening the door to a more secular society.[24]

At the same time, printing strengthened governance and organizations. Where before policies had been spread by word of mouth and handwritten documents, printing made it possible for much more detailed documents to be distributed.

The first print shops made their profits by publishing and selling books, many of which were sold to universities. Since it was relatively cheap to add more copies to a print run, printers also sold books about science to the public. This practice fostered scientific discovery both inside and outside university walls. Not only did information become widely available, but it was consistent and reliable: every reader got an identical copy of it. Books helped power the Scientific Revolution, which in time gave birth to the Industrial Revolution. The Industrial Revolution, in its turn, directly created social phase changes. Printing's structural transformations were trickle-down, in that it took three hundred years for some of its most powerful effects to be fully felt.

A REVOLUTION BY DESIGN AND COMBINATION

This brings us to the Industrial Revolution, when structural transformations that had been accumulating and combining and recombining for hundreds of years abruptly spilled out across the entire society, giving rise to societal phase change. The Industrial

Revolution was driven by the development of a number of general-purpose technologies and numerous inventions—steam and internal combustion engines, electricity, and later semiconductors and computers.

According to the complexity theorist W. Brian Arthur, combining ideas is the fundamental process that drives the creation of inventions:

> I realized that new technologies were not "inventions" that came from nowhere. All the examples I was looking at were created—constructed, put together, assembled—from previously existing technologies.[25]

Economic historians talk about three phases of the Industrial Revolution. The first began around 1760 and was based on the steam engines that powered the early factories and made rail transportation possible. The second phase of the Industrial Revolution began in the late nineteenth century, facilitated by electricity and the ability it created to deploy small amounts of mechanical power directly at the point of use. Its third phase, which is often referred to as the Computer or Information Revolution, began about 1960. It depended on computer and semiconductor technology.[26]

The structural transformations that accompanied the Industrial Revolution fall into three general categories: how we worked, how we used physical space, and how the economy was organized. Looking at textile production is a good way to get a feel for the types of structural transformations that resulted from the social phase change that occurred as a result of the First Industrial Revolution.

Between 1750 and 1850, industrial production in Britain increased by around a factor of 10, a rate of growth of about 2 percent per year.[27] Before industrialization, jobs (in the sense of going to a workplace and being paid for performing a set task) were few and far between. Most people farmed. Many people were self-employed or worked in small groups. In Britain, large numbers of textile workers worked in a cottage industry, working at home to produce thread with spinning wheels and weave fabric on handlooms.

Cottage industry workers could not compete with highly productive factory workers. Inventions such as the spinning mule increased productivity by a factor of 100.[28] The effects were devastating. In 1820, an estimated 170,000 workers in Lancashire County were employed in handloom weaving. Within thirty years, two-thirds of those jobs had vanished. By 1871, only 10,000 were employed in cottage industry.[29] People flooded into cities in search of work. The population of Manchester grew sixfold between 1771 and 1831.[30] Men, women, and children toiled in the factories in unsafe and brutal working conditions for fourteen hours a day, six days a week. They lived in industrial slums within walking distance of the factories. The industrial city, a new physical form, was born.

Over time, big companies with major factories requiring large capital investments and mass channels of distribution began to employ a growing percentage of the workforce. Companies developed hierarchical management structures.[31] The job, an artifact of the social phase change created by the steam engine, began to evolve, from inhuman drudgery to something better. Jobs in the United States also followed this trajectory. In the early 1800s, more than 80 percent of the American labor force had been self-employed or worked for small enterprises. By 1900, about 55 percent of the labor force had jobs, a percentage that rose to 85 percent by 1960.[32]

When people use the term "good job" today, they are usually referring to one that pays a good salary, is secure, and comes with health insurance and retirement benefits.[33] Those jobs are hard to find today, and they were rare before the 1950s.[34] But much of the second half of the last century was a golden age of good jobs that were powered by the rise of labor unions. In 1935, when Congress passed the National Labor Relations Act (NLRA) to protect workers' rights to collective bargaining, there were about 3 million union members in the United States.[35] By 1940, union membership had grown to around 14 million, topping out at around 22 million in 1980.[36] At one point, unions represented more than 30 percent of the nation's wage and salary workers.[37]

During their heyday, unions pushed hard for health care and retirement benefits, establishing the benefit patterns that spread throughout industry. For a time—almost half a century—the good job defined workers' identities, provided them with self-esteem and a gateway to the middle class, and played an important role in reducing income inequality.[38]

A product of social phase change, the good job has been with us for less than seventy-five years. As we discuss in chapter 6, the new economic and work structures that have been unleashed by the Autonomous Revolution pose an existential threat to it. For all our leaders' efforts to bring them back, good jobs are rapidly disappearing—and income inequality has returned to levels that haven't been seen since the Gilded Age.

The steam engine and electricity also triggered structural transformations driven by thought. The commercial successes of railroads and manufacturing businesses did much to reinforce the free-market ideas of the eighteenth-century economist Adam Smith. At the same time, the exploitation of the proletariat by the capitalist classes that occurred during the Industrial Revolution gave fuel to Marx's Communist philosophy.

The Industrial Revolutions also gave rise to a Transportation Revolution, which fundamentally transformed the physical infrastructure of our society. Before the advent of the automobile, the trolley, and the railroad, cities were structured around the most prevalent form of interconnection: walking. Gross population densities were rarely less than 35,000 residents per square mile. City neighborhoods were diverse, with few or none devoted exclusively to commercial, office, or residential functions. Work and living spaces were often integrated, with family members and apprentices living above or behind the shop or workplace. During the Industrial

Revolution, the slums built to house workers almost always surrounded the factories they served.

Cities were unhealthy places. The coal fires used to heat homes and power the engines of production blackened the skies. Sewage systems were grossly inadequate. And then there were the horses: the streets were filled with manure, flies, and the carcasses of overworked animals that died in their traces. In New York, horses produced 1,500 tons of manure a day, and in 1880, the City removed 15,000 dead horses from its streets.[39]

By the middle of the nineteenth century, the compact structure of the city began to change. Metropolitan Boston grew from a tightly packed merchant city of 200,000 residents in 1850 to an industrial metropolis of more than a million residents within a radius of 10 miles by 1900. This growth was made possible by public transportation—the horse-drawn coach, the horse-drawn trolley, and, later, electric trolleys, subways, and commuter railroads.[40] These improved methods of transportation allowed more affluent city dwellers to escape the noxious and noisy urban cores and live in the green and spacious suburbs that sprang up along the railroad tracks. Eventually businesses and factories would decamp to the suburbs as well.

The automobile freed Americans even more. People no longer had to live near railroad tracks, and businesses had the freedom to locate wherever they chose. By the 1950s, cities became less the anchors of metropolitan regions than their hollowed-out centers— the proverbial holes in the doughnuts. Suburbs that had once been inextricably tied to cities via railroad and trolley lines and jobs were no longer just subsets of the urban world, but self-supporting communities. People no longer had to go to cities to shop, work, go to the movies, see a doctor, or eat in a nice restaurant, as these functions and amenities were now available elsewhere. Populations spread across the rural landscape, and cities were increasingly abandoned to the poor.

While many urban areas have enjoyed significant revivals over the past several decades, the structural transformations that have been unleashed by the Autonomous Revolution will almost certainly transform them again. As more of our work, play, and social interactions shift to virtual space, our physical environments will surely change as well.

The Industrial Revolution brought with it hierarchical, top-down organizations. Until the mid-1800s, businesses were able to operate fairly effectively by relying on market mechanisms to coordinate their production activities. According to Alfred Chandler, "[I]n the textile industries long after the 1840s, the basic functions of marketing, production, finance, and purchasing remained under the control of different men often in different enterprises who barely saw one another."[41]

Over time, businesses required more complex and expensive machinery. Products became more complex as well. Individual components were assembled into subassemblies, and then those subassemblies were combined with others in the manufacture of a complex machine like an automobile. In order to reduce coordination costs, Henry Ford built the massive Rouge complex, where raw materials came in the front door and finished automobiles left by the back.

As manufacturing processes and supply chains became more complicated, they required more direct management. The railroads led the way in confronting this challenge. Railroads were capital intensive, complex, and difficult to operate efficiently. They were accident-prone. With operations spread across broad geographies, it was difficult to know where capital assets, such as railcars, were located.

Telegraph lines were strung along rail tracks partly because they served as the backbone of the information system that enabled managers to keep track of equipment. They also helped to coordinate rail schedules and avoid head-on collisions in systems that ran on single tracks.

The difficulty in managing the railroad systems is perhaps best illustrated by an 1855 report that noted that the cost of freight per mile was less on systems that were 50 miles in length than on those that were 500 miles or more in length.[42] Running the railroads effectively required administrative structures, internal controls, standard procedures, good communication, and professional managers. The management model that the railroads developed was quickly adopted by other businesses.[43] Vertically integrated, professionally administered firms grew to massive scales, dominating markets.[44]

Today, in the early years of the Autonomous Revolution, the forms of organizations are changing again. Some hugely profitable corporations employ relatively few full-time workers, drawing instead on the services of people who work in the "gig" economy. Others are in the process of replacing their human workers with robots. Some service providers are moving their whole operation into virtual space, because they no longer need physical places of business to accommodate their customers and their workers are mostly robots.

ACCELERATING TRANSFORMATION

There is now talk of a Fourth Industrial Revolution.[45] However, those words do not fit the future that we envision. Industrial Revolutions have been about physical products that are produced by physical machines and distributed by physical trucks, trains, and ships, in environments controlled by human hands and minds. The Autonomous Revolution is about autonomous workers, autonomous systems, and of a life lived sometimes in the physical world, sometimes at the intersection of the virtual world and the physical world, and at other times completely in virtual space. Humans controlled the machines that replaced their muscle power, but the autonomous machines that we have created will increasingly control us.

Perhaps the most important difference between the next societal phase change and those of the past will be the rapid rates of change we are about to experience.

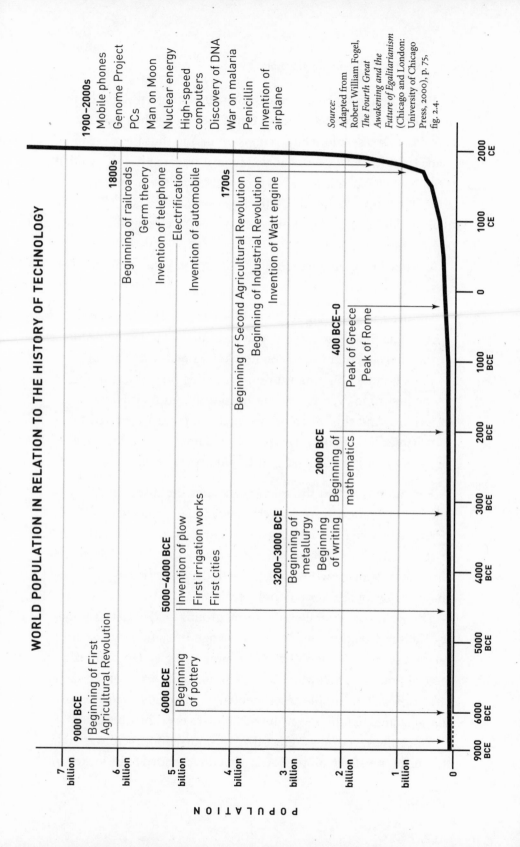

WORLD POPULATION IN RELATION TO THE HISTORY OF TECHNOLOGY

1900–2000s
Mobile phones
Genome Project
PCs
Man on Moon
Nuclear energy
High-speed computers
Discovery of DNA
War on malaria
Penicillin
Invention of airplane

1800s
Beginning of railroads
Germ theory
Invention of telephone
Electrification
Invention of automobile

1700s
Beginning of Second Agricultural Revolution
Beginning of Industrial Revolution
Invention of Watt engine

400 BCE–0
Peak of Greece
Peak of Rome

2000 BCE
Beginning of mathematics

3200–3000 BCE
Beginning of metallurgy
Beginning of writing

5000–4000 BCE
Invention of plow
First irrigation works
First cities

6000 BCE
Beginning of pottery

9000 BCE
Beginning of First Agricultural Revolution

Source:
Adapted from
Robert William Fogel,
*The Fourth Great
Awakening and the
Future of Egalitarianism*
(Chicago and London:
University of Chicago
Press, 2000), p. 75,
fig. 2.4.

POPULATION

7 billion
6 billion
5 billion
4 billion
3 billion
2 billion
1 billion
0

9000 BCE
6000 BCE
5000 BCE
4000 BCE
3000 BCE
2000 BCE
1000 BCE
0
1000 CE
2000 CE

Population growth is a useful proxy for getting a feel for the rate of progress and change across culture because, when population densities increase, more interactions occur and thus there are more chances for knowledge exchange. Modern research has shown that these "knowledge spillovers," as economists call them, spur innovation.[46] Geoffrey West, a theoretical physicist at the Santa Fe Institute, has demonstrated that innovation super-scales in cities as their populations increase.

"It's like being on a treadmill that keeps on getting faster," West says.

> We used to get a big revolution every few thousand years. And then it took us a century to go from the steam engine to the internal-combustion engine. Now we're down to about 15 years between big innovations. What this means is that, for the first time ever, people are living through multiple revolutions. And this all comes from cities. Once we started to urbanize, we put ourselves on this treadmill. We traded away stability for growth. And growth requires change.[47]

For more than ten thousand years after the discovery of agriculture, population grew at a very slow rate. A good guess is that it increased by a factor of about 100 times in those ten thousand years, or at a rate of 0.05 percent per year—a very slow rate of growth.[48] That slow rate of growth correlated with the slowly emerging social phase change of the Agricultural Revolution.

During those ten millennia, social groups tended to be stationary. Cultural patterns tend not to change in stationary societies. People use the same tools, have the same living systems and commercial practices, follow the same religion, and carry out the same ceremonies. There is little experimentation. Members honor the past, and unchanging mores exert broad controls over their behavior.[49]

Since there was not a great deal of innovation, there were few structural transformations. Social structures tended to be locked in for long periods of time, changing only under extreme duress, such as invasions or natural disasters. Since there was very little change going on, coping with change was greatly simplified.

Then, about 250 years ago, the Industrial Revolution released the flood of innovations depicted on page 35. As the chart shows, the number of innovations is closely associated with the steep rate of population growth of about 1 percent per year.[50]

Others have come up with different proxies for measuring rates of change. Henry Adams, the nineteenth-century historian who was a grandson and great-grandson of two American presidents, used the power generated from coal as a way to measure progress during the Industrial Revolution. He estimated that power output doubled every ten years between 1840 and 1900, a compounded rate of progress of approximately 7 percent per year. In 1919, Adams was lamenting the impossibility of keeping up intellectually with that rate of progress.[51]

One could select other proxies for rates of change, such as the speed of transportation. A human being walks at 3 miles per hour, a horse trots at eight. In 1848, the world record for rail speed reached 60 miles per hour.[52] If that progression had taken place over two thousand years, it would equate to a rate of change of about 0.03 percent per year. Today commercial aircraft carry passengers at speeds approaching 600 miles per hour, a rate of progress of roughly 2 percent per year over the railroad.[53]

Another way to think about rates of change is to consider that the Agricultural Revolution took place over ten millennia and five hundred generations, while the Industrial Revolution has been with us for only about two hundred years, or ten generations. We anticipate that a great many of the effects of the Autonomous Revolution will be experienced in just two generations. The disruptions ahead are epochal, and we're not going to have much time to adjust.

In changing societies, governance systems come under stress. There is a tendency to pay less attention to authority. Conduct tends to be based on expediency rather than reason. Mores and moral codes lose their sway. If change results in chaos, authoritarian regimes often seize control.

In 1922, William Ogburn introduced the idea of cultural lag.[54] Cultural lag occurs, he said, "when one of two parts of culture that are correlated changes before ... the other part does."[55] Ogburn pointed out that severe conflicts could result when this occurs, even to the point of causing a revolution. In 1936, as Europe was sliding toward war and America was still locked in the Great Depression, he wrote that "there is no great harmony in culture. The times seem out of joint."[56] They were.

Rates of technical progress today are much greater than those observed by Ogburn. The most difficult challenge we will face is negotiating the tensions created by the headlong pace of technological change. At no other time in the history of humanity have we had to deal with such rapid rates of technological change, such radical social dislocations, and such a great degree of cultural lag.

CHAPTER THREE

SUBSTITUTIONAL EQUIVALENCES

The Drivers of Societal Phase Change

LET'S BEGIN LOOKING at substitutional equivalences with an example of a structural transformation that might seem on its face to be an unlikely driver of societal phase change, but that nicely illustrates the substitutional equivalences that power it: bank robbery.

Robbing banks at gunpoint is dangerous work that frequently results in long prison sentences or getting shot or killed. And the returns on the investment get lower all the time. Gone are the days when Willie "the Actor" Sutton could rob one hundred banks for a collective haul of $2 million—$30 million in today's dollars.[1] Because of the use of credit cards, banks no longer keep huge hoards of cash on hand; the average bank robber today makes off with only about $5,000 per heist. But it is still true that it makes sense to rob banks, because, in Sutton's famous words, "that is where the money is."[2] The modern, high-return way to rob a bank is to steal small amounts of money from thousands of customer accounts using computer zombies. The process is managed remotely, preferably from a foreign country that turns a blind eye to cybercrime.

Information Age tools made this possible. First, banks provided millions of customers with relatively insecure systems that allowed them to transfer money in and out of their accounts via the Internet. Then, in the late 2000s, low-cost versions of Zeus malware—a

Trojan horse that runs on Microsoft Windows—became available.[3] Cybercriminals planted it on bank customers' computers and used it to collect their account information, track their keystrokes, and discover their passwords.

A crime organization called Citadel set up a "botnet" ring that consisted of 1,500 servers around the world. Those servers, the virtual equivalents of Mafia consiglieri, managed 1.2 million computers on which Zeus-based malware had been installed. Taking a little bit of money at a time, Citadel stole an estimated $500 million.[4] To stop them, Microsoft engineers joined forces with cyber-trained investigators in the FBI, who coordinated their efforts with eighty international partners. In 2015, Dimitry Belorossov (a.k.a. Rainerfox), a Russian citizen, was arrested in Spain. One of the key technologists behind Citadel,[5] he was tried, convicted, and sentenced to four-and-a-half years in jail. Setting aside the respective lengths of their prison sentences, Sutton and Belorossov couldn't be more different, even though they both worked in the same profession.

Information Age tools had reached a high level of sophistication with respect to data capture and manipulation. Simultaneously, the banking environment had created millions of points of attack. A critical point was passed and a new type of bank robbery was created, for which we had few law enforcement techniques to defend ourselves. What we know about armed robbery gives us very little insight into how to deal with cyber-theft.

The rules and the tools had changed; local police were of little or no help. At first, even national and international law enforcement organizations were stymied. Putting an end to this new kind of heist required cyber-trained investigators, help from Microsoft, and the efforts of numerous international partners.

THE POWER OF SUBSTITUTIONAL EQUIVALENCE

Substitutional equivalence is the engine that drives societal phase change. Throughout history, new ideas, new technologies, and new inventions have enabled humanity to construct new forms of institutions, new types of relationships, and new kinds of space that replace former ways of doing things. However, we immediately add that these substitutional equivalents are not the same as what they replace. Typically, they work more efficiently in some manner and often include new features. But they operate using new rules, tools, and processes.

When new methods and forms perform in an almost identical way to what they replace, they are substitutionally equivalent, but a structural transformation has not necessarily happened. For example, if you replace a handwritten ledger with a spreadsheet, you are substituting a more useful and efficient method of bookkeeping for an old one, but a structural transformation has not occurred—the spreadsheet is merely a new medium for the same information and it is put to the same use. The same rules apply. But if the intelligent technology–powered substitution enables the creation of a new institutional form that follows a different set of rules and performs in a different fashion from the old one, then a structural transformation has taken place. Add up enough of them, and you have a social phase change.

Seventy-five years ago, most consumer transactions were paid for with cash. Today, most of us use credit or debit cards. Things are very different when one pays with a credit card instead of cash, for both the buyer and the seller. When you use cash, the merchant gets his money instantly, which he then deposits into his bank. When you pay with a credit card, he gets his money from the bank that is associated with the card. If a cash-using customer comes up short, the merchant doesn't let her take the product home. If the credit card–using customer is short on cash, the merchant doesn't have to know or care. Why? Because unless the customer is committing credit card fraud, the merchant knows he will receive his money.

Cash is anonymous and, unless the police have arranged to give you marked bills, it is virtually untraceable. When you use a credit card, you give up a great deal of privacy, because the system can track your spending. Though the buying power of cash may change with the broader economy, when you use a dollar to buy something that costs a dollar, you pay a dollar for it, and the merchant receives a dollar. When you buy that same item with a credit card, you may opt to borrow the money and pay interest on it. The merchant may receive a little less than a dollar because the credit card system charges him a fee for its services. Using a credit card is different from paying with cash, but we use it to perform the same functions. Indeed, the credit card has rendered cash obsolete in many ways. In that sense, it is substitutionally equivalent.

To repeat the list from chapter 1, three types of substitutional equivalences are powering the Autonomous Revolution:

1. *Information Equivalence.* In which the information underpinning an institution can be used to restructure that institution

2. *Intelligence Equivalence.* In which traditionally human acts and capabilities, both intellectual and manual, can be replaced by computer-based operations

3. *Spatial Equivalence.* In which activities that are traditionally based in the real world, such as social interactions, commerce, entertainment, meetings, even travel, now operate in the virtual world

Now let's take an in-depth look at each of them.

INFORMATION EQUIVALENCE

Intelligent machines have created numerous forms of substitutional equivalence.

The effects of the structural transformations that we are experiencing in our business and economic institutions and in our work and home environments are primarily being driven by information and intelligence equivalences. Information equivalence is so prevalent in our institutions and affects such a large swath of our economy that we will begin there.

Our institutions are composed of information and physical processes. For example, a farm has a very large physical component and a fairly small information component, whereas a bank has a very large information component and a relatively small physical one. In the most extreme case, a modern social network such as Facebook manages more than 2 billion users on six continents with just 4,000 or so employees, who are based in a handful of buildings. When you add intelligent machines to institutions where the information component is dominant, dramatic changes take place. The plumbing profession will likely stay pretty much the same throughout the Autonomous Revolution, but retail banks (which are really information systems in disguise—"information proxies") will change beyond recognition.

Regarding the phrase *information proxy*, think of an office building and its contents—desks, paper files, computers, networks, and people. This structure is really an information storage and processing network. Information is stored on computer and paper files and in people's brains. Information is exchanged over a digital network, by moving paper files from desk to desk, and in face-to-face conversations. Intelligent machines and people process it.

If an information system can gather this information by itself, store it in a computer-readable form, process it using simple rules or via artificial intelligence algorithms, and respond without human involvement, then the office building and its contents can be replaced by a rack of computer gear. There is no need for people, file cabinets, desks, or more than a few square feet of physical space. As mentioned before, many customer call centers today already fit this description.

The physical structure, its contents, and its people are information proxies. The substitional equivalent is a rack of computer gear.

A retail store is an information proxy combined with a physical delivery system. When consumers go to Walmart, they engage in a number of information exchange processes. Customers find out what items are available and at what prices. They may want to inspect the merchandise to determine its quality and try it on to make sure it is the right size. When customers make a purchase, they pay cash or provide credit card information. Then they carry the merchandise to their car to complete the physical delivery process.

Retail shopping is being replaced by informational and spatial equivalences. Instead of going to the store to shop, cyber-shoppers get product, price, and availability information online. They can even try on an item of clothing virtually, using digital imaging. The computer takes their credit card information (an intelligence equivalence of what a flesh-and-blood retail clerk does), and FedEx or UPS provides delivery.

For many commodities, the retail substitutional equivalence of the future will consist of shopping online with rapid delivery by autonomous vehicles from large warehouses located near urban centers. The same functions will be carried out, but will use entirely different tools, rules, and processes.

Surprisingly, many institutions that do not appear to be heavily dependent on information content for their success are, in fact, quite vulnerable to disruption by information equivalent infrastructures. For example, on the surface, the hospitality industry would seem to be dominated by physical infrastructure. But the industry depends on two very important information components: the idea of a hotel and brand awareness. In the past, when travelers thought about where they would stay while visiting a distant city, the mental model that they called up was a hotel. The second important information component had to do with trust. Consumers assumed that if they stayed in a branded hotel, they would experience a certain level of quality. The Airbnb model has changed the rules and tools by substituting a different set of information equivalents for those assumptions. Now travelers think about staying in the homes of total strangers. And they trust a computer system—Airbnb—to find them one that is clean, safe, convenient, and fairly priced.

The extent of the transformation that takes place as a result of information equivalence depends, first, on the amount of functionality that can move from one information equivalent structure to another. Second, the new information equivalent infrastructure must offer a significant perceived benefit. And third, the technology has to be in broad enough use that a large portion of the user base can move to the equivalent information infrastructure. For example, before a virtual currency can achieve broad use, large numbers of merchants have to be willing to accept it as a form of payment.

While tomorrow's restaurants, plumbers, and landscapers will promote their businesses via social media, bill their customers electronically, and make use of digital tools in their operations, the essence of their businesses will likely remain the same. But some kinds of institutions are almost totally information proxies in disguise. Retail, banking, finance, and monetary systems are examples of institutions with extremely high information proxy content. One would expect them to be significantly transformed.

INTELLIGENCE EQUIVALENCE

Advances in artificial intelligence, deep learning, neural network processing, and big data have unleashed the forces of intelligence equivalence. Machines are now capable of intelligent behavior. In many applications, they can substitute for humans' brains, minds, and senses.

For more than one hundred years, technologists involved in computation have speculated about and attempted to construct machines that would exhibit intelligent behavior. In 1914, the Spanish engineer Leonardo Torres y Quevedo demonstrated a mechanical device that could play simple king rook chess endgames.[6]

In 1921, the Czech author Karel Capek wrote *R.U.R. (Rossum's Universal Robots)*, which introduced the word *robot* to the world.[7] Reading this prophetic play, written almost one hundred years ago, is a startling experience. Its disillusioned workers, displaced by robots, could equally well be members of today's middle class.

In 1950, Alan Turing, one of the early investigators of machine intelligence, proposed a simple test to determine whether a machine could "think." Now known as the Turing Test, it is a protocol in which three terminals are set up in isolation from one another, two operated by humans and one by a computer. One of the humans asks the computer and the other human a series of questions. If the questioner can't tell which respondent is human and which is a machine after a certain number of tries, then the computer is said to have intelligence. By 1966, Joseph Weizenbaum, author Davidow's first boss, had developed a program called ELIZA that appeared to pass the test.[8]

In the nearly seventy years that have passed since the creation of the Turing Test, artificial intelligence has passed through cycles of excitement and disillusionment. At a 1956 Dartmouth conference, where the term *artificial intelligence* was coined, Marvin Minsky predicted that the problem would be solved within a generation.[9] He was wrong. Most early attempts to mimic intelligent behavior were based on systems that ran according to more and more complex sets of rules. But it turns out that it is both very difficult and very expensive to write rules that can cover every possible situation that a computer might find itself in. A real breakthrough would occur if machines could learn from their experiences and then reprogram themselves, without human assistance. This is precisely what has been happening in the past few decades.

In 1997, Deep Blue, a chess-playing computer developed by IBM, beat the Russian grandmaster Garry Kasparov in a six-game match.[10] Kasparov said that he had sensed a thinking presence inside his computer opponent. Then, in 2016, Google DeepMind's artificial-intelligence program, AlphaGo, defeated Lee Sedol, a Go champion, 4–1. Go is a more difficult game for a computer to play than chess, and AlphaGo's victory is perhaps the best harbinger of what is to come. While Deep Blue relied on hard-coded functions written by human experts for its decision-making processes, AlphaGo used neural networks and reinforcement learning. In other words, its system studied numerous games and played games against itself so it could write its own rules.[11]

The lesson here is that it is now possible to use inexpensive computer power to develop intelligent processes. Until recently, intelligent systems learned how to behave in specific situations. When presented with a new situation, they would have to learn how to behave from scratch. Being able to generalize a response based on past experience comes very close to cognitive behavior—a once-impossible barrier that now appears to be crumbling. *The Economist* recently reported that certain computers, trained to play a number of games, have been able to come up with viable strategies for playing different games they have never seen before.[12]

The semiconductor industry has only just begun to unleash the power of Moore's Law (the regular doubling of semiconductor chip performance) on neural networks. Google's DeepMind system used Nvidia's newly announced P100 chip, containing 1.5 billion transistors, to power its system. The chip enabled Google to build neural networks that were five times deeper than in the past—and the deeper the networks, the more intelligent the behavior.[13] The key point here is that neural network systems will benefit from high rates of progress in the semiconductor industry. In the years to come, each generation of machines will be cheaper, faster, and more capable than the one that came before.

A second key advance is the amount of data we have at our disposal. The numbers of data sets that can be used to train new systems will grow exponentially.

Finally, we are continually learning how to design better software.

The implications of all of this intellectual equivalence are staggering. Financial firms have hundreds of routine processes that can be automated. So do many other businesses. For example, WorkFusion makes a software that studies what employees do when they manipulate data on their computers and then assesses which tasks can be automated and which can be outsourced. Though its ostensible purpose is to help workers become more productive, over time, it's easy to imagine how this process will replace them. When this happens, human work will have been absorbed into a workerless world—an archetypal example of intelligence equivalence.

Workers whose jobs are being transferred overseas have often complained that their companies force them to train their replacements. With services such as WorkFusion, employees are training invisible robots to replace them—an indignity that is no less infuriating for being invisible.

Machines are only going to get smarter. Suppose for a second that today's intelligent machines are only capable of doing the work of a person of average intelligence, someone with an IQ of 100. Then imagine that, thanks to Moore's Law, the technology in those machines improves by 40 to 60 percent per year. Suppose that this rate of technological progress raises the machine-equivalent IQ by 1 point per year. In a decade, those machines would have a machine-equivalent IQ that would empower them to do the work of more than 75 percent of the U.S. population.[14]

In fact, machines with the equivalent of 110 IQ points are here already. In certain applications, even the minds of highly educated doctors are no longer needed. In 2013, the FDA approved Johnson & Johnson's Sedasys machine (since discontinued), which delivered sedatives to patients automatically, eliminating the need for an anesthesiologist.[15] An emerging field in radiology is computer-aided diagnosis (CADx).[16] A recent study published by the Royal Society showed that computers performed more consistently and accurately in identifying radiolucency (the appearance of dark images) than radiologists by almost a factor of 10.[17]

In 2014, the authors of this book took to the pages of the *Harvard Business Review* to warn about the growing numbers of Zero Economic Value citizens (ZEVs)—many of them possessing high skill levels—who will never find meaningful employment again, because they will keep losing the race with robot/artificial intelligence. We'll discuss this sobering challenge in more depth later. For now, it's important to know that many systems in use in the business world already incorporate both information and intelligence equivalent processes. Larger and larger numbers of worker-less environments will be the inevitable result.

SPATIAL EQUIVALENCE

Spatial equivalence is familiar to all of us. One form of it is social networking: Facebook, Instagram, Twitter, LinkedIn, Reddit, YouTube, and many more platforms now claim billions of users. Facebook alone has around 2 billion users worldwide. China has some 597 million social media users.[18]

Social networks—which we'll discuss in chapter 8—provide a new way to organize affinity groups and an inexpensive way to communicate with them. But they have also transformed the social contract in often disturbing ways—such as the surrender of privacy and the proliferation of false information.

A second major form of spatial equivalence is online gaming, with its hundreds of millions of participants. It has largely replaced not only traditional board games but even, in extreme cases, outdoor recreation. It has brought with it a unique set of challenges, including compulsive and addiction-like behaviors. The power of these games will only increase with the rise of virtual reality, 3-D imagery, and more powerful computation engines. Gaming is also spreading its influence into other forms of recreation, increasingly bringing group participation, virtualization, and 3-D imagery to the rest of the Web, television, and film.

Already we are constantly interacting with virtual environments. While meeting someone in virtual space has become the social equivalent of meeting someone for a cup of coffee, the experience is not, in fact, the same. Moreover, human interactive experience must exist in time—and the amount of our time is necessarily limited.

Thus, as our time in virtual space increases, the time we spend in the real world must decrease.

Many businesses now function primarily in virtual space. Google, Spotify, and Netflix are examples. When those businesses did not exist, some form of their services existed in physical space. People read printed newspapers, went to record stores to buy music, and to Blockbuster and other video stores to buy or rent movies. Before VCRs became common, they went to the movies.

The implications of these shifts are still not fully known. Even the rules of this new world are, as yet, only partially written. In the meantime, the lure of the virtual world—and the risk of severe and unintended social consequences that our immersion in it might bring—only increases. We will also look more deeply into this matter in chapter 8.

Substitutional equivalences put pressure on every corner of modern life. Understanding how they operate will be vital to determining how we should respond. For that reason, in the pages that follow, as we consider the various cultural aspects of the Autonomous Revolution, we will refer to substitutional equivalences regularly and will provide examples of how to respond to the challenges they present.

CHAPTER FOUR

PRODUCTIVITY WITHOUT PROSPERITY

The Emerging Era of Non-Monetizable Productivity

TO UNDERSTAND WHERE WE ARE GOING, we need to revisit the events of the past and see them through the lens of our new understanding of social phase change. Consider the Industrial Revolution, which has given us numerous general-purpose technologies, among them the steam and internal combustion engines, electricity, wired and wireless communications, and computers—technologies that have found their way into every corner of our lives and transformed our society in fundamental ways.

Those inventions raised worker productivity and drove economic growth. They lifted millions out of poverty and created a vibrant middle class. They also had displacement effects that caused considerable pain. For example, in early nineteenth-century England, the Luddites, skilled weavers who had lost their livelihoods to the new textile mills, sabotaged machinery. Many cottage industries and artisanal trades and crafts vanished. But ultimately, the creation effects of the new technologies tilted the scales in the other direction. Thousands of jobs were lost, but millions of new ones were created.

The intelligent machine, the general-purpose technology of the Autonomous Revolution, is similarly driving large increases in productivity and unleashing huge displacement effects. Unlike its counterparts from the Industrial Revolution, its job creation effects have been small and tend to flow to a specialized group of technocrats.

The technologies of the past created massive amounts of what we call monetizable productivity—that is, improvements in productivity that significantly increased gross domestic product (GDP). By comparison, the technology of the future is generating large amounts of non-monetizable productivity—improvements in productivity that in many cases drive GDP down instead of up. Despite this difference, techno-optimists (including many economists) have argued that the ultimate impact of intelligent machines will be similar to those of past general-purpose technologies.

We believe, however, that things will be different this time. The structural transformations unleashed by intelligent machines are already rendering many of the economic rules and social processes of the past obsolete. We will have to search for, and put into place, new rules to deal with the future.

To understand what's different, let's take a closer look at two general-purpose technologies: the internal combustion engine and the semiconductor. As we all know, the impact of the internal combustion engine was particularly dramatic. It not only furthered the evolution of transportation but also rewrote the rules of the modern world and in the process transformed the physical infrastructure of society.

Now, as the internal combustion engine—and very likely the traditional automobile—fast approaches obsolescence, it is time to better understand those rules and what is likely to replace them.

Let's start with the history. In theory at least, the internal combustion engine has been around for nearly a millennium. For example, a firearm is a very simple application of the principles of internal combustion. In the 1600s, Christiaan Huygens, a Dutch polymath, built a version of an explosion engine that used gunpowder and a cannon barrel.[1] The first commercially successful internal combustion engine (actually a converted steam engine) was invented by Étienne Lenoir around 1859, and the first modern internal combustion engine, using compressed fuel and pistons, was built by Nikolaus Otto in 1876. Crucial figures in this early story are Gottlieb Daimler and his partner Wilhelm Maybach, and Karl Benz, who developed four-stroke and two-stroke motors, respectively, in the 1870s. Then, in 1885, Benz took the pivotal step of putting his engines into carriages and selling them. The Automobile Age had begun.

By 1910, several dozen automobile companies around the world were selling a few hundred thousand trucks and automobiles to industries and wealthy consumers. A leading innovator during this era was Henry Ford, who not only designed an elegantly simple automobile with standardized parts but also adapted Eli Whitney's rifle production technology of seventy years before to build his car with unprecedented speed, efficiency, reliability, and low cost. Suddenly, automobiles were available to the common worker.

In 1914, Henry Ford shocked the industrial world when he doubled the pay of his highly productive assembly-line workers to $5 a day.[2] Ford reasoned that a higher-paid workforce would be able to buy more cars and thus increase his business.[3] Others followed suit.

The market for automobiles was elastic. The Model T Ford went on sale in 1908 for $950; due to productivity improvements, its price had dropped to $269 by 1923.[4] In 1909, Ford produced 10,666 vehicles; in 1923, the company sold more than 2 million.[5] By 1927, the Ford Motor Company had sold 15 million of its Model T "flivvers."

As a spillover from their explosive success, automotive companies also created a large demand for other products and services that employed millions of workers—steel, coal to make the steel, glass, rubber, machine tools, auto dealerships, gas stations, oil fields, mechanics, and so on. Thanks to the roads they required and the access to the countryside they created, automobiles helped to establish suburbia—which kicked off the home construction boom that followed. They made possible a new form of retail distribution, the shopping center.

The workers in all these new jobs—the rising middle class—purchased homes, appliances, and clothes, creating still more jobs and more consumers. The virtuous circle this created was classic capitalism in action, and arguably the greatest achievement of the Industrial Revolution.

Of course, the internal combustion engine also unleashed the forces of Joseph Schumpeter's creative destruction. Most notably, the engine replaced the horse. In 1870 there was one horse for every five citizens and 27 percent of farmland was used to grow feed for horses used for transportation.[6] According to historian Joel Tarr, "in 1880 New York and Brooklyn were served by 427 blacksmith shops, 249 carriage and wagon enterprises, 262 wheelwright shops, and 290 establishments dealing in saddles and harnesses." Most of them vanished.[7] Add together all the other cities and farms in the United States and around the world and the losses are not at all insignificant.

But whatever the personal costs to those farmers, merchants, and tradespeople, the automobile generated more than enough economic opportunities to make up for the displacements. Similar displacement/creation stories could be written about the steam engine, electricity, and all of the other technologies of the Industrial Age.

SILICON SOCIETY

Now let's consider the technology that enabled the third phase of the Industrial Age: semiconductors.

As a historical phenomenon, semiconductors emerged—despite the interruption of a world war—incredibly quickly. In the 1930s, two scientists at Bell Telephone Laboratories saw a demonstration of how an insulator made of silicon, when "doped" with certain impurities, suddenly became a semiconductor. By applying voltage to junctions, the flow of electical current could be turned on and off.

This would enable engineers to design systems that encoded ones and zeros—the binary numbers used in computers.

Intrigued, the two scientists, Walter Brattain and John Bardeen, made plans to develop a commercial application. But it wasn't until 1946 that they were able to return to the project. With the advice of a particularly brilliant scientist at the Labs, William Shockley, they created a solid-state device that could replace the fragile, fifty-year-old vacuum tube (which, in turn, had replaced the electro-mechanical switch). They called this tiny device a transistor.

So fast was the development of this technology that, within a decade, technologists had discovered ways to manufacture hundreds of transistors on flat sheets (the "planar" process), which when wired together created integrated circuits. And just a decade after that, those integrated circuits, much miniaturized and adapted to different purposes (memory, logic, etc.), would be interconnected to create a computer on a single chip: the microprocessor, arguably the greatest invention of the century.

Today, the typical microprocessor contains more than 1 billion transistors, making it the most complex device in general use in human history. These chips, like Henry Ford's flivvers, drove large increases in what we call monetizable productivity. Monetizable productivity raises the dollar output that each worker produces per hour of work, increasing GDP and enabling employers to pay them more for their efforts.

When integrated circuits first appeared in volume in 1961 as a substitute for large, slow, unreliable, and power-hungry vacuum tubes and bulky individual transistors, the worldwide electronics market was $29 billion.[8] Today, it is $1.5 trillion—growth by a factor of 50. The integrated circuit made existing products better. Mainframe computers became less expensive, much faster, more reliable, substantially smaller, and more energy-efficient. As a result, the mainframe computer business expanded rapidly. IBM's revenue increased from less than $2 billion in 1960 to more than $26 billion in 1980, a

14 percent growth rate.[9] In the form of the microprocessor, the integrated circuit also spawned industries and applications that had never existed before—including cellular communications, personal computers, tablets, and the Internet of Things.[10] New jobs followed.

Today, the worldwide market for smartphones is approaching a half-trillion dollars.[11] For personal computers and laptops, it's about $200 billion.[12] IHS Markit, a technology consulting firm, forecasts that the installed base of Internet of Things devices will reach 75.4 billion units by 2025, or about ten devices for every person on the planet. Estimates of the potential economic impact of these devices and associated services fall in the wide range of $2.7 to $6.2 trillion.[13]

Just as remarkable is that the semiconductor industry was able to achieve this mind-boggling level of growth while experiencing precipitous declines in the price per transistor. The price of a transistor in 1965 was about $8; today, it is just one-millionth of a cent.[14]

As costs fell, the world was flooded with cheap transistors and the market, being elastic, found new ways to use them. Initially, semiconductor dollar sales grew by more than 20 percent per year while the industry doubled the densities of the circuits every two years—following the so-called Moore's Law.[15]

The key point is that prices did not fall to zero, even though catastrophic price wars swept through the industry, squeezing margins to the bone. One-millionth of a cent per transistor may be an incredibly low price (with an even slimmer margin), but it can generate billions of dollars of income if the market simultaneously expands by factors of a billion.

And that is just what the market did. In fact, the market for semiconductors expanded so rapidly that one producer, Intel, eventually became the most valuable manufacturer in the world. The newspaper industry would be delighted to experience a similar fate. All it needs is a billion times as many readers.

The most important point of all is that in the semiconductor technology, creation dominated substitution. Yes, the semiconductor triumphed over the clunky vacuum tube, but that was only the beginning. By the mid-1960s, semiconductor technology was already creating industries that never would have existed without it—ultimately billion- and trillion-dollar ones.

One of the defining characteristics of the monetizable productivity increases of the past was that they created even larger increases in the value of the GDP. According to the economist Robert Gordon, U.S. productivity grew at an annual rate of 2.82 percent between 1920 and 1970.[16] During that same interval, GDP increased by more than 3.2 percent.[17] When GDP grows faster than productivity it generates a demand for more workers. Thus, the old productivity created not only more dollars of economic output but also jobs. Even more importantly, it created good times. Per capita GDP grew about 2 percent per year during that same half-century,[18] and each generation earned about 50 percent more income than the one before. Workers' sons and daughters were almost certain to enjoy higher living standards than their parents.

The productivity that Gordon is talking about is *labor productivity*, which is measured by dividing the GDP by the total hours worked by all workers. At best, this calculation is a proxy for real productivity; at worst, it sorely underestimates it. For example, economists point out that it does not take into account quality improvements. Take the impact of Moore's Law: If the price of a personal computer stays the same but next year's model runs four times faster, processes twice as quickly, and has three times the memory, the labor productivity number would stay the same, even though the customer is getting a lot more for the dollar he or she spends.

There are other problems with this metric as well.

Take the notorious case of Turing Pharmaceuticals. Martin Shkreli, the founder of Turing, purchased the U.S. marketing rights to the drug Daraprim (pyrimethamine) in 2015. This sixty-year-old drug is critical for the treatment of toxoplasmosis. Turing raised its price from $13.50 a pill to $750—more than a 5,000 percent increase. The result was a giant scandal, Congressional hearings, and more. Eventually Shkreli went to prison (for different reasons, but his notoriety didn't help his case). But on paper, Shkreli's move was a huge success: if one could get one's hands on the precise data for a labor productivity calculation, it would probably show that Shkreli's workers became 25 to 50 times more productive at a stroke of the pricing pen.[19]

Another example that makes one scratch one's head is illustrated by a discussion that coauthor William Davidow had in the 1970s with Robert (Bob) Noyce, the inventor of the integrated circuit and the president of Intel. Bob was complaining that the financial analysts who followed the company were criticizing him because employee productivity was not growing. Bob justifiably pointed out that the number of transistors being produced by each Intel employee was growing at a rate of about 40 percent per year, but that prices were falling so fast that the dollar output per employee was not growing at all.

This was an early glimpse of a structural transformation that is now inescapable: productivity at Intel was obviously climbing rapidly and consumers were benefiting from it—but by traditional measures, those productivity increases weren't being converted into dollars. That is, Intel and the rest of the semiconductor industry were experiencing non-monetizable productivity improvements. What began there has now spread to much of the world's economy—and that process will define the Autonomous Revolution.

Most economists, policy makers, and politicians still take it as an article of faith that increased productivity leads to a prosperity whose benefits are broadly shared. That assumption is baked into neoclassical economic theory and the current approach to economic policy. But the social phase change that drives non-monetizable productivity should make us question that assumption.

In the past, when we were fighting a recession or an economic slowdown, the Federal Reserve would reduce interest rates. One reason they did this was to spur capital investment to raise productivity, which was presumed to be monetizable. But suppose the rules don't work that way anymore. Suppose that a lot of that capital investment is used to finance the growth of non-monetizable productivity that actually slows economic growth. Non-monetizable productivity may be one of the reasons that the low interest rates of the past decade have had a smaller than anticipated effect on the overall economy. Societal phase change might be rendering the old rules for economic policy obsolete.

PROGRESS WITHOUT PROFIT

The challenges that non-monetizable productivity poses for the middle class in the world's developed countries will soon spread to emerging economies as well. The middle class is working better and smarter than it ever has, but it's not getting any wealthier.

In the years to come, we will have to accept that not all productivity is created equal. The productivities to which we are all accustomed—that is, monetizable productivities—brought with them expansions in the GDP and a prosperity that was widely shared. By comparison, much of the productivity of the future will be non-monetizable. Its effects may in fact slow down GDP growth and drive middle-class wages down even further. And the ratio between non-monetizable and monetizable productivity will only increase.

For the past 250 years, the Industrial Revolution has created a deluge of monetizable productivity increases that were collectively responsible for one of history's greatest economic free lunches. Things got better for almost everyone—the poor, the middle class, and the rich. The fact that most people were doing better, generation after generation, helped foster a national unity of purpose. While productivity increases led to job losses in some areas, they stimulated economic growth in others—which led to new opportunities and ultimately created far more jobs than had been lost. This consistent return on investment gave birth to a wide array of new industries and services, all of which needed workers. A second, but just as important, benefit of all this was that the new technologies replaced muscle power with mechanical power, freeing workers from much of the backbreaking labor that ruined bodies and shortened life expectancies.

Non-monetizable productivity has different effects. The technologies driving it are intelligent machines, artificial intelligence, high bandwidth communication, low-cost sensors, lifelike visual displays, and speech recognition and control. These technologies can substitute for the human brain and mind, the senses of vision, touch, and smell, and give us new ways to interact with people and our surroundings.

These technologies greatly increase the output of goods and services even as they reduce costs. Substitutional equivalents of some products and services are being produced and scaled with almost zero cost. New business models follow—and in many cases the products are given away for free.

An everyday example that we now take for granted is email. It not only reduced the cost of sending a letter to nothing but also made it possible to send that letter to scores, even hundreds, of people at the same time—also for free. Today people get more mail (email, e-catalogs, and physical mail) than ever. Our non-monetizable mail productivity has shot through the roof. The direct effect is that postal service employment has dropped by almost 30 percent.[20] But email caused other displacement effects as well. For example, "mail" changed form.

Envelopes, stationery, and photocopies went away. So did the file cabinets that stored the paper correspondence. The greeting card industry is a $7 billion business.[21] It would likely be much bigger now, but email made it easier not just to send creative invitations and greeting cards, but to buy them and keep track of the occasions that they mark. Employment at Hallmark is down by more than half, from 22,000 to 10,500.[22]

Another big difference from the old economy is that when replacement institutions emerge in the Autonomous Economy, the new business forms are frequently supercharged substitutes for the old ones. They rarely have the secondary effect of creating new industries.

In the case of email, new displacement businesses have emerged. Paperless Post and Evite provide very good e-invitation services. Similarly, Jacquie Lawson Inc. has a great catalogue of e-birthday, thank you, and congratulation cards. But to the best of our knowledge, email has not created large numbers of new jobs in new markets. The email equivalents of the smartphone or the highways that carried Henry Ford's cars have yet to emerge.

In the next chapter we will be discussing the potential impact of the Autonomous Economy on finance. We hypothesize that in the future everyone will be able to get better financial services for less money; but the bad news is that those higher-quality services will employ just half as many people as they do today. Good for consumers, but bad for bank and credit card company employees.

If half of the 8 million people who are currently working in financial services lose their jobs, what new industries will be created as a result? If the price of those high-quality services declines by 50 percent, will the market expand to offset the decline?

The media business has already experienced job losses at that scale, and very few of those jobs have been replaced. It does not require much imagination to envision this happening nearly everywhere.

PROGRESS WITHOUT PEOPLE

Now, let's look more specifically at intelligent machines and how they create non-monetizable productivity.

1. *The intelligent machine is an efficiency engine.* It substitutes, displaces, and is remarkably devoid of new opportunity creation effects. It does not create millions of new jobs in other areas of the economy as the semiconductor and automobile did. Rather, by improving itself and extending

its intelligence to other products and services, it will likely do just the opposite: remove millions of existing jobs and replace them with other intelligent machines.

2. *The intelligent machine replaces the human brain.* These intelligent, largely autonomous machines will have a large impact on the brain-based services segment of the economy. Services are the growth segment of the economy and currently employ 80 percent of the workforce.[23]

3. *The markets that intelligent machines affect the most are in many cases inelastic.* Even though prices will drop, unit sales will not increase significantly as, for example, they did with the automobile. Back then, when prices of Ford's cars dropped, sales increased by a factor of 200. With semiconductors, they increased by factors of a billion and more. But in the case of news, if the price of a newspaper drops to near zero, people with limited time will not buy or read 100 times more news. Similarly, we will not file more personal tax returns if the price of getting tax help declines.

The impact that autonomous productivity will have on the overall economy depends on the size of the markets it affects and the size of the productivity increases it causes. But as we will see, both are very large.

Consider the intelligent machine at work. The newspaper industry, in which coauthor Michael Malone is a fourth-generation participant, is a good place to start.

As early as the 1980s, newspapers were losing as much as 1 percent of their readership per year to television and the emerging Web. But, thanks to increasing advertising revenues and subscription prices, those losses weren't showing up on the balance sheets. Then, between 2003 and 2012, in the face of competition from such Web-based competitors as eBay and Craigslist, newspaper advertising revenue plummeted from $46 to $22 billion, even as online ad revenues grew from $1.2 billion to $3.4 billion.[24] Total weekday newspaper circulation dropped from around 62 million to 45 million, a 25 percent decline; to hang on to the readers that remained, many papers slashed subscription fees. Meanwhile, newspaper jobs declined from around 450,000 to 250,000, the lowest level in nearly eighty years.[25]

Today, former full-time reporters struggle to make their livings as freelance writers, searching for jobs in the gig economy. "No one I know has a job anymore," Tina Brown, the former editor of *The New Yorker* and *The Daily Beast*, observed. "They've got gigs" and are living "on what's left of their 401(K)s."[26] In most cases, displaced reporters earn far less than they did when they had full-time jobs.

Some reporters now find themselves in direct competition with intelligent machines that are capable of writing simple stories about sporting events and financial news. Yahoo and the Associated Press use WordSmith, produced by Automated Insights, to get the news out fast.[27] The value of the work those reporters did is being set by the cost of the writing done by intelligent machines.

Even though newspapers have a fraction of their former readership, everyone still gets the news. Many get it for free over the Internet (much of it, ironically, from those same dying newspapers), and it is more timely, often uses multimedia, is continuously updated, and offers links to endless quantities of supporting information for those who want to dive deeper. If those quality and service improvements had occurred in the past, readers would have been charged more for them and advertisers would have purchased more space at higher rates. Newspaper revenues would have increased substantially. But with the arrival of the Internet and, increasingly, artificial intelligence, the opposite has occurred.

Based on a purely economic calculation, the advertising dollars per employee in the industry fell from $102,000 to $88,000 over that nine-year period, a decline in advertising productivity of about

1.5 percent per year. But from a consumer's point of view, that same era was characterized by better-quality news services, produced by 44 percent fewer people—a productivity gain of about 4.5 percent per year.

The real productivity was much greater, because the news was produced with a lower level of capital investment, distributed at a lower cost, and consumed less physical material. If all these factors were taken into account, the real increase in productivity would probably be in the range of 5 to 7 percent.

Of course, new Internet news services have appeared, and some of them have thrived. For example, in 2015, the *Huffington Post* reported revenues of $146 million and BuzzFeed $100 million.[28] But those figures are insignificant when compared to the $24 billion drop in advertising revenues that their newspaper counterparts suffered. It is hard to see how newspapers will ever make up the difference.

A FEW VERY PRODUCTIVE WORKERS

Many economists still insist that new technologies create new opportunities to make up for displacement effects. They also point out that the resources freed up as a result of productivity increases are used to create new opportunities in other areas of the economy.

Would that those truisms were true. In the old economy, they were. To understand why that is no longer the case, we need to take a closer look at the new opportunities that are actually being created.

One fact is obvious: the intelligent machine is helping to create new and vibrant companies such as Amazon, Facebook, and Google. These companies have grown rapidly, are very profitable, and are extremely productive.

Amazon had sales of $89 billion in 2014 and employed 154,000 people, an output of about $578,000 per employee.[29] The comparable number for Walmart was $219,000. So, from an economic point of view, Amazon employees were more than 2.5 times as productive as Walmart's. Customers get lower prices because Amazon is so efficient. But the market for the products Amazon sells is not that elastic. Customers will not purchase 2.5 times more toothpaste, so employment in retail is bound to fall.

In 2013, Google had about 50,000 employees and generated revenues of about $55 billion in sales—an output of roughly $1.0 million per employee.[30] In the traditional economy, a company with similar sales would have about 250,000 employees. The numbers for Facebook are similar ($800,000 per employee in 2017).[31]

Netflix's productivity numbers dwarf Google's. In early 2019, the company generated revenue of more than $8 million per employee.[32] Using intelligent machines, Netflix and the rental kiosks of Redbox displaced Blockbuster, which at its peak in 2004 had 60,000 employees and 9,000 stores.[33] By comparison, that year Netflix had approximately 1,000 employees.[34]

So while it is true that these companies are creating new jobs, it is also true that they have displaced many times more jobs.

As uncomfortable as it may be, it is important—especially at a time of such sweeping change—to accurately define the challenges we are confronting. Robert J. Gordon points out that between 1970 and 1996, productivity experienced a marked slowdown. Further, he states, "In the past decade, productivity growth has been even slower than it was between 1970 and 1996."[35]

But if our analysis is accurate, the reality is just the opposite: in fact, productivity in many areas of the economy is growing rapidly when measured in terms of the goods and services produced per unit of labor. It is just that this increased productivity is no longer registering in the form of growing markets and more money in the pockets of workers or even their employers. Businesses are being forced by competition, or by the fact that their business models have changed, to sell their products and services at reduced prices. As a result, they cannot monetize the effects of their productivity increases. They are reducing their workforces in response—at best, rehiring workers as part-time contractors—and paying less to the workers who remain.

The problem now facing the entire economy is very similar to the problem Bob Noyce wrestled with forty years ago as president of Intel. His employees were becoming 40 percent more productive each year when output was measured in terms of transistors produced per employee. Unfortunately for Bob, his prices were under great pressure as his factories and those of his competitors flooded the market with transistors. In the end, Bob and his competitors were saved by an explosion in demand from the creation of brand-new industries—such as the personal computer. There likely won't be a similar rescue this time. There is no evidence that the Autonomous Revolution will duplicate that kind of market creation.

Historically, per capita GDP has been one of the key metrics that policy makers use to assess and manage the health of the economy. Rising GDP was tightly correlated with the quality of life for average Americans. When GDP rose, they could pay for college educations for their children, save money for retirement, purchase more goods and services, and have access to better health care.

That connection has been broken. Today, per capita GDP could be flat and the quality of people's lives could still be improving. The reason is non-monetizable productivity. If we get a lot of valuable services for cheaper or for free, people can be living higher-quality lives even if their income is not increasing.

Suppose you get your news and entertainment free. Suppose you do not have to visit the doctor as often because a virtual doctor takes care of you. Suppose low-cost virtual travel substitutes for going there. Suppose you can get rid of your car because work and shopping come to you. Well, in those cases you might be able to live better on less income. In a world in which everything else is being redefined, our definitions of quality of life have to change as well.

Simon Kuznets, who developed a system of national accounts, is considered to be the father of GDP. He received the Nobel Prize in Economics for his work, which took place during the 1930s. During that time, Presidents Hoover and Roosevelt were working to combat the Great Depression but had only fragments of indirect data, such as freight car loadings and stock prices, with which to evaluate the effectiveness of their new policies.[36] The measurement schemes Kuznets devised helped them develop more finely honed approaches.

But Kuznets was well aware of the limitations of his system, and in 1934 he warned Congress that "The welfare of a nation can, therefore, scarcely be inferred from a measurement of national income as defined above."[37] The increasing scale of non-monetizable productivity adds an exclamation point to Kuznets's warning.

If Kuznets were alive today, he might point out that, while it is easy to take a dark view of non-monetizable productivity, we should also be jubilant about the abundance it implies. He might point out that the problem is not with this new economic force, but with our perception of it and with our increasingly obsolete economic value system.

We need new tools to guide economic and government policy. We need a better metric for economic health and quality of life than GDP. We have been trained to believe that increasing incomes are essential if we are to improve our standard of living. That perspective is baked into that anachronistic value system. As a result, our media is full of dour stories about how middle-class incomes have not increased in recent decades and how income inequality has grown. But suppose we chose instead to measure middle-class incomes in terms of the quantity and quality of services we could purchase. From that perspective, we would be *celebrating* the effects of non-monetizable productivity.

Suppose that the cost of education, health care, entertainment, transportation (because of autonomous vehicles), and food (produced by synthetic biology) all declined dramatically by a factor of 2. In that scenario, how much would we notice if our incomes decreased by 25 percent?

One deeply concerning issue with phase change is that people will evaluate the future using the perceptions and values of the past. In that case, their intuition will fail them. Good news would be perceived as bad—and the "medicine" applied would be toxic.

SEARCHING FOR NEW METRICS

In the face of the current shift in the nature of productivity, we no longer have an accurate measure of success. Benefits indexed to obsolete forms of economic measurement will need to be re-indexed. And those new measurement systems will have to reach beyond the system of national accounts that Kuznets helped establish if we are to truly determine "the welfare of the nation."

Recently, the Skoll Foundation became a major backer of an effort to create a Social Progress Index that uses fifty factors to evaluate the quality of life in various nations and geographies.[38] The index takes into account things like access to health care, water and sanitation, environmental quality, advanced education, and personal safety. The United States ranks high on the index, but other countries, such as Canada, Iceland, and many Northern European countries, rank higher.

On another index, the Quality of Life Index, the United States ranks as number 2 for purchasing power, but number 9 on overall quality of life, and at just 50 for safety.[39]

One of the unwritten rules of business is "Be careful what you measure; you may get many things you do not want." Just ask Wells Fargo, which put in a finely honed measurement system to drive its employees to cross-sell its financial products. To meet those new goals, employees opened 3.5 million false customer accounts and have been accused of forcing customers to purchase unnecessary auto insurance. Wells got the cross-selling it measured—along with class-action lawsuits, shareholder lawsuits, and increased regulation by the Federal Reserve.

The use of obsolete measurements will drive the wrong kinds of economic policies and decisions. If the U.S. government doesn't change what it measures, it will continue to get a lot of the things it doesn't want, such as increasing income inequality and the death of the "good job."

Things really are different this time. The Autonomous Revolution is changing the very definition of quality of life. We are going to need a new set of monetary, fiscal, and social policies to deal with its effects. We will also need new measurement systems and metrics that will ensure that we will be happy with what we get.

CHAPTER FIVE

COMMERCIAL TRANSFORMATION

Rewriting Business and the Economy

INFORMATION, INTELLIGENCE, AND SPATIAL EQUIVALENCES are re-shaping commerce and the economy at large. Tom Goodwin's now-famous observation encapsulates just how thoroughly the rules are being rewritten:

> Uber, the world's largest taxi company, owns no vehicles. Facebook, the world's most popular media owner, creates no content. Alibaba, the most valuable retailer, has no inventory. And Airbnb, the world's largest accommodation provider, owns no real estate. Something interesting is happening.[1]

The worlds of business and finance are changing rapidly: online retailing, the sharing economy, freemium business models, stream-ing media, crowd-sourcing, peer-to-peer lending, virtual curren-cies. All this and more, and the Autonomous Revolution has hardly begun. New forms of business, driven by these opportunities, plus an explosion of new enterprises made possible by autonomous ve-hicles, big data analytics, artificial intelligence, and the Internet of Things, are waiting in the wings.

The Autonomous Revolution will challenge every enterprise, big and small, to rethink the correct calculus of employees versus ro-bots, internal operations versus crowd-sourcing, custom operations versus open-sourcing. How disruptive these transformations are at any given moment will depend on the complex interrelationships between the technological state-of-the-art and the social and political environments.

From our point of view, the four most important commercial trends are:

1. *Virtualization.* Many information-intensive service businesses that currently employ more than 80 percent of the workforce will virtualize. Some will melt away like ice in the physical world and adopt fluid forms as applications executing on smart devices.

2. *Networking.* New businesses will appear in the sharing economy, where core groups of permanent employees will leverage the efforts of much larger groups of work-for-hire contractors and content creators to build valuable businesses and vast fortunes for insiders. These businesses will be extremely capital-efficient, but will employ few people and have limited spillover effects.

3. *Displacement.* Many of these new businesses will be displacement businesses, meaning that they will take the place of the old ways of doing things without creating enough new opportunities to offset their displacement effects.

4. *Non-Competition.* Monopolies will become more prevalent and will be well-positioned to stifle their competition while exploiting their customers, contractors, and most replaceable workers.

In attempting to understand the commercial repercussions of societal phase change, it is important to remember that businesses today exist on a continuum. Some, such as restaurants and plumbing contractors, have low information content. Taking advantage of the benefits of information equivalence will have little effect on their forms and functions. They will be able to plan their work more effectively and will need fewer administrative employees. If they are restaurants, they may see a considerable expansion of their take-out operations, thanks to apps like Grubhub; but they will still have dining rooms and kitchens, in which people peel mountains of onions and grill steaks to order. Plumbers will still weld pipes. At the other end of the spectrum, the greatest impact of information equivalence will be felt in the service industries.[2]

Many service businesses, such as airlines, have both large information and large physical components. They will make use of autonomous workers to deliver higher-quality, lower-cost services, but, to an outside observer, the changed businesses will appear very similar to what existed before. Airlines are already using lots of autonomous workers. We interface with them when we check in using our credit cards or when our phone dings us with a message that our flight has been delayed, but airlines are still defined by the cities they serve, the uniforms of their cabin crews, and whether their seat pitch is 29 or 34 inches. Because these types of business are so strongly anchored in the physical world, the effects of the structural transformations may not be immediately apparent. But the processes embedded in the businesses will be starkly different as robots replace more and more of their human workers.

Other businesses, such as media companies and financial institutions, are mostly pure information-processing systems in disguise. Many of them are building equivalent business structures on top of new platforms in virtual space—on the Internet, in smartphone apps, and in the Cloud. A large percentage of them are displacement businesses. Apple Music, Spotify, and Pandora have grown into multibillion-dollar enterprises, while CD sales have fallen from $27 billion in 1999 to $15 billion in 2014 and are still plummeting, and chain record stores like Virgin Records and Tower have disappeared. While these streaming services provide a valuable service to customers, they have eliminated far more jobs than they've created, directly or indirectly, and they have greatly reduced the flow of revenue to artists.

Consumers now take photographs with their phones, store and share them with Snapchat, Flickr, and Photobucket, and use services such as Shutterfly to make albums for friends. At the same time, Kodak, whose scientists invented digital photography in the 1970s, has been driven into bankruptcy.

Think of the changes of form that took place in these businesses as a result of structural transformations. CDs and DVDs sold through retail outlets became bits that traveled down wires and through the air. Newsprint, printing presses, and newsstands are no longer needed. We still take photographs, but none of us purchases film or picks up prints at our local drugstores.

The transitions to these new business models occurred because the new services are more appealing to customers and can be produced very inexpensively. As a result of the low production costs, many things that customers once paid money for are now available for free. The rules these businesses operated under are different as well. Many adopted the freemium business model. They give away their services in order to capture the customer's attention, which they then sell to advertisers.

A second wave of business virtualization is now starting to materialize. Instead of swallowing whole industries in one gulp, these new business forms chip away at them. Targeted applications take over small parts of the industry. Companies then combine these small applications to offer broader and more sophisticated services. This has already happened in the travel industry and it is beginning to happen in finance. The same type of thing will happen in other markets.

Eight million people work in the financial industries, almost 5 percent of the country's workforce. Leading up to the financial crisis in 2008, the sector generated between 30 and 40 percent of domestic corporate profits. After falling precipitously, to 10 percent of profits in 2008, the sector clawed back up to the 20 percent level, where it stands today.[3] Its lush profits and functional inefficiencies make it an ideal target for information equivalent services. That said, banks, credit card systems, financial advisory services, and so on will not go away. But their forms will change so completely that they will effectively become a different industry.

FROM PLASTIC TO CYBERSPACE

Financial, banking, and credit card institutions perform a number of valuable services:

1. They hold and protect customers' assets.
2. They serve as trusted intermediaries that move money and assets between accounts, match sources of capital with users, and match buyers and sellers.
3. They manage risk.
4. They provide advice and manage assets.
5. They maintain a ledger to keep track of account activity.

Some financial entities do a few of these things; full-service banks do them all. All such businesses have information equivalents that can be moved to virtual environments. When this happens, autonomous people-less systems will take the place of service systems that used people to perform transactions and make judgments. By examining some of the shortcomings of the existing systems, we can develop a better feel for why and how these changes will come.

Credit cards are a perfect example of a business segment that is ripe for displacement by substitutional equivalent structures. They are very expensive for both consumers and merchants, highly vulnerable to theft and fraud, and complex and slow for the transaction clearing process.

In 2015, Americans charged $3.2 trillion on their credit cards and

$2.6 trillion on debit cards.[4] Users paid $90 billion and merchants around $60 billion in transaction fees.[5] Credit card holders paid an additional $65 billion in interest at a rate of approximately 16 percent.[6] One would think that, with $5.8 trillion of charges plus an additional $215 billion in fees and interest flowing through it, the system would have armed cyber-guards standing at every cyber-portal. But in fact, the credit card system has a long history of not paying adequate attention to security risks. According to Donn Parker, one of the nation's early experts on computer crime, the credit card companies initially worried that if they added even basic security features (such as PINs) to their credit cards, it would slow consumer adoption.[7] The companies assumed that losses would be so small that they could easily be absorbed as a cost of doing business.

This is a typical example of how intuition fails us when phase change is involved. How could someone in the 1960s possibly have conceived of bots that did not yet exist, stealing tens of millions of credit card numbers using the Internet, which also did not exist, by monitoring customer key strokes on personal computers that would not appear until the 1980s? The culture that believes that fraud losses are an acceptable cost of doing business still prevails, and the results are pouring in. Thieves stole information on 40 million credit card accounts at Target, 56 million accounts at Home Depot, and 94 million at TJX, the parent of the Marshalls and T. J. Maxx chains.[8] Even the little guys suffered. Malware installed on cash registers at Arby's, a relatively small fast-food chain, resulted in the theft of credit and debit card information for 355,000 customers.[9] In 2015, credit and debit card fraud reached almost $22 billion.[10] Ten percent of Americans have been directly affected.[11]

One of the worst security breaches in consumer information history was reported on September 7, 2017, by Equifax, after thieves gained access to the records of 143 million Americans. The breach was discovered on July 29 and it took Equifax more than five weeks to inform consumers. Only 209,000 of those records contained credit card numbers, but the information on the other 143 million accounts will aid thieves in their efforts to commit consumer fraud.[12]

The credit card network consists of a number of layers. Those layers involve the merchant, the acquirer (the company that signed up the merchant on the system), the credit card network (Visa, Mastercard, American Express, Discover, etc.), and the bank that issued the card. The 2-percent fee the merchant pays is divided between those service providers. Even though transactions are authorized almost instantly, the actual payment process is slow. Frequently it takes three days for a transaction to show up on a cardholder's account, because transactions are batch processed as they pass through different layers of the system.[13]

Information equivalents already exist that can save cardholders and merchants much of the $215 billion they pay in fees and interest. These systems can be made so secure that a lot of the $22 billion in losses due to credit card fraud can be eliminated. Increasing confidence in the system would restore another source of lost revenue— the 63 percent of consumers who have experienced fraud and use their cards less often as a result.[14]

In China, India, and many developing economies, this replacement is well under way. In some of these countries, credit cards never really became established, because merchants lacked point-of-sale machines and customers didn't have bank accounts and credit. Now mobile payment systems supplied by the likes of Alibaba and Tencent are filling in the gap. Mobile payments in China reached $9 trillion in 2016, compared to just a little over $100 billion in the United States.[15]

But numerous mobile payment platforms—PayPal, Venmo, Popmoney, Snapcash, and so on—are now vying for Americans' business.[16] These platforms are frequently inexpensive and are tailored to individuals' needs. Snapcash is a payment system designed to allow Snapchat users to "quickly and easily exchange money— such as splitting the bill at a restaurant or paying someone back for concert tickets."[17] Popmoney enables individuals who are online to send money to one another for a fee of $0.95 per transaction.[18] Customers of Ally Bank pay nothing to use the service.[19]

The financial services area is a seething cauldron of innovation, as venture capitalists, entrepreneurs, existing financial firms, and platform providers such as Apple and Google pour billions into financial technology (fintech). There are more than 4,000 fintech start-ups around the world.[20]

Let's take a look at some of the other services being offered that are chipping away at the industry: managing assets, managing hedge funds, and transferring money.

Managing assets for clients is a big business. Registered investment advisers manage more than $2 trillion in assets.[21] These advisers typically charge a commission of 1 percent of the assets they manage.[22] Some of them invest clients' money in actively managed funds that charge additional fees.[23]

Hedge funds manage another $3 trillion.[24] In a fee structure called "two and twenty," hedge fund managers typically charge clients 2 percent of the assets under management and 20 percent of the capital gains. Managers of other types of assets manage trillions more with a wide range of fee structures. BlackRock, the world's largest asset manager, manages more than $5 trillion in assets and offers a wide range of financial products.[25] The top fifty money managers in the United States control more than $25 trillion.[26]

This market creates a lush target for businesses hoping to replace human managers with automatons and move money management services to virtual space. A 0.1 percent reduction in fees would save investors $25 billion, and many of the automated systems charge as little as 0.5 percent. Vanguard uses robo-advisers to manage $4.2 billion in customer funds for a fee of just 0.3 percent of assets. There are lots of other choices if you don't like the Vanguard robot. For example, in some cases Betterment will charge customers even less. Small accounts can choose Wealthfront.[27]

Tellingly, 80 percent of the investment products managed by humans perform the same or worse than those managed by robots.[28] Needless to say, as those robots get smarter and more efficient, they will be even more competitive. And hardworking robots will be happy to earn a 0.25 to 0.5 percent fee. This is good for consumers, but thousands of jobs and billions of dollars in fees will vanish.

Transferring money between parties and countries has been a profitable business for financial institutions for hundreds of years. Many innovations are occurring in this space with a goal of making these systems more convenient, secure, and less expensive.

For as long as banks have existed, customers have searched for ways to reduce charges and eliminate the hassle in making payments. In 45 BCE, Cicero, who lived in Italy, needed Greek money to pay for his son Marcus's education in Athens. Cicero had an Italian friend Atticus, who was owed money by Xeno, who lived in Greece. So, Cicero avoided getting bankers and money changers involved by paying money to Atticus, who then told Xeno to pay for Marcus's education.[29]

More than two millennia later, Patrick and John Collison stand ready to help modern-day Ciceros who are frustrated by complex international payment processes. Their company, Stripe, offers users a customizable payment platform that they can tailor to their needs, significantly reducing the hassle involved in conducting business across national borders.[30] The Collisons, brothers from rural Ireland who just crossed their thirtieth birthdays, are two of the world's youngest billionaires. Their company has fewer than a thousand employees. It had fewer than one hundred as recently as 2014.[31]

WHEN MONEY GOES VIRTUAL

Then there are cybercurrencies such as Bitcoin. Bitcoin has proved that extremely secure, anonymous, inexpensive, and fast payment systems can be implemented using distributed ledgers, a system in which multiple copies of the same ledger are stored on geographically dispersed systems. The ledgers are virtually impossible to hack, because there are so many of them—thousands in Bitcoin's case. If a hacker penetrated one of them to steal something, he would also have to figure out how to alter the records on the thousands of other systems.

By comparison, the single-copy ledgers that banks use to keep track of bank accounts and credit card transactions are much less secure. In payment systems based on distributed ledgers, only the source of a payment is identified; no account information is ever revealed to the payee. This makes it virtually impossible to acquire information from a payee, such as Arby's, to access money from a payer's account.

Transactions using blockchain technology (a form of distributed ledger technology in which data can only be added to databases and not altered or deleted) can also be made very secure and anonymous. In the case of Bitcoin, a cryptographic algorithm is used to ensure that Bitcoins are transferred from the correct payer's wallet to the correct recipient's wallet.[32]

In the credit card world, the typical fee for transferring money is about 2 percent of the size of the transaction, and a merchant will typically have to wait one to three days before money is deposited in its account. Things are very different with Bitcoin. The charge for the transfer is based on the length of the message required to specify the transfer and the current value of a Bitcoin. The fee is constant (typically 0.1 percent of the value of a single Bitcoin), whether one is transferring one dollar or a million. The transfer time can also be speeded up. Users willing to pay higher fees can usually get a transfer completed in two block times, or about twenty minutes. One of the features that Bitcoin users especially like is that, since users in different countries are all using the same currency, there are no charges associated with currency conversion.

In contrast to Bitcoin, even the most secure traditional systems are vulnerable. Hackers have attacked the SWIFT system by stealing the credentials of bank employees. Eighty-one million dollars was stolen from accounts at the Bangladesh Bank, and the hackers might have gotten access to $1 billion more were it not for a typo—the hackers misspelled "foundation" as "fandation," attracting the attention of the New York Federal Reserve.[33]

There are also many practical problems associated with Bitcoin, and for that reason Bitcoin itself will probably have a limited impact. But the blockchain technology it gave the world will be used in many applications with the goal of making transactions more secure. It is highly likely that new virtual currencies using blockchain will be more broadly adopted in the future.

Millions of dollars of Bitcoins have already been stolen from users. The attributes of the technology described above regarding the speed, security, and anonymity of the transfer process make it inherently more difficult to solve Bitcoin thefts. If a thief figures out how to get access to an individual's Bitcoins they can transfer them securely and quickly, leaving no tracks to follow.

JUST BETWEEN US

Peer-to-peer lending and investment groups are springing up all over in virtual environments, with each of them focusing on a different market niche. The Lending Club, Prosper, and Upstart make loans to consumers while providing investors with higher returns and borrowers with lower interest rates. OnDeck, Kabbage, and Funding Circle focus on small businesses and other investment groups' mortgages.[34]

Peer-to-peer lending platforms use their Internet presence to attract investors who are seeking higher interest rates than they can get from bank CDs or by investing in bonds. They attract borrowers by offering lower interest rates or by making loans that banks are not interested in pursuing and they use automated systems to evaluate the creditworthiness of borrowers.

Many banks have found lending to small businesses unattractive. The ten largest banks loaned $72.5 billion to small businesses in 2006 but that number declined to $44.7 billion by 2014.[35] As a result, small businesses have been flocking to peer-to-peer lenders. In many cases, those small businesses generated most of their sales over the Internet. Peer-to-peer lenders who could monitor online businesses and their payment activities were in an excellent position to evaluate their receivables and consequently their loan risk.

Other new ways will be found for peer-to-peer lenders to manage risk. FICO scores will continue to be used, but a great deal of public information is available that correlates with credit risk as well, much of it accessible on social networks. Information about schools attended, area of study, academic performance, and work history all give clues about creditworthiness for both lenders and merchants. Then there are reviews by customers, who discuss their experiences in dealing with a business. Yelp-like systems can be employed. A business that gets lots of good reviews is probably a lower-risk customer.

The industry is small but rapidly growing. Lending Club, the U.S. leader, originated around only $8 billion in loans in 2015.[36] But one market research firm estimates that the worldwide market will grow faster than 50 percent per year and approach a half-trillion dollars in just five years.[37]

As one might expect, entrepreneurs are offering peer-to-peer lending platforms for sale. A company can paste its name on the white-label product and become its own peer-to-peer lender.[38] Using a white-label platform, a company in need of credit could borrow money directly from consumers and become its own bank.

All of these platforms will create alternate sources of credit and investments for consumers and businesses. To compete, banks will offer some of their own peer-to-peer services.

THE VIRTUAL TELLER

At present, the effects of most of these developments on the financial industry have been small. In many cases, the applications are great in theory but do not work all that well in practice. Smartphones use near-field communication systems to talk with in-store payment systems. Sometimes those systems mesh perfectly and at other times they don't. Frustrated customers then return to the old methods of doing business. It will take a number of years to perfect these applications so that they are simple, robust, widely accepted, and convenient.

We tend to forget that the first major credit card, Diners Club, appeared in 1950, and that it took until 1970 before the market began to really scale. Many different groups—consumers, banks, and merchants—had to adopt the technology before it would be broadly accepted. For similar reasons, the virtualization of finance will also take some time.

One of the bigger challenges these new systems face is the existence of legacy systems that use such things as credit card terminals. Mobile payment systems, such as Apple and Android Pay, use them now—but the systems supplied by the likes of Alibaba bypass them entirely. Eventually the legacy systems will be phased out altogether.

The future of virtualization in finance will progress as service providers glue together individual pieces and create broader and more comprehensive sets of consumer services. Those integrated services will run on mobile computing platforms; eventually they will do to cash, credit cards, payment systems, credit facilities, loyalty and gift cards, coupons, boarding passes, and event tickets what the smartphone did to the iPod.

We are beginning to see early signs of this integration. Only 2 percent of transactions in Sweden are made with cash. Nine hundred of its 1,600 banks keep no cash on hand and do not take cash deposits. Many are getting rid of ATMs.[39] Half of the country's population has used Swish, a mobile phone application, to make payments. The country is well on its way to becoming a cashless society.

The banks of the future will be bits floating in cyberspace, their only real-world avatars the mobile payment systems that reside on customers' smartphones. Customers will get their financial advice from a robot whose software is maintained in one of the world's financial centers—London, New York, Tokyo. If they need a loan, there will be seamless interfaces to peer-to-peer lenders. They might choose to have their assets denominated in some form of cyber-currency.

What we have just outlined is speculation. What is certain is that the cumulative effects from these structural transformations will drive us down this path. We may get only a fraction of the way there, but our guess is that we will go all the way there and then much further. New forms using new tools following different rules will emerge.

The reason we choose to look at the financial industry in such detail is that it is a collection of service businesses that are, for the most part, information proxies. The transformation that will take place in other service businesses with high information proxy content will be similar.

A SHARED FUTURE

Many of the most disruptive new business models will emerge in what has been called the *sharing economy*.

Information equivalence is the primary driving force behind the sharing economy, which is also known as the *shareconomy*, *collaborative consumption*, *collaborative economy*, or *peer economy*. All of these terms are used to describe a broad range of economic activities.[40]

Arun Sundararajan does an excellent job of characterizing this phenomenon in his book, *The Sharing Economy*.[41] The sharing economy, he writes, is market based and facilitates the efficient exchange and sharing of goods, services, and human skills. It is crowd-based and not organized around corporate hierarchies. Its supply of labor and capital comes from decentralized sources and exchange is generally mediated by third parties. Full-time jobs frequently get replaced by contract work. Individuals migrate from being employees to "entrepreneurs."

The sharing economy will have great impact in areas where expensive, privately owned assets are underutilized. Automobiles are one such asset. Privately owned automobiles spend as much as 95 percent of their time parked.[42] That means the average car is driven approximately nine hours a week. A number of sharing services have emerged with a goal of monetizing those idle hours. Uber and Lyft are already household names. The twentieth-century relic Zipcar is now owned by Avis.[43] New aspirants keep emerging. Getaround allows neighbors to rent cars from other neighbors by the hour, while a competing service, Turo, focuses on longer-term rentals.[44]

Turo's website claims that owners can cover their monthly car payments by renting their cars for as few as nine days a month. It claims to operate from 4,700 cities, provide owners with liability insurance, and deliver cars directly to their renters.[45] BlaBlaCar, a European service, allows its more than 35 million members to locate other members who are going where they want to so they can hitch a ride.[46] Looming in the future, when the self-driving car arrives, are driverless types of Uber services. The vision is that you will be able to summon a car using your smartphone. It will pick you up, drive you to where you are going, and then speed away to pick up the next passenger.

Car sharing is one of the growth industries of the future. GM estimates that 5 to 6 million people globally already share cars and that that number will grow to 20 to 30 million in the next few years.[47] To capitalize on this trend, GM has launched its Maven car-sharing service, which allows part-time workers in the gig economy to rent a car when they need it to do such things as delivering groceries to paying customers.[48] Maven competes with Mercedes' Car2Go, which "allows customers to take cars one-way inside of a set perimeter and charges by the minute."[49]

Our first thought is that these services compete with cabs and limousine services, but that may be overlooking the depth of the structural transformation. Jeremy Rifkin has speculated,

"Twenty-five years from now, car sharing will be the norm, and car ownership an anomaly."[50] That trend is already under way. Only 78 percent of millennials own cars, compared with 91 percent of the older generations.[51]

Think of what might happen to the automotive manufacturing, services, insurance, and parking businesses if car ownership declined by 25 percent, 50 percent, or even more.

A MATTER OF RATIOS

Office space, temporary accommodations, and vacation rentals are another area where capital assets are underutilized, and the sharing economy is ready to help.

If you are looking for vacation rentals, Airbnb is just one of many services that you can use. Tripping.com has more than 8 million vacation properties listed. Tripping.com competes with Flip-Key, Roomorama, VacayHero, and Wimdu.[52] ShareDesk lets you find on-demand workspace in more than four hundred cities.[53]

A sharing economy service or equivalent exists for just about anything you can think of. That includes sharing people as well. If you want to hire freelance labor for everyday work, TaskRabbit is operating in approximately thirty cities. If you are interested in food delivery, Postmates might be a better alternative.

Sundararajan's book on the sharing economy carries a subtitle, *The End of Employment and the Rise of Crowd-Based Capitalism*. The implication is that, as more work migrates to the sharing economy, it will be less valuable.

Part-time workers now perform jobs that once came with salaries, health care, and other benefits. A part-time Uber worker displaces the fleet taxi driver. A skilled union electrician suddenly finds himself doing part-time work via TaskRabbit. A lot more people are going to be working in the gig economy.

But perhaps the most significant phenomenon of all is what we would call the hub-and-spoke business model, in which a small, highly compensated core group works for a company that organizes the work of hundreds, thousands, and tens of thousands of subcontractors.

Uber has about 12,000 employees and contracts with approximately 1.5 million drivers worldwide—a 100 to 1 ratio.[54] Facebook tops that, with about 25,000 employees and approximately 2 billion active users who provide the company with monetizable content for free, a ratio of 8,000 to 1.[55]

These companies illustrate another of the important commercial trends identified at the start of this chapter: that the sharing economy will drive the transformation of a whole range of commercial enterprises. In some cases, businesses that were capital-intensive will become applications. A hotel is capital-intensive, but Airbnb is an application. Hertz and Avis have large investments in their fleets and pay a lot of money for rental locations and parking lots. Getaround and Turo make use of idle assets, parked cars owned by individuals, and do not have lots of leases to worry about.

Companies that leverage idle assets put great competitive pressures on established companies that own them. Hotels will not go away. Many people will never use shared office space or even consider sharing a stranger's car. But new business models will exert price pressures on many capital-intensive businesses, making it much more difficult for them to grow and compete.

From a commercial and social point of view, the hub-and-spoke model of business in the shared economy may be of greater significance than the asset-sharing aspect. It might be said that the "secret sauce" of the shared economy is the principle that the more workers you can outsource, the better it will be for the owners and senior management.

A permanent employee is a double-edged sword. Loyal, skilled, and committed employees are a great asset. No business can succeed without them. But they are also an expensive burden. Companies have to provide them with health insurance, retirement benefits, vacations, time off for emergencies, and pay them when they come to work, even if there is no work to do. So, in a sense, the Uber and TaskRabbit business models are ideal for employers. The beauty of it is that the free market sets the value of the work done by the non-core employees. Since the company takes a cut of what the contractors make, its fixed costs are very low.

WHEN SUCCESS MEANS SMALLER

In 1997, Clayton Christensen published one of the most influential business books of all time, *The Innovator's Dilemma*. He describes how the very processes that enable market leaders to succeed also set them up for failure when disruptive new products and technologies appear. A common reason is that the market for a new service is too small to meet its needs for growth, so the large company doesn't pay much attention to it—until that market explodes, led by a suddenly powerful new competitor. And then it is too late.

In 1994, when Amazon still only sold books, it probably made a lot of sense for Walmart to keep investing in big stores that sold everything—especially since books were probably not a very important product category for its customers. But in hindsight, it is obvious that Walmart should have taken Amazon on directly from day one. It is the same with new technologies. In retrospect, record companies made a serious mistake when they licensed their music to iTunes and other streaming services. But at the time they saw them as providers of incremental revenue, not as direct competitors. Newspapers probably should have competed directly with Craigslist when they put their content online, but they thought of themselves as purveyors of journalism instead of advertisements.

In coming years, equivalences will power the innovator's dilemma across broad swaths of the economy. But this time things will also be different, because many of the businesses that will replace existing ones will make markets *smaller*. The great new businesses will be shadows of the ones they replaced. Newspapers were big businesses, but the online news services that replaced them employ fewer people and make less money. An application that facilitates the direct transfer of funds will generate less revenue per customer than a credit card company does.

Management will increasingly be bringing a hard-to-swallow message to shareholders: "The investments we are making in this new technology are massive and will allow us to be the leader in a new form of our old business. Unfortunately, the company will be much smaller as a result. You should support our decision to shrink the company, because if we do not take control of the shrinkage, we will be even smaller and less relevant. Or dead." If the shareholders balk, management can point to Sears, Blockbuster, and Toys "R" Us to make their point.

The right strategy for businesses going forward is to attempt to anticipate the effect of the equivalences and to make the commitment to be the leader in the new form of the existing business, even if that business cannibalizes the existing one. In many cases, the new form of business may depend on a new platform—a smart device like an iPhone, an online retail platform like Amazon, a blogging platform like Pinterest, a peer-to-peer payment system, a virtual currency, and so on.

If a business can figure out how to maintain its leadership on these new platforms, its chances of surviving the phase change are greatly increased.

BIG BAADD COMPANIES

In recent years, the public, business leaders, and government officials have become increasingly concerned about the monopoly power of the platform companies—Facebook, Apple, Google, and Amazon. In the words of *The Economist*, these companies and their like are being accused of being BAADD—big, anti-competitive, addictive, and destructive to democracy.[56]

In addition, gaming platforms, which we will discuss further in chapter 8, are accused of using operant conditioning techniques to create addictive behaviors in their users in order to dominate their attention.

The complaints against the behavior and power of dominant platform providers are legion—and growing. Unlike publishers, they do not take responsibility for their content. As a result, they empower trolls and fake news, and enable foreign powers to interfere with elections. They spy on individuals using GPS, Internet cookies, and other techniques to generate advertising revenue. They subtly (and not-so-subtly) steer customers to their own proprietary offerings, putting competitors at a disadvantage. One could go on, but it is safe to say that the monopolies arising in our phase-changed world are no better-behaved than the trusts that arose in John D. Rockefeller's time.

A phenomenon called "network effects" has been powering monopolies in the virtual world. The term refers to the fact that, as networks add nodes, their power increases. These effects have been with us for a very long time—since long before the Internet. Coauthor William Davidow was first introduced to network effects when he was eight years old and his mother told him stories about her own childhood in Reading, Pennsylvania. Three telephone companies served the city. If you were on one network, you could not talk with someone who subscribed to another. Ultimately, one network got ahead in the number of subscribers, and pretty soon, if you wanted to talk with most of your friends, you had to be on that network.

In short, network effects occur because each new user added increases the value of the network to other users. Network effects powered Microsoft's dominance in personal computer applications. As more and more people used its Word program to generate documents, it became easier and easier to exchange documents with others. As a result, it became more desirable to be a Word user.

Similarly, as applications for the iPhone became available, the iPhone became more appealing, and Apple sold more of them. And as Apple sold more iPhones, more and more application providers were motivated to produce applications for it. Today, there are more than 2 million iPhone applications.[57]

The issue of greatest concern is the platforms themselves. In many cases, either it does not make sense or it is extremely difficult to have numerous competing platforms. Today, we essentially have one major social network, Facebook, a dominant online retailer and search engine with Amazon and Google, and two mobile operating systems, Apple's and Google's Android. These BAADD guys are finding all sorts of creative ways to exercise market power, control suppliers, and limit consumer choices.

The platforms have aggressively supported the idea that information, though valuable, should be free. Publishers lacked the market power to resist the trend and, to remain relevant, gave away much of their content, while the platforms made money selling advertising attached to it. Put simply, ads moved from the pages of publications to the servers at Google—and so did the revenues they represented.

Other less publicized battles are being fought as well. Amazon's battle with Hachette is but one example. Amazon's share of online sales grew from 25 percent in 2012, to 33 percent in 2015, to 43 percent in 2016. In 2016, Amazon accounted for 53 percent of the growth in online sales.[58] In books, it accounts for 41 percent of all new book purchases, 67 percent of e-book sales, and 64 percent of online book sales.[59] Fifty-five percent of shoppers start their searches for online purchases on Amazon.

Amazon has made attempts to use its market power to set consumer pricing. For example, Amazon wanted to cut the prices on Hachette's e-books from $14.99 to $9.99, dividing the revenue three ways—30 percent for Amazon and 35 percent each for the author and publisher.[60]

Hachette balked and Amazon retaliated, according to Hachette, by failing to keep Hachette's print books in inventory, which slowed their delivery time from days to two to four weeks.[61] Authors were so disturbed that more than nine hundred of them signed an advertisement in the *New York Times* to protest.[62]

Now, $9.99 is probably an okay price for an e-book (customers certainly like it better than $14.99); but what is not okay is the leverage a company like Amazon will have as its market share grows. In the future, a more powerful Amazon might be able to push that price all the way down to $2.99 and take half. At that point, authors, most of whom are already struggling, might have to supplement their income by flipping burgers.

One of the most concerning aspects of platforms is that they, too, are linked together by network effects. If you control a mobile platform, it gives you the leverage to control a payments platform that uses it. In the case of Amazon, control of a retail platform sets the company up to control a delivery platform.

Smaller businesses that might have been successful if those network effects were weaker get sucked up in the vortex. In many cases, the entrepreneurs of smaller companies feel that if they do not let themselves be acquired, the giant suitor will develop its own competing application and drive them out of business. That is what happened to Snapchat. The company reportedly turned down a $3 billion offer from Facebook. So Facebook added popular Snapchat-like offerings to its own messaging applications—such as new camera filters and a sharing feature called Stories.[63]

Snapchat still managed to go public in 2017 at $17 per share, at a market cap of about $20 billion.[64] But since that time its stock has struggled, and there are many concerns about how the company will fare over the long term in the platform wars.

Instagram was sold to Facebook for $1 billion.[65] Google bought YouTube for $1.65 billion, and Amazon acquired Zappos, the online shoe retailer, for $1.2 billion.[66] In a less connected world, these businesses might have made the decision to remain independent. They might have grown and become competitors with the companies that bought them. Instead, they ultimately served only to further consolidate industry control for an established giant.

In the larger picture, network effects may be slowing down the growth of the economy—or at least that is what some economists speculate. The claim is that big business has become so powerful that we are experiencing a slump in start-ups. Today, companies that have been in business less than a year account for only 8.1 percent of the total number of businesses—as opposed to nearly 15 percent in 1980.[67] Because small businesses have been one of the engines of growth powering the economy—and a major source of new jobs—the concern is that this shortage of fast-growing new start-ups will retard overall economic growth.

The commercial transformation driven by societal phase change is creating a very different business environment. Regulations designed to deal with virtual world issues will be significantly different than regulations designed to solve physical world problems. Of those new issues, the platform monopoly issue is the one of greatest concern to us.

In the physical world, it is pretty easy to agree that it only makes sense to have one electric, gas, or water platform company serving the needs of the community. Increasingly, there is discussion about regulating broadband Internet services in a similar way as a public utility.

But broadband is different. Electricity, gas, and water are consumed directly; the consumer controls and owns the application layer associated with them. For example, the application layer for electricity is the light bulb, for gas the furnace, and for water the shower or faucet.

But in the virtual world, broadband is pretty useless unless it is bundled with the application layer. Try using the Internet without the apps on your smartphone, Google, or Facebook. In order for the free market to work well from the consumer's point of view, there have to be viable choices from a competitive market, and this goes not just for the broadband supplier but also for the application layers.

We are just now waking up to the threats posed by the BAADD guys. Congress is starting to investigate their effects. Europe is substantially ahead of the United States in its thinking. In 2017, Google was fined $2.7 billion by E.U. antitrust regulators for unfairly recommending its platform services over those of competitors.[68] In 2018, Google got hit again when it was fined $5 billion for forcing Android users to preinstall Google's search engine, Chrome.[69]

As the power of the platform companies increases, as more and more platforms come under the control of a few providers, and as the public and regulators become more aware of platform power and the difficulty in making virtual markets truly competitive, there will be more and more pressure to treat the BAADD guys as if they were public utilities.

The commercial transformations discussed in this chapter will present us with many challenging but solvable issues. One of the most difficult will be how we deal with jobs—or the lack of them—in the future. In the next chapter we will look at how phase change has affected work and jobs in the past and how it will likely do so in the future. We will suggest how we can best respond.

To successfully deal with some of the other issues presented in this chapter, we will have to constantly look through the lens of "phase change"—or, in the words of the old Apple ad, we will have to "Think different."

When the telephone and other ways to use electricity were invented, the companies that supplied those services were private enterprises, not regulated utilities. If we were capable of converting them into utilities in the early twentieth century to better serve the public interest, we should be capable of defining the new utilities of the future, perhaps creating them from existing private enterprises, and in the process determining effective ways to regulate their behavior.

This chapter also raised the issue of the few who control these new enterprises becoming very wealthy by living off the labors of part-time, contract—"gig"—workers. The Autonomous Revolution will tend to increase this wealth concentration and exacerbate wealth disparity. If you believe wealth concentration is a problem, and we do, there are tax solutions to this problem.

Again, the new forms of the Autonomous Revolution will require new rules and tools. If we try to deal with the new forms using only the existing methods, significant problems will arise. If we experiment, debate, and search for creative solutions to the challenges, we will find them.

Ultimately, this chapter is a story about abundance. Numerous new, better, and less expensive products and services will be available that will materially improve our lives. But to benefit from them and reduce their undesirable side effects, we are going to have to think differently—and take action, starting *now*.

CHAPTER SIX

THE DEATH OF THE GOOD JOB

The Nature of Work in the Autonomous Revolution

ONE OF THE MOST FRIGHTENING EFFECTS of the Autonomous Revolution is that the new technologies that are replacing the human mind are rapidly creating a widespread shortage of traditional work—from service and blue-collar jobs through positions traditionally held by professionals. For now, though, most of the impact is being felt by blue-collar and entry-level white-collar workers. The "good job," that gateway to and mainstay of the middle class for nearly three quarters of a century, is in steep decline.

The immediate consequence of this has been large numbers of people living lives of despair. Job loss may already be a major contributor to the increasing rates of opioid addiction, fatal overdoses, and suicides—and, for the first time in American history, a decline in life expectancy among white males. In the long run, it could spark a wholesale breakdown of civil society. Democracy is struggling. Hate crimes are on the rise. Our politics are as polarized as they've been since the Civil War.[1]

We believe that the free market should be given a shot at solving the problem of creating good jobs, but it is highly unlikely, for reasons that we will detail below, that it will be able to deal with this problem on its own. We had better prepare ourselves to consider the alternatives, not excluding direct government subsidies to the growing ranks of the permanently un- and under-employed.

During its heyday, the good job was one of history's most powerful weapons for reversing income inequality. Powered by the good job, between 1950 and 1980 family income grew faster for the bottom 60 percent of the population than incomes for the top 20 percent. In particular, income for the poorest quintile increased by 144.1 percent, while the top quintile grew at less than 100 percent and the top 5 percent by just 73.3 percent.[2]

But that situation has been reversed, owing in large part to job capture by autonomous workers.

The autonomous economy employs an endless supply of virtual workers—robots and computers—whose capabilities are increasing at astounding rates and whose costs are declining almost as quickly. When middle-class workers in more and more job categories demand higher pay, virtual workers are happy to step in and take their place for next to nothing.

Our economy is now bipolar, with a traditional economy at one end and a virtual one at the other. The traditional economy is biased toward inflation. The economy at the other end, the Autonomous Economy, is biased toward deflation.

The traditional economy provides us with most of the basic necessities of life—food, shelter, health care, clothing, transportation, and energy. Money spent on these necessities accounts for almost 80 percent of middle-class expenditures.[3] And the costs of all of them are rising.

Between 2012 and 2014, the median home price rose by 17.3 percent, while weekly wages rose by only 1.3 percent.[4] According to the U.S. Department of Agriculture, food prices rose 31 percent between 2005 and 2014, or about 8 percent more than inflation.[5] The cost of health insurance has risen by more than 54 percent in the past five years.

The middle class is mired in this bipolar trough. Real median household income is below the level it was in 2000—$56,671 versus $57,372.[6] Since 2000, the number of lower-income families has increased from 31 percent to 34 percent of the population, while the number of middle-income families has declined from 45 percent to 43 percent. The average weekly hours worked by production employees has declined from 38.8 in the 1960s to 33.7 today. Inflation-adjusted annual earnings for production employees peaked in the 1970s and is down by 14.6 percent.[7] The bottom 50 percent of U.S. taxpayers, approximately 68 million people, had an average adjusted gross income of about $14,800.[8] Those incomes are supplemented by transfer payments on the order of $13,000 per household.[9]

Nobody knows how many autonomous workers are now on the job; all we have is guesses and estimates. But the estimates of the job losses that are to come are staggering. A recent study by Frey and Osborne looked at 702 occupations and concluded that 47 percent of American jobs might be automated in the future.[10]

McKinsey estimates that 85 percent of the simpler business processes can be automated. Many of those processes are in companies that provide services. Using automation, one European bank was able to originate mortgages in fifteen minutes—instead of two to ten days—cutting origination costs by 70 percent.[11] A more recent study by McKinsey estimates that 400 to 800 million jobs around the world will be lost to automation by 2030.[12]

In 2011, W. Brian Arthur was probably the first person to describe the Autonomous Economy. He called it the "Second Economy" and pointed to air travel as a quintessential example of it. As he explained it, thirty years ago, when you arrived at an airport for a flight, you would present a paper ticket to a human being at a counter. That person would register you on a computer, notify the flight that you'd arrived, and check in your luggage.

Today, you walk into an airport and look for a machine. You insert your frequent-flier card or credit card, and, in just three or four seconds, the machine spits out a boarding pass, receipt, and luggage tag.

What interested Arthur about the latter scenario "is what happens in those three or four seconds. The moment the card goes in, you are starting a huge conversation conducted entirely among machines—talk that used to take place between people. Once your name is recognized, computers are checking your flight status with the airlines, your past travel history, your name with the TSA, and no-fly lists. They are checking your seat choice, your frequent-flier status, and your access to lounges."[13]

Now to the sobering part: a sidebar in Arthur's article speculates that by 2025, the output of this Second Economy will be equivalent to the output of the traditional First Economy in 1995—$7.6 trillion, according to a McKinsey estimate.[14]

If the Second Economy achieves that rate of growth, it will be doing the work of approximately 50 million workers.[15] To put that number in perspective, the current total civilian labor force in the United States is about 160 million workers.[16]

Of course, the McKinsey numbers are a guess. Nobody knows precisely how many jobs will be superannuated. But to argue about the correct number or the precise timing is to miss the point. Arthur's estimate points out that the effects of the Autonomous Economy will be very large.

Three factors affect the decline of the good job and work in general.

1. People are no longer required to perform a wide range of functions. This is the structural transformation Arthur described. In the case of the airline jobs he discussed, the form of the business stays the same, but autonomous workers replace employees and their good jobs.

2. The second change, driven primarily by substitutional equivalence, results in new forms of businesses replacing older forms. Netflix's replacement of Blockbuster is such an example. Instead of distributing DVD discs in physical

stores, Netflix streams video over the Internet. Most of Netflix's business now resides in virtual space, and much of its work is done by computers. Tens of thousands of Blockbuster jobs were destroyed and not replaced, and thousands more spillover jobs (in construction, to build new offices; in retail and food service, to serve new workers; in logistics, to move those physical DVDs around) will never be created.

3. The third change is that Information Age tools make it possible to forecast workloads and schedule workers instantly. As a result, companies now use part-time workers in place of full-time employees. They are cheaper and receive fewer, if any, benefits.

The path to the Level 5 Autonomous Vehicle, or aCar, the robot-controlled vehicle that is being developed by Google and many others, provides a concrete way to speculate about the future.[17] Numerous companies aspire to have these vehicles on the road before 2030.[18]

The aCar will make travel safer, cheaper, more enjoyable, and efficient. It will make the nation more capital-efficient and increase its productivity. It will free up as many as 100 million parking places—nearly 800 square miles of space.[19] Unfortunately, it will probably also eliminate a huge number of jobs, cause markets to shrink, and exert downward pressure on wages. These deflationary effects are a result of numerous non-monetizable productivity gains—and they are a microcosm of our virtual economic future. Similar scenarios are being played out in numerous other economic sectors—finance, entertainment, education, media, health care, and so on.

The path to the aCar began in a boring way; all of us have watched it progress over the last quarter century. Cars were gradually equipped with cruise control, engine computers, Bluetooth connections, satellite radios, GPS and Internet mapping services, and emergency services. Consumers love the convenience these technologies provide. Suddenly, we can avoid traffic jams, stay in constant touch with our jobs and families while driving, and never get lost.

More and more technologies are being added: back-up cameras, distance sensors, lane sensors, and so forth. Cars can squeeze into tight parking spaces by themselves and are running into fewer things. The most advanced cars can drive themselves onto freeways, requiring help from their drivers only when they get into difficult situations.

Meanwhile, broadband communications and social networking have made ride and car sharing and other new transportation paradigms more efficient. Suddenly the full-time jobs of 250,000 U.S. taxi and chauffeur drivers are at risk of being taken away by 400,000 mostly part-time drivers for Uber, Lyft, and other services.[20]

Cab companies are already having a difficult time competing. That's not surprising: cab fares in Los Angeles are $2.70 per mile, while Uber charges about $1.00.[21] The oversupply of Uber drivers drives down the price of the service and the value of the work done by drivers. There are other economic impacts as well. Some consumers are discovering that using Uber and occasionally renting a Zipcar or Car2Go is so convenient and cost-efficient that they can get rid of their own cars altogether and just ride and rent.

From the protests of cab drivers, you would think the sky had fallen. Yet in comparison to what is about to come, the economic impacts of all of this have been relatively small. Not for long: the Level 5 aCar will be the game-changer.

Strictly speaking, not much would change—at least initially—if consumers simply purchased self-driving vehicles to replace their existing automobiles, essentially hiring a robot to chauffeur them around. But people who have studied the problem believe another scenario will emerge.

In the autonomous transportation vision of the future, customers will be able to summon a vehicle on demand using their cell phones—a driverless Uber, so to speak. Car ownership will be expensive by comparison.

According to the American Automobile Association study, in 2013 the average annual cost of owning a car driven 15,000 miles per year was $9,122, or 60.8 cents per mile.[22] Of this, ownership costs—depreciation, insurance, registration fees, financing fees—come out to approximately $6,000 per year or 40 cents per mile. Operating costs—primarily gas, maintenance, and repair—are roughly $3,000 per year, or 20 cents per mile.

A study has estimated the cost per mile for using a shared vehicle to be just 41 cents, thus saving the average user about 20 cents per mile. These savings result primarily from the shared costs of ownership. The user who drives 15,000 miles per year would save about $3,000 for every vehicle displaced. Even more remarkable, the same study estimates that a special-purpose vehicle designed for short trips of a few miles could deliver a driverless service at the cost of just 15 cents per mile—just a quarter of the current rate.[23]

Moreover, an MIT study concluded that a shared fleet using one-third the number of vehicles currently owned by individuals would provide three-minute wait times during non-peak traffic environments and maximum wait times of fifteen minutes during peak periods.[24] For many people, fifteen minutes is about equal to the time it takes to get to the parking lot and get in their car.

OUT OF THE DRIVER'S SEAT

What are some of the impacts of such a structural transformation?

Americans own approximately 260 million vehicles.[25] If shared vehicles replace 30 percent of them, and each of those 78 million retired vehicles saves consumers the estimated $3,000, then $234 billion less would be spent on transportation. That's the good news. The bad news is that this would cause about 1.5 million jobs to disappear in automotive related industries—manufacturing, service, insurance, and so forth.

The effects of autonomous vehicles will also be felt in wider swaths of the economy. Level 5 Autonomous Trucks—aTrucks—will move goods faster, more efficiently, and more safely than trucks driven by people. There are 3.5 million professional truck drivers in our country, and about 8.7 million people employed in the trucking business.[26] Many of them will be displaced. If just one-quarter of them are, that's more than 2 million jobs.[27]

No doubt autonomous vehicles will also drive down the costs of delivery services. The business model for groceries, retail stores, and many commodity products will consist of large automated warehouses that deliver products ordered over the Internet to the customer's home or to a convenient location for pick-up within a few hours. Some stores will disappear; others will be transformed into showrooms.

Approximately 15.7 million Americans currently work in the retail sector.[28] By making delivery more convenient and cost-effective, the autonomous vehicle will spur the growth of virtual retailers, which need only about a third as many employees as brick-and-mortar stores to generate the same volume in sales.[29] So, every 10 percent increase in market share by virtual retailers will eliminate on the order of 1 million traditional retail jobs.

Earlier we discussed the structural transformations that are coming in the financial industry. Today, 8 million people are employed in what the government calls "financial activities."[30] As the retail bank changes form and becomes an app on our iPhones, and as robo-advisers take over more and more highly paid financial consultants' jobs, we may see as many as half of those jobs melt into cyberspace. The total number of estimated job losses due to the aCar and the virtualization of finance comes to 8.5 million.

Lost jobs have a multiplier effect. When manufacturing jobs decline in the auto industry, jobs vanish up and down the supply chain as well. People who lose jobs purchase fewer retail goods and eat out less—so a host of service jobs are lost as well.

Estimates vary dramatically about the size of this multiplier effect. One frequently cited Silicon Valley study estimated that every new high-tech job created 4.3 additional jobs in local goods and services.[31] Economists refer to such job additions as the spillover effect.[32] So when a high-tech company hires one new employee, other companies in supporting businesses hire 4.3 more workers, for a total of 5.3 new jobs. Another study found multipliers of 4.6 in automobiles; 2.5 in communications; 1.9 in construction; 1.6 in wholesale trade, transportation, and business services; 1.1 in hospitality; and 0.88 in retail trade.[33]

If we assume that the multiplier works both ways and and pick a fairly conservative multiplier of 2.5, then the total jobs lost would be 2.5 times 8.5 million—or 21.25 million jobs. Thus, the total job loss comes out to about 15 percent of the existing workforce.[34]

Admittedly these numbers are guesses. The aCar effect and the impact on financial services jobs could be larger or smaller. But in looking at just these two areas, we already have identified more than 40 percent of the 50 million jobs that W. Brian Arthur estimated would be absorbed in the Second Economy.

These new business forms substitute for the old ways of doing things. A truck still arrives but it has no driver. We still get our financial advice, but it comes in an email or over the Internet instead of from someone who meets with us in a well-appointed office. It is hard to conceive of these substitutions having the kinds of job creation effects that occurred when the Model T Ford replaced the horse and the semiconductor replaced the vacuum tube.

ERASING EMPLOYMENT

The aCar effect will be repeated across hundreds and very likely thousands of similar scenarios as more and more jobs move from the physical to the virtual economy. People have already been squeezed out of some job categories. For example, in the past a travel agent would use a computer to contact an airline to reserve a place for a passenger and then send the passenger a paper ticket. In 1996, airline customers gained access to reservation systems through Expedia and other online services—and soon after, travel agent employment began a precipitous decline. Employment in the industry peaked at 172,000 in 1999 and declined by 30 percent over the next five years.[35] In 2016, industry employment stood at approximately 65,000, a decline of 62 percent.[36] No one expects those jobs to come back.

This is a good example of the rapid rates of change that occur during transitions to the virtual economy. The decline in travel agent employment of approximately 6 percent per year is about three times the rate of decline in farm employment experienced over the course of 140 years.

Today there are 1.2 million professionals engaged in tax preparation.[37] As more and more tax data flows in electronic formats, many of those jobs will vanish. The system will become increasingly people-less as electronic systems suck in data and automatically prepare the returns, file them electronically, and directly deduct tax payments from bank accounts—while at the same time, the Internal Revenue Service replaces more and more of its auditors with robots. Tens of thousands of tax preparation (and tax compliance) jobs will almost certainly vanish into cyberspace.

Utilities are automating as well. Today, there are 15,600 meter readers. As Internet-enabled meters replace existing stand-alone versions, remotely accessed people-less utility billing systems will emerge.[38] So most of those jobs will also disappear.

The relentless reality is that machines are only going to get smarter.

The legal profession is now a target for attack. Venture capitalists are pouring money into legal tech. Ninety-six million dollars was recently invested in Zapproved. JPMorgan uses COIN to review documents that in the past required legal aides to expend 360,000 hours of work per year. CaseMine, an Indian company, is building systems to aid in document discovery.

A large number of things that government bureaucrats do are done by the book. If a machine can beat a Go champion, it can easily learn how to play many bureaucratic games.

According to the most recent data, labor productivity is growing at a 1.3 percent annual rate, which means that about 2 million workers are displaced every year by productivity improvements.[39] In a traditional economy, where every $150,000 in growth creates a new job, the GDP would have to grow by about 1.7 percent per year to absorb those displaced workers. The good news is that our economy is currently growing at more than 3 percent, so jobs are being created and unemployment has dropped below 4 percent.

Now imagine that our entire economy looked like Amazon, Google, Facebook, and Netflix, companies that are highly productive thanks to virtualization and intelligent machines. Those companies require $600,000 to $1 million increases in income to create a new job, not $150,000. GDP would have to grow at a rate of between 6.8 percent and 11.3 percent to absorb all those displaced workers. No modern developed economy has ever maintained that level of growth. While those companies may create dozens of billionaires and hundreds or even thousands of millionaires, they cannot save the middle class.

Consider what we might call the "Amazon Effect." The Internet has made shopping more efficient and created more competition— and that has driven consumer prices down. But this transformation has had little or no effect on per capita sales. Monthly retail sales adjusted for both inflation and population growth are below where they were prior to the 2008 recession—$165 billion versus $168 billion—and have increased by just 0.6 percent per year in the last fifteen years, or about 10 percent.[40] Meanwhile, employment in the retail and wholesale trades dropped from about 21.2 million jobs in 2000 to 19.9 million in 2010.[41] New technology is not creating new jobs in retail.

What is particularly disconcerting about this jobs scenario is what is missing compared to the past. Two hundred years ago, when jobs were vanishing in agriculture, they were on the rise in manufacturing. Then, as the latter area matured, new jobs were created in the service industries.

Eighty percent of the workforce, 104 million all told, now work in services. But as more and more of those jobs are automated, we need a new area of economic growth to absorb those excess workers. Unfortunately, that area appears to be the burgeoning workerless segment.[42]

Many of the proposals for bringing back the good job involve investing in infrastructure and creating more manufacturing jobs. But here is the challenge: there are only 6.9 million jobs in construction and 12.5 million jobs in manufacturing, a total of about 19.4 million. Because the ratio of manufacturing and construction jobs to service sector jobs is one to five, every 1 percent productivity increase in the service sector would require a 5 percent increase in manufacturing and construction employment to offset its effects.

As pointed out earlier, thanks to non-monetizable productivity, we suspect that productivity increases in the services area have been understated. If productivity growth in services, when measured in terms of output rather than dollars, is more like 3 percent per year, then manufacturing and construction jobs would have to increase at a 15 percent rate to offset its effects, which is significantly less likely to happen than a 5 percent growth rate.

Some might say that our pessimism strikes a discordant note at a time when unemployment numbers are as low as 4 percent and companies are struggling to find skilled workers. Perhaps it does; we would like to believe that we are giving too much weight to our anecdotal observations. But those low unemployment rates have come after unprecedentedly high levels of deficit spending since the 2008 financial crisis. Currently deficit spending is running at a rate of 5 percent. During the fifty years before the economic crisis of 2008, that number averaged around 3 percent and only exceeded

5 percent one time, in 1983.[43] We believe that the current level of deficit spending is unsustainable and that it is masking the job displacement effects of the Autonomous Revolution.

BUILD FOR THE TWENTY-FIRST CENTURY

What then should we do? Unfortunately, there is no silver bullet. The problem demands a number of different actions.

Certainly reducing burdensome regulations, creating a more rational tax structure, better educating our citizens, and increasing investment in science and technology are crucial. But even if we could muster the political will to do those things, all of them taken together would still not be sufficient.

Fortunately, we will have a lot of construction to do. We argued above that it will be difficult to create enough new manufacturing and construction jobs to completely offset the effects of the Autonomous Revolution, but aggressively building infrastructure will certainly help. We believe that we have greatly underestimated the amount of infrastructure that will have to be built to support society in the future.

The reason for our underestimation is that every time humans have made significant advances in the ways we interact, connect, and transfer information to one another, we have transformed the physical infrastructure of society. The transition from tribal cultures to agricultural communities depended on the development of better modes of transportation—wagons drawn by horses and oxen and ships that could transport goods. Cities would never have been viable without the means to get food and energy (firewood at first, and later coal and other petroleum products) in from the countryside and the goods that they manufactured out to distant markets.

The railroad created densely populated industrial cities and the hub-and-spoke pattern of suburban infrastructure, in which homes were built along railroad lines. The automobile created a more sprawling, two-dimensional suburban infrastructure, in which homes, businesses, and shopping centers could be located anywhere a car could reach. A lot of the economic and employment growth of the post–World War II period was created by building those highways, shopping centers, and detached houses.

Just as in the past, our new ways of connecting will necessitate a new kind of physical infrastructure. We will need to do much more than repair and update our bridges, roads, pipelines, and electrical networks.

To understand why, consider that the physical infrastructure of today's society evolved in response to basic information transfer problems. In order to efficiently exchange the information necessary to buy and sell goods, produce things of value, learn, or be entertained, people had to gather in physical places.

Our existing infrastructure assets, and the business processes supporting them, can be seen as information transfer proxies. As noted earlier, consumers go to retail stores in part to find out what is available at what prices—in other words, to get information. Workers go to office buildings to gain access to files and communicate with co-workers. Walmart stores and office buildings are essentially giant file cabinets.

But modern information and communications technologies increasingly remove the need for such proxies. To name some obvious examples, eBay, Google, Wikipedia, Amazon, and Orbitz have each in their own way reversed the traditional requirement that the customer or user must travel—to a garage sale, library, bookstore, or travel agency—to obtain a product or service. Information transfer processes are already efficient enough to allow stores to come to shoppers, files to laptops, and work to workers. And we are only at the beginning of that evolution.

At one time, Internet visionaries believed that people would choose to work remotely and live anywhere they chose. But a different scenario now seems just as plausible, which is that more and more people will choose to live in more densely populated areas that are served by intelligent public transportation. This could create an apartment construction boom. The cities of the future may come to look and feel more like the old cities that Jane Jacobs celebrated and mourned in her book *The Death and Life of Great American Cities* half a century ago—lively, diverse federations of mixed-use neighborhoods, but powered by twenty-first-century infrastructure.

The amount of construction required to create this autonomous country of the future is massive. The American Society of Civil Engineers (ASCE) has estimated that the country has a $3.6 trillion backlog and it is planning to spend only $2 trillion by 2020.[44] Completing the projects identified by the society in a five-year period would require spending an additional $300 billion a year, or about 2 percent of GDP.

The projects identified by the ASCE represent only a fraction of what has to be done to create a robust twenty-first-century infrastructure. Providing 100 million households with FTTH (fiber to the home) would require an investment of between a quarter and a half-trillion dollars—and that's just the tip of the iceberg.[45] Massive investments in public transportation are needed—things like high-speed rail, and possibly even hyperloops that would allow trains to travel at the speed of sound.[46] Substantial portions of our cities and suburbs will need to be retrofitted or rebuilt from scratch.

In the 1960s and 1970s, when the 41,000-mile Interstate Highway System was being completed and the suburban population was burgeoning (it almost doubled between 1950 and 1970), construction spending ran 10 to 11 percent of GDP.[47] It falls in the 5 to 6 percent range today,[48] so it could easily double.

Creating the construction boom of the future would undoubtedly involve government subsidies and programs similar to Eisenhower's Federal-Aid Highway Act of 1956.[49] It would also involve tax incentives to encourage entrepreneurs to build the right kinds of infrastructure.

These arguments about construction obviously go against the

notion that white-collar work bolstered by a college education will be the best defense against the depredations of job loss due to robots and artificial intelligence. In fact, building and trades, traditional blue-collar work, could well turn out to be the Last Stand of the Good Job.

Another opportunity lies in entrepreneurship. New companies are the major source of new jobs in the U.S. economy. Unfortunately, new business formation has dropped to a forty-year low that is about 25 percent behind its best year.[50] Our lawmakers hardly seem to have noticed that fact—after all, small start-ups are too busy to do much lobbying on their own account, even if they could afford to. Because of that, legislators typically ignore entrepreneurs or freight them with company-killing regulations. But an economy that actively cultivated new company creation might be able to generate hundreds of thousands of those start-ups per year—and generate 1 or 2 million new jobs.[51]

BEYOND A FREE MARKET

As far as we can tell, the ideas above exhaust the free-market solutions that will have a major impact on the problem. Finding ways to better compensate large numbers of content providers will also help, but they are unlikely to create millions of high-paying jobs. If the goal is to create more meaningful work and raise the income levels of the less fortunate 60 percent, it will have to involve government programs, direct subsidies, and some form of income redistribution.

One of the most creative and well-thought-out proposals for addressing this issue that we have seen comes from the arch-conservative writer Charles Murray, who has proposed basically terminating all welfare programs and replacing them with a basic income of $13,000 per year for all citizens over the age of twenty-one. Everyone would be required to spend $3,000 on health insurance. Payments would start to taper off after someone was earning more than $30,000 per year.[52]

Murray argues that the savings resulting from the elimination of entitlements would be enough to finance much of the plan.

One of the most common objections to universal basic income (UBI) proposals is that they undermine the self-esteem and personal identity that comes with having a job. Opponents of UBI paint pictures of twenty-one-year-old white males living in cheap apartments, hooked on opioids, playing video games ten hours a day, and contemplating suicide. But as Murray points out, the plan would not incentivize unemployment, because everyone would still have to work to live at a comfortable level. And since everyone would receive payments, there wouldn't be a stigma attached to them.

Another approach to consider is a version of the French solution—cutting the workweek. Let's talk a little history and Information Age reality. The workweek has been declining for many decades. In the early 1800s, it was seventy hours. It fell to fifty hours in the early 1900s and then to forty hours.[53] For a large number of Americans, the less than thirty-five-hour workweek is already a reality. Part-time employees now make up 18.5 percent of the workforce, up from about 16.6 percent in the year 2000.[54]

Of course, creating jobs with shorter workweeks and less pay would not put more wealth in the hands of the less fortunate 60 percent. Some kind of income subsidy would still be needed. Possibly the government could consider subsidizing the first twenty hours of work that employees perform with direct cash payments. Those subsidies could be reduced if a worker worked more than, say, thirty hours per week.

Perhaps the greatest opportunity for creating meaningful work will be to find ways to pay people who do socially useful work that today has no monetary value. Consider people who pay others for childcare during working hours, or families who pay thousands of dollars per month to a service provider for an infirm adult who lives in an adult care facility. If those children or elderly persons are cared for by family members at home, that same work is done for free.

Is there a workable alternative that monetizes the last scenario? It would be difficult to figure out how such a system might work—much less administer it. But it is easy to argue that doing socially useful work benefits society and, by freeing talented workers, also benefits the economy. Here is a perfect opportunity for creative minds to come up with a workable solution.

There is so much that is unknown. And there is always the possibility that the free-market optimists are right. So let's by all means keep pushing the free-market solutions and pursue an aggressive construction agenda. If we do the right things to prepare for the Autonomous Revolution, construction could easily hit 10 percent of GDP. But let's also start experimenting with some of the subsidy approaches as well. The experience we gain will help us avoid some mistakes if we have to roll them out in a bigger way. Let's also search for ways to pay people for performing socially useful work.

The one thing that is certain is that phase change will alter the rules. The sooner we confront the problem—and learn the new rules—the sooner we will uncover workable solutions.

LIBERTY AND PRIVACY

Escaping the Algorithmic Prison

IF SOME LATTER-DAY PATRICK HENRY were to stand up in Congress today and reprise his "Give me liberty or give me death" speech, the target of its invective would likely be the rulers of the Internet.

The liberation Henry demanded in 1775 was not just from England. After the Revolutionary War had been fought and won, he refused to attend the Constitutional Convention, lest a too-strong national government become as tyrannical as that of King George III. To counter the fears of Henry and other anti-Federalists, a Bill of Rights was appended to the Constitution that explicitly upheld individuals' rights of worship, a free press, trial by jury, the right to petition the government, and so on.

In the world of the Autonomous Revolution, the most insidious threats to our liberties are posed not by governments (in democratic countries, at least), but by the commercial enterprises and groups with social, political, and belief agendas that are increasingly reading our files and our minds, predicting and seeking to influence our behaviors, and controlling our actions and access to information and opportunities.

When James Madison drafted the first ten amendments to the Constitution, incursions on human liberties occurred in physical space. In response, property lines could be drawn on maps. Doors had locks. Prison was a place that you were taken to in handcuffs. Trials took place in courtrooms, where defendants were represented by attorneys and judgments were rendered by juries of their peers.

It is fair to assume that if Madison had known about information and spatial equivalences, his Bill of Rights would have been more expansive. If he had been able to imagine virtual space—the space created on the Internet by institutions such as Facebook, Google, and Amazon—he would have demanded that liberty and freedom be guaranteed there, too. If he had anticipated that individuals would be tried and convicted in absentia by invisible algorithms, he would have searched for a way to prevent that. If he had understood the ability of commercial enterprises and groups with social, political, and belief agendas to influence and control human actions and behavior, he would have found ways to constrain the behavior of these commercial shadow governments.

Societal phase change has altered both the form of unreasonable search, commercial punishment, and the nature of imprisonment. It is almost impossible to get a fair trial in virtual space, and when it's over, you might not even know the verdict or understand that you have been imprisoned. All that you will know is that many of the things that you are reaching for are always just beyond your grasp—such as that great new high-paying job that no one will interview you for.

And you may be completely guiltless: imagine the loan company that thinks you are late on a car payment that in fact was lost in their system due to a software upgrade. In response, the loan company remotely disables your ability to start your car. Picture the virtual hassle as you argue over the phone with an unsympathetic automaton.

In what follows, we will discuss these new threats to liberty and the new processes that are empowering them. We will explain why the currently proposed solutions to them are doomed to be ineffective. We will make the case that if we are serious about maintaining our privacy and freedom, we will have to consider adopting a different business model for the Internet. And we will describe how that business model should look.

Our discussion will focus on trends that are already occurring in the free market and that we believe pose the greatest threats to the liberties of individuals living in liberal democracies. For those who live under authoritarian regimes like those in China, Russia, and Iran, or in formerly democratic countries that have taken an authoritarian turn, such as Turkey and Hungary, the more pressing concern, obviously, is government surveillance via virtual technologies of the sort that Orwell feared. If you are a Uighur living in Xinjiang in northwestern China, where your ID card indicates your "reliability status" and CCTV cameras surround you and record your face and license plate wherever you walk or drive, we understand that our focus on commercial institutions may seem naïve.[1]

Even democratic governments are undertaking activities that should be raising alarms. The use of metadata to track our phone calls; the increasing use of automated number-plate recognition (ANPR) by local police departments to track our movements; the use of Cellebrite services by ten thousand law enforcement agencies to analyze what we do on our smartphones; artificial intelligence software that predicts where crimes might be committed and who might commit them; and numerous other spy tools are all deeply troubling.[2]

You would also be right to be concerned about the next advances in emotion detection, in which the same cameras used to track and recognize your face are enhanced to detect your emotions. By analyzing the narrowing and widening of eyes, a grimace, the tightening of the jaw, a smirk, or a smile, they will be able to tell whether someone at a party rally is a supporter of a totalitarian regime or a dissident.

You should also be deeply concerned that in 2014 Facebook filed for a patent on an "emotion detection" technology that will likely be used to influence and control your behavior. After all, leveraging the individual's emotional state is the key to creating emotional contagions that create fashion trends, polarize countries, and empower authoritarian regimes.[3]

Fortunately, to date the misuse of these technologies has affected only a relatively small percentage of the citizens of democracies, and the protests against them have been appropriately vigorous. But the life of virtually every citizen in these democracies has already been affected by the misuse of personal information by private industry. We have been so numbed by the wondrous applications and so value the free services we are being offered that we have come to passively accept and ignore the massive exploitation of our daily lives.

The cry of a modern-day Patrick Henry protesting the commercial misuse of our personal information would be "Give me liberty or give me intolerable inconvenience." For as we will see, if we do not do something radical to change the vector we are on, we will be condemned to a life of constantly erasing cookies to protect our privacy, discovering misleading information about ourselves that has been distributed across the vast Internet universe, and then engaging in frustrating, time-consuming, and often expensive exchanges, probably with machines, to get the information corrected.

When new tools made it frictionless to collect information about us and to parse it to not only know what we are thinking now but also how we are likely to behave in the future, a critical tipping point was passed. Some of the factors involved were:

1. The dramatically reduced cost of collecting data on individuals over the Internet

2. Having knowledge of customer location because low-cost GPS was integrated into smartphones

3. Being able to identify individuals, track their movements, and analyze their emotions using facial recognition software and low-cost cameras[4]

4. The willingness of individuals to freely post information about themselves on social media

5. The widespread access to public records

6. The development of artificial intelligence tools that empower the owners of big data to look into our minds, influence our thoughts, predict our behavior, and motivate us to act in specific ways

Nowadays, if you want to shop anonymously, you should probably wear a face mask. Otherwise, shopping malls and retail stores will track your every move around the store. They ostensibly do so for security reasons, but they also derive a commercial benefit from the intrusion.[5] Fifty-nine percent of fashion retailers in the UK use video data to determine such factors as what items or point-of-sale advertisements best grab customer attention.[6]

When you visit Internet sites, cookies and tracking pixels are installed on your computer or phone. Using these pixels, advertisers can determine how many people see their ads and visit their websites, how long they spend looking at advertisements, and what motivates them to make a purchase.[7] Companies using this technology are asked to voluntarily comply with the industry's Online Interest-Based Advertising Accountability Program and inform users that they are being tracked. This is accomplished by displaying a small blue triangle on their ads.[8] In theory, this gives the consumer a heads-up, so he or she can opt out of the program. But few consumers notice the blue triangle or know what it means, and fewer still know how to opt out—and companies are quite content to keep them ignorant.

Cookies have multiple purposes, many of them beneficial for the customer. They allow sites to recognize return visitors and customize what they are shown. They can also be used to track their users' activities. At any given moment, a lot of sites can be watching. In one case, a reporter discovered that 105 different Internet companies tracked his behavior over a thirty-six-hour period.[9]

Some sites will aggressively load your browser with cookies.

Dictionary.com, which claims to be the world's leading online source for English definitions, has been known to cram two hundred tracking cookies onto a user's browser just because that user wanted the definition of a single word.[10] Even if the user employs DoNotTrackMe plug-ins, companies have found ways to create "flash cookies" in Adobe's Flash player to overcome that defense.[11]

The Internet will get even more intrusive in the future. It is highly likely that Internet service providers such as Comcast and Verizon, which can already capture data on every site you visit on the Internet, will be allowed to sell your personal information without your permission.

And that is only part of the problem. Increasingly, you don't even need to log onto the Internet to make your personal information available to the Web. Stanford faculty member and former Microsoft executive Mike Steep recently conducted a test to see what happened to his data. He placed a couple of posts on social networking sites, joined friends for dinner at a Palo Alto restaurant, and bought an item at a CVS drugstore. Then, using a special auditing tool, he tracked what happened.

Within the first ninety days, those four pieces of data proliferated into 500 records on corporate servers scattered around the world. The CVS visit, he found, had been scraped by Apple and then used by Facebook. Within six months, the footprint of these minor events had grown to 1,500 entries—"all items I never entered on an order form," says Steep. "If you think there is privacy anymore, you are dreaming."

NOWHERE TO HIDE

The erosion of our privacy has been growing for many years. It began to gather momentum as credit rating agencies—Experian, TransUnion, and Equifax—along with companies like Acxiom and ChoicePoint, grew their massive databases. Acxiom, for example, looks at 50 trillion data transactions per year and maintains a database on 500 million consumers worldwide, with about 1,500 pieces of information per person.[12]

When Reed Elsevier purchased ChoicePoint (LexisNexis Risk Solutions) in 2008, it became public that the service had 17 billion records and had sold information to 100,000 clients.[13] Some of the information it had was of value to the government, but federal law didn't allow government agencies to collect it themselves. No problem: it was perfectly legal for them to purchase that same information on the commercial market, which is one reason that seven thousand of ChoicePoint's customers were government agencies.[14] You can be sure all of those numbers have grown in the years since.

Which isn't to say that the government has subcontracted all of its information-gathering; it still does plenty of surveillance itself. All of us have watched spy movies in which a bug is planted in someone's phone or a camera is hidden in a chandelier—but who would have thought that those secret microphones have already been installed in countless homes and that the secret agents who did it were the homeowners? Many of us were surprised to learn that the CIA can and does hack into "endpoints" like smartphones and watch and listen to their owners through their microphones and cameras. Using a tool called Weeping Angel, a TV can be put into a fake "off" mode and turned into a listening device.

"Smart speakers," such as Amazon's Alexa-equipped Echo, are always listening for the next command and they can easily be hacked.[15] As IoT devices that can see, hear, and monitor surrounding activity proliferate, the NSA's job gets easier and easier.

We could go on for pages, but the key point is that it now costs just fractions of a penny to monitor our Internet behavior and track us in physical space. Using that information, companies, institutions, and the government can learn about our tastes, discover our thoughts, and predict our behavior. And they can use those same tools to shape our thoughts, manipulate our elections, control our behavior, motivate us to act, and deprive us of our freedoms.

WHEN CUSTOMERS BECOME PRODUCTS

Another critical tipping point that enables companies' new business models turns traditional commerce upside down. Increasingly, users of media are no longer customers so much as they are products.

The transition point between customer and product is fuzzy, with no bright demarcation line. Think of it this way: in the past, people used to subscribe to newspapers and magazines. They paid modest amounts; subscription revenues accounted for only about 20 percent of newspaper companies' income.[16] Advertisements paid for the rest.

Of course, the subscribers were always part product, since advertisers paid publications for their subscribers' attention. Publications also supplemented their advertising revenues by selling subscriber profiles and mailing lists. But the information about their customers that publications captured was typically very coarse and circumscribed. A media company could tell you that a customer lived in a particular zip code, that the average income level in that zip code was $100,000 per year, and that voters from that zip code were predominantly Republican. But that was about it. From that limited information, you would have to infer whether the individual in question was a likely customer. The poor quality of this kind of information led to the famous quote by John Wanamaker, "Half the money I spend on advertising is wasted; the trouble is I don't know which half."[17]

This is very different from knowing, as is the case today, what the customer reads, where he shops, whether her friends also shop at a particular store, what his friends like and purchase, and that she has been searching the Internet for low prices on a particular brand of luxury car. Of particular import is that today's technologies allow advertisers to glean granular data about the tastes and buying motivations of individual customers, not just the broad strokes of their demography.

Needless to say, the value of the information that businesses could collect increased dramatically when this transformation hit—at the same time that the cost of collecting it plummeted. That enabled businesses to sell valuable access to targeted customers at very attractive prices. For example, researchers from Ohio State University discovered that click-through rates increased by 670 percent when ads were behaviorally targeted. The targeted ads also appeared to have a positive effect on consumers' psyches, making them more likely to purchase.[18]

As media businesses came to understand this, their consumers transitioned from being mostly customers and somewhat products to being mostly products and somewhat customers who could be sold to advertisers and other businesses at a steep profit. The result of the structural transformation was a brand-new phenomenon: widespread implementation of free or "freemium" business models,[19] in which a service is provided for free, though the hidden price is the customers' privacy.

The freemium model has, in fact, been around for a very long time. In an obvious example, commercial radio and broadcast television have depended upon it for years. Customers get to listen to and view programming for free, while making themselves into a captive audience for the advertisers who pay for it. But there is a big difference between the freemium business models of the past and those of today.

In the past, the quality of the information sold to advertisers was pretty bad. For that reason, it was not especially valuable. By comparison, the information sold today is very good and actionable, and is thus worth a great deal more. Also, the services and content provided to users in the past were good but not great. Today, you can still get all of those legacy services. But on top of that, you now get access to vast libraries of past content. On YouTube you get content packaged to match not just your demographic but also your specific needs and interests. To top it off, you get access to history's largest indexed library. Virtually all human knowledge is at your fingertips. In short, the freemium business model went from being limited and of low quality to being as good as it can get.

The reader may feel that consumer information is the product being sold by these new companies ... but we believe it is more accurate to say that the consumer himself or herself is the real product because, as a result of the sale of information, the consumer has surrendered his or her privacy—and with it, a piece of personal sovereignty.

In this new world, perhaps the best way to think of the customer is as a personal information production factory. By searching the Internet, posting on Facebook, clicking on websites, and driving a car to a specific location, the customer produces actionable and hence monetizable personal information product. To carry the metaphor further, the customer uses his or her own capital equipment (computer, smartphone, or automobile) to produce the tracking information being sold by commercial companies. In some cases (Facebook, Instagram, Twitter) they even produce the content themselves, in the form of their posts.

If I own a factory in the real world, I get to sell my product at the price I choose. If I put my product on the shipping dock and you steal it, I can have you put in jail.

Compare that to the freemium business model that now prevails in the virtual world: Internet companies take the valuable personal information product that users leave on their shipping docks and do not pay them anything for it beyond the services or content they have already used or seen. When they sell that information to a third party for a lot of money, the producer of that information does not get to share a penny.

The reason Facebook and Google are so profitable is that they are skillful at arbitraging the difference between the price they paid for the personal information product—zero—and the price at which they sell that product to advertisers. Because that later transaction is largely invisible, the information producers feel they are getting a good deal.

By turning the customer into the product, commercial enterprises have built massive databases with two basic objectives: first, to influence the choices that consumers make; second, to exert control over them and motivate them to take certain actions. When companies target ads at potential customers and decide what information to provide, they are using their massive databases to help influence consumer choices. When companies use the information in databases to decide not to sell you automobile insurance or not to tell you about a job you might want to apply for, they are using information to control consumers. If they decide to tell you about a certain product but not about a competing one, they are attempting to channel and control your actions.

If you are concerned about your liberty, you should be deeply concerned about the growing number of these databases and the ways they can be used to restrict your choices.

INVISIBLE PRISONS

Companies and the government use algorithms to make important decisions about us. Employing massive data files, they profile us and predict our tastes, spending habits, and even our creditworthiness and moral behavior—and take actions accordingly.

As a result, some of us can no longer get loans or have trouble cashing checks. Others are being offered only usurious credit card interest rates. Many have trouble finding employment or purchasing health insurance because of their Internet profiles. Others may have trouble purchasing property and insurance of all kinds. Algorithms also select some people for government audits, while subjecting others to gratuitous and degrading airport screenings. In fact, millions of Americans are now virtually incarcerated in what can only be characterized as *algorithmic prisons*. They are still able to move about in the world but can no longer fully participate in society. They are virtual prisoners.

The FBI has 100,000 names on its no-fly list; about 1,000 of them are U.S. citizens.[20] Thousands more are targeted for enhanced screening by the Transportation Security Administration (TSA). By using data, including "tax identification number, past travel itineraries, property records, physical characteristics, and law enforcement or intelligence information," the TSA's algorithm predicts how likely a passenger is to be dangerous.[21] The agency then acts accordingly.

In the past, it was possible to sneak around the edges. Unfortunately, the Internet has perfect recall and X-ray vision. Most of us have done dumb things that we would never do again. Some of us have said things in private that we would never discuss in public. Some of us have made racist and misogynistic comments on chat boards. We might have been trolling, or maybe we were spurred on by other commenters on the site.

Then there are those nude photos we might have sent to a lover. Or the drunken debauchery of a frat party. We might have posted something regretful on Facebook the morning after we got overly aggressive while engaging in consensual sex. After a tough day at work, we might have railed against our boss and even mused about hurting him. If we lost our job, we might have visited an anti-capitalism website. Maybe we are a Muslim and spent time checking out an ISIS website. We might have even sent a message to a recruiter. Perhaps we did a lot of those things before we were twenty-five years old—and now years have gone by and we are looking for a job.

Suppose one of those algorithmic prisons has a lot of 100 percent factual information about us, including "made threatening comments about his boss," "thought about joining ISIS," "may have forced himself on a woman," "may be alcoholic." We suspect that information would put us at the bottom of the candidate list of any job opening for which we might apply.

Algorithms constrain our lives in virtual space as well, whether we have done anything regrettable or not. They analyze our interests and select the things we see. In doing so, they limit the range of things to which we might be exposed. As Eli Pariser puts it in his book *The Filter Bubble*, "you click on a link, which signals your interest in something, which means you are more likely to see articles about that topic" and then "you become trapped in a loop."[22] You are being shown a distorted view of the world. In a very tangible sense, you are the subject of discrimination.

If you're having trouble finding a job as a software engineer, it may be because you got a low score from the Gild, a company that predicts the skills of programmers by evaluating the open-source codes they have written, the language they use on LinkedIn, and how they answer questions on software social forums.[23]

Algorithmic prisons are not new. Even before the Internet, credit reporting and rating agencies were a power in our economy. Fitch's, Moody's, and Standard and Poor's have been rating business credit for decades. Equifax, the oldest credit rating agency, was founded in 1899.[24] But the new software, combined with the pervasiveness of the Internet and the latest data analysis tools, represents a whole new level of control.

When algorithms get it right (and in general they do a pretty good job), they provide extremely valuable services. They make our lives safer by identifying potential threats to our society. They make it easier to find the products and services we want, increasing the efficiency of businesses. For example, Amazon constantly alerts me to books it correctly predicts I will want to read. But when algorithms get it wrong, inconvenience and sometimes real suffering follows.

Most of us would not be concerned if ten or a hundred times too many people ended up on the TSA's enhanced airport screening list, so long as an airplane hijacking was avoided. Similarly, in times when jobs are scarce and applicants many, most employers would opt for tighter algorithmic screening. After all, there are lots of candidates to survey, and more harm may be done by hiring a bad apple than by missing a potentially good new employee. Meanwhile, avoiding bad loans is key to the success of banks. Missing out on a few good clients in return for avoiding a big loss is a decent trade-off. That is, until the person who is inconvenienced or harmed is us. As the cost of surveillance gets cheaper and the tools more pervasive, the likelihood of that happening is increasing.

The federal Consumer Financial Protection Bureau lists more than forty consumer-reporting companies. These are services that provide reports to banks, check cashers, payday lenders, auto and property insurers, utilities, gambling establishments, rental companies, medical insurers, and companies wanting to check employment histories. The good news is that the Fair Credit Reporting Act requires those companies to give consumers annual access to their reports and allows a consumer to complain to the Consumer Financial Protection Bureau if he or she is being treated unfairly.[25] But how many of us want to spend time regularly checking reports from two score companies and then filing paperwork with the Consumer Financial Protection Bureau to appeal an injustice?

Even if an algorithmic prisoner knows that he or she is in jail, that person may not know why or who the jailer is. Unable to get a loan because of a corrupted file at Experian or Equifax? Or could it be TransUnion? This person's personal bank could even have its own algorithms to determine a consumer's creditworthiness. Just think of the needle-in-a-haystack effort consumers must undertake if they are forced to investigate dozens of consumer-reporting companies, looking for the one that threw them behind algorithmic bars. Now imagine a future that might contain ten or maybe a hundred times as many algorithms that pass judgment upon you.

It is impossible to fathom all the implications of algorithmic prisons. Yet one thing is certain: even if they do have great economic value for businesses and make our country somewhat safer, many of us will be seriously harmed as algorithmic prisons continue to proliferate . . . and still more of us will experience great frustration.

The Fifth Amendment guarantees American citizens due process in physical space. But what due process standards apply to algorithms? The Fifth Amendment also ensures that we are not tried twice for the same offense. But if there are hundreds of sites out there, they could all be trying and punishing us for the same "crime."

The Sixth Amendment guarantees citizens a fair trial. But most algorithms base their decisions on economic rationales. If mistakes are costly, then the algorithms will err on the side of caution, reversing one of the most fundamental principles of common law, Sir William Blackstone's formulation: "It is better that ten guilty persons escape than that one innocent suffer."[26]

Attempting to free yourself from algorithmic prisons could make you resemble the tragic protagonist of Kafka's *The Trial*. How do you correct a credit report or get your name off an enhanced screening list? Each case is different. The appeal and pardon process may be very difficult—if there is one—and you might have to repeat it at each of the offending companies. And before everything, you need to realize that you actually *are* in prison.

Bruce Schneier's recent book *Data and Goliath: The Hidden Battles to Collect Your Data and Control Your World* addresses a host of potential protections for consumers, including protecting whistleblowers, making vendors liable for privacy breaches, and passing laws that protect certain categories of personal data—financial data, health care information, student data, video rental records, and so on. Individuals should be entitled to know what data is being collected about them, he writes, and how the algorithms that pass judgment actually evaluate that data.[27]

Transparency is good in principle, but it doesn't solve the problem on its own. Just envision yourself going through pages of disclosures every time you visit a website to determine what data is being collected on you and whether or not you agreed to that collection. Think of the time it would take merely to understand the algorithms. Then imagine the frustration that would occur as companies continually modify their policies.

Schneier does offer users practical advice on some of the steps they can take to deflect or foil surveillance—including configuring your browser to delete cookies every time you close it, closing your browser numerous times a day, and entering random information onto Internet forms to confuse Google profiling.

These solutions offer an excellent early glimpse of the nature and magnitude of the threat. But most of them are hard for regular, trusting, law-abiding people to implement in the course of their daily lives. People want to use email and the Internet without having to worry constantly about guarding the gates to their lives. We need a practical solution that is simple and puts the user back in control.

DEFENDING PRIVACY

Throughout this book, we have argued that phase change creates new rules and new institutions. In many cases, we will need to establish new laws and regulations to control the behavior of those new institutions.

One example of this is the General Data Protection Regulation (GDPR) that the European Union put into effect on May 25, 2018.[28] The rule requires opt-in consent from users before data can be collected; that "by-default" sites use the highest possible privacy settings; and that personal data be made more difficult to tie back to an individual, either by using pseudonymization or a stronger form of encoding anonymization. Users must be informed of how long their data will be retained and be given the right to be digitally "forgotten." Controllers would also be forced to design data protection into all systems by default, thus reducing the chances of theft.

If the United States were to adopt its own version of GDPR, it would certainly help. Until then, users will have to do a lot of work themselves to ensure they are protected. On a website run by Oath, the media firm created by the merger of AOL and Yahoo!, a user is asked for consent to "use your . . . data to understand your interests and personalize and measure ads." If the user does not agree, he or she has the option to follow links . . . only to then discover that had they agreed, the user would have granted Oath permission to share their data with more than one hundred ad networks.[29]

It is highly likely that the GDPR will be improved and strengthened in the coming years. After all, it superseded weaker legislation—the Data Protection Directive—implemented in 1998.[30] So one approach to solving the problem is to chip away at it, every decade or so bringing out a new version of the GDPR. In all likelihood this will be the chosen solution.

Still, we would argue that the GDPR is an all-too-typical example of using Industrial Revolution rules to deal with Autonomous Revolution issues.

If we really want to solve the problem of Internet privacy, we have to engage in phase-change solution thinking. What is really broken here is the defective freemium business model of the Internet—and the way to solve that problem is to give the user complete ownership and control over his or her data.

One way to do this would be to create information fiduciaries that would hold individuals' information. Think of the fiduciary as a personal information safety deposit box that can be unlocked only if the holder supplies a key or knowingly withdraws the information and sends it to the desired recipient.

These fiduciaries would have the right to collect all the personal information they can from legal sources. The owner, in turn, would have complete control over who can access the information stored with a fiduciary.

The fiduciary would organize the information by tiers or levels. The first level would be pretty innocuous stuff, while the highest level would be highly sensitive kinds of information that an owner would permit only a limited number of institutions to view.

The individual—the owner—would have the right to examine the information in his or her file at any time. For simplicity's sake, the owner might opt to use only one fiduciary, and he or she would have the ability to work with that fiduciary to correct any misinformation. Should the owner choose to release information to an Internet site, it would be illegal for that site to sell it or provide it to a third party.

Here is the way such a system could work. Suppose an information owner wants to get free services from Google. He or she would agree to provide Google with First Level information in return for its services. Google might deem the owner's First Level information not valuable enough to warrant those services and ask for Second Level information as well, or, if that's not acceptable, propose a fee, say $5 a month.

Perhaps an auto insurance company wants access to the owner's Fourth Level information to determine what price it will give her on her insurance. She could agree to give the company access, but it would not have the right to use that data for any other purpose.

We suspect the fiduciaries of the world would love this business model because they would charge information users for access to the information.

A NEW KIND OF PRIVACY SERVICE

What would it take to begin this transformation of the privacy model? It would begin by turning companies such as Equifax, Experian, TransUnion, Acxiom, and ChoicePoint into those fiduciaries. Even a company like Google or Facebook could establish and offer fiduciary services.

What about the algorithmic prisons? Suppose one of those prisons was very good at analyzing credit risk, and a lot of banks wanted to use its services. A bank could agree to pay the prison for analyzing a person's private information. With the explicit permission of that person, the bank would get access to his or her information from their information fiduciary. Once the prison had performed this task for the bank, it would by law erase the information and not use it for any other purpose.

This concept of an information fiduciary would have an added benefit: it would offer a high level of protection against illegal search and seizure by the government. The government could not buy our information on the open market. Instead, it would be required to obtain a search warrant to look at the information stored with the fiduciary.

Of course, this is a radical idea. Many people—and institutions—will object to it. But think about it this way:

Our current situation just happened. No one really understood what was going to transpire, so we just sat back and watched. Now we are stuck with a system that has some very undesirable aspects. But suppose for a moment that, at the turn of the twenty-first century, the visionaries of the Internet had appeared before Congress and said:

> As we go through the process of adapting to phase change, we have a choice between using our old rules to chip away at the problem or adopting a radical new approach that can cure it. We believe the right approach is the radical one, because our individual liberties are too precious to put at risk.

Had that occurred, had new institutions based on the new rules been instituted, the Internet would have evolved very differently from what it has become today. Had the freemium model never been allowed to emerge, many of our current threats to privacy might be all but unknown.

Purging the existing model as we have suggested above would be gut-wrenching and extremely difficult, but we believe it offers the best solution to the problem. But other approaches would also greatly improve the situation.

There is a lot of hard work to be done, but if we commit to aggressively attacking the problem we can have our privacy and our liberty for years to come.

CHAPTER EIGHT

WITHIN THE CHIMERA

Living in a Virtual World

VIRTUAL SPACE, which once seemed so benign, has proved to be a treacherous environment. People who venture too far into it have been known to die from exposure—some after just 24 hours. Others have survived for as long as 650 hours (twenty-seven days!) before their hearts gave out.[1] In China, the government has shut down thousands of Internet cafes and required game developers to install anti-addiction safeguards.[2]

It's not just gamers who lose themselves in the Internet. Other regular visitors to virtual spaces become addicted to, among other things, pornography, gambling, shopping, and the search for companionship. The darker corners of the Web are clearinghouses for child exploitation, illegal and black-market goods, and terrorism. Images and experiences one might encounter once in a lifetime (or never at all) in the physical world can be witnessed and experienced hourly on the Web. Among its shadier denizens are con artists, anarchists, and spies, all waiting to pounce on the naïve, curious, and lost.

Yet all of us spend more and more of our time in virtual space, seemingly oblivious to its dangers. We think of the Web as a place to meet new friends and reconnect with old ones, to get our news, search out any information we want, and be entertained for free. We take great pleasure in many of our online experiences—and we should. But we shouldn't delude ourselves that what's good about the Web is safely walled off from what's bad. The borders of the bright Web are poorly guarded, and the dark Web regularly makes incursions into it. Most of all, we must realize that virtual space is unnatural. It is an addictive environment for which we are maladapted.

Many of us are hooked on physical activities like exercise. We love the endorphin afterglow and the deeply satisfying sense of relaxation that follows a workout. But exercise has limits that are built in. We can work out for only so long before exhaustion sets in and forces us to quit. Most of us know that if we push past that point, we risk injury and threaten our health.

No such limits exist in the virtual world. We don't run out of breath or get a cramp in our side; our heart rate never exceeds a safe level. We haven't evolved the same warning systems for our brains and endocrine systems that we have for our muscles and hearts and lungs. No matter how many adrenalin bursts or hormonal surges we experience, we don't know when to stop.

Environments and experiences shape our personalities, and our experiences in virtual space are sculpting and resculpting the minds and personalities of hundreds of millions of us. More and more habitués of virtual space are exhibiting behaviors associated with addiction and obsessive-compulsive personality disorder. Some actually meet the clinical criteria for those dysfunctions. Young people, who literally grew up on the Internet, are especially susceptible. According to a recent article in *The Atlantic*, "The arrival of the smartphone has radically changed every aspect of teenagers' lives, from the nature of their social interactions to their mental health."[3]

In other words, visitors beware.

WHEN SPACE HAS PURPOSE

The natural environment exists, but if it has a long-term purpose, it is known only to God. It was not created to serve us; it is just there.

The virtual world, in contrast, is purposeful. Many who designed its features had business goals. The most popular applications, the places where users spend most of their time, have a commercial purpose. They were designed to sell us products and services, command our attention, control our actions, and invade our privacy. As part of the bargain for using them, consumers are provided with valuable services—news, maps, email and photo-sharing services, access to social groups, and more.

Our bodies, senses, brains, minds, personalities, and social and governance systems evolved over millions of years, enabling us to survive and thrive in physical space. About 3 million years ago, our ancestors invented the first stone tools.[4] Starting around twelve thousand years ago, numerous important inventions followed in rapid succession—agriculture, the wheel, bronze and iron tools. All of those new tools and knowledge created the structural transformations that gave birth to the societal phase change of the Agricultural Revolution.

Over time we learned how to build comfortable shelters, speed our travel, and produce the comforts of everyday life. The goal was to blunt nature's control over us and shape it to better serve our needs. When it became too cold, we learned to tame fire. If rain did not fall, we diverted a stream. We built walls and roofs to protect us from the elements. We created institutional tools as well: businesses and government organizations. Over time, those institutions sought to control more of our lives and behavior.

The commercial world doesn't control our bodies so much as it does our desires—overtly, by enticing us with better products and services, and covertly, by associating itself in our minds with more primal passions and loyalties: sex, family, and patriotism. Its effectiveness has particularly evolved over the last century. At first, loyalty programs were launched and aggressively expanded to reward repeat customers with discounts, prizes, and big rewards, such as free trips. In some cases, deceptive offers were used to get customers hooked. Then, in the post–World War II era, advertisers took a crucial leap and made the first crude attempts to program consumers' minds.

In 1957, the social critic and journalist Vance Packard published a book with the provocative title *The Hidden Persuaders*. The cover illustration showed a fishhook with its barb sunk into a shiny red apple. Packard's frightening message was that the unscrupulous ad men of Madison Avenue were using applied psychology to manipulate the irrational parts of consumers' psyches. Americans found Packard's book convincing—so convincing, in fact, that it sold more than 3 million copies.

Packard's bête noire was a psychologist and corporate consultant named Ernest Dichter, often called the father of motivational research. In 1960, Dichter came out with his own book, *The Strategy of Desire*, in which he explored the emotional resonances of material objects. Consumers didn't need to be manipulated, he argued. When they were properly presented, products sold themselves. (Decades later, Dichter's insights into the mind of the consumer inspired many of the advertising pitches that were featured on the television show *Mad Men*.)

Both men's pronouncements about the human psyche were based on a rudimentary understanding of the brain. As neuroscientists have learned more about the brain's pleasure centers—and especially its response to rewards—marketing techniques have grown even more sophisticated. But until recently, those techniques were constrained by the limitations of physical space.

Then, with the best intentions in the world, computer scientists created virtual space. At first, it served primarily as a vehicle that facilitated communication (ARPAnet), a new tool to share information between government agencies, universities, and defense contractors. But as it expanded its reach to more than half the world (via the World Wide Web), new capabilities were added.[5] It became multidimensional and tangible, a place where we can learn, socialize, be entertained, and shop. Today, we can feel the heat of battle in a single-shooter video game. We can visit distant places instantly, without sitting for hours in a cramped seat on an airplane or experiencing jet lag. At the Jet Propulsion Laboratory, scientists can walk on Mars unencumbered by space suits.

Large expanses of cyberspace still solely serve the needs of its visitors. But the vast majority of it was intentionally designed to serve the needs of the commercial interests that created and maintain it, and that are continually devising new ways to dominate our attention and control our behavior. What they created surpasses even Ernest Dichter's wildest dreams.

The creation of the Internet is a structural transformation that has created new tools and new rules. The substitutional equivalence of virtual and real space not only facilitates information exchange, social experience, and commerce but also blurs the boundaries between the imagination and reality. And it does it intentionally. As they say in Silicon Valley, it's a feature, not a bug.

HITTING THE LEVER

Let's look at how virtual space became purposeful and then examine some of the consequences, beginning with operant conditioning.

If B. F. Skinner were alive today, he would recognize the rat-like behavior of Internet addicts. Back in the 1930s, the Harvard psychologist held that an animal's behavior is heavily influenced by its experience and conditioning, and that all creatures—including humans—are inclined to do what the world rewards them for doing.

To test his theories, Skinner invented the "operant conditioning" chamber, or Skinner Box, in which he put pigeons and rats. This cage's artfully designed food dispenser was controlled by an array of lighted buttons. When one of them lit up a certain color, pushing or pecking the adjacent lever caused a drawer to open that was filled with food. Eventually, through a process of trial and error and trial and reward, the animals learned to recognize and respond to the cues.

The same thing happens with social networkers, hunched over keyboards and oblivious to the flesh-and-blood people surrounding them. Couples in restaurants ignore each other while checking their smartphones for messages, and players of massively multiplayer on-line role-playing games (MMORPGs) become so absorbed in their play that they collapse from fatigue. The Internet is the ultimate Skinner Box, in which hundreds of millions of users peck keys in search of rewards—game points, engrossing bits of information, or a potential new love object.

Neuroscience has given us an understanding of the neurochemistry underlying operant conditioning. We know that animals' brains are primed for pleasure, and that pleasure is accompanied by the signature release of the chemical dopamine, a neurotransmitter. Recent research into drug and gambling addiction has shown that the brain responds to all pleasures in a similar way, whether the stimulus is a cash reward, a line of cocaine, the victory bells that ring when a slot machine hits the right combination, leveling up in a video game, getting a thumbs-up on Facebook, or receiving an alert on a smartphone that your stock shares just went through the roof.

Dopamine can kick in at any stage in the reward-seeking cycle. In the late 1990s, Wolfram Schultz, a psychologist at Cambridge who was working on biochemical explanations for Skinner's findings, discovered that when monkeys were given a cue and then a reward, at first dopamine neurons would be activated only after the reward was dispensed. But when the monkeys learned that the reward always followed the cue, the cue itself served to activate the dopamine. This helps explain why so many of us constantly check our smartphones: just the anticipation of a new text message or email is enough to give us a squirt of dopamine excitement.

Apparently, it goes even deeper than that. New research using MRIs has shown that sustained exposure to technology actually re-wires the brain's circuitry. Gary Small, a psychiatrist at UCLA, has found that self-described Internet addicts feel a pleasurable mood burst or "rush" just from booting up their computers.

The Internet and cellular communications are ideal vehicles for operant conditioning. SMS (Short Messaging Service) arrived on the scene in 1984.[6] But using phone keyboards to type messages was an arduous task. When the Blackberry with its tiny QWERTY keyboard arrived in 1999, the messaging floodgates opened.[7] Within a few years, people were continually checking their phones for good news and alerts. The last barrier was breached with the arrival of ubiquitous touch pad smartphones.

Operant conditioning environments are everywhere in virtual space. Many of them started by accident. In an effort to make their games, Internet sites, and user experiences more engrossing, designers used A/B testing, presenting two flavors of an experience, to see which one the customers liked best. Most designers did not understand what they were doing in explicit terms, but they were testing for dopamine response.

As more and more business environments moved to the Internet and its experiential bandwidth began to fill up, companies had to compete harder for customers' attention. The best way to keep a customer on their site, they learned, was to engineer a quasi-addictive experience. Today, the designers of those experiences are no longer innocent. They know precisely what they are doing and how to accomplish their goals.

The real pioneers in this endeavor were Las Vegas casinos, which perfected video slot machines in 1976.[8] The idea was to get slot players into "the zone," a state of mind in which "time, space, and social identity are suspended in the mechanical rhythm of a repeating process."[9] As one player put it, "You're in a trance, you're on autopilot. The zone is like a magnet, it just pulls you in and holds you there."[10] Many of the techniques that the casinos used have been adapted to the Web.

Let's examine those techniques in more detail. Casinos began by designing and building physical spaces that satisfied people's desire to be "together and yet separate." The gambling rooms provided a combination of darkness and enclosure—and, with no clocks present, timelessness.[11] If you visit Pinterest and look at the "epic" home video game room designs that users post, they look a lot like casino environments.[12]

The next thing the casinos did was to create more productive gamblers—that is to say, gamblers who produced more profits for the casino. They did this by accelerating the rate of play, extending the duration of play, and increasing the amounts of the bets. Pace was critical to keeping players in the zone. Speed didn't tire them—rather, it helped them better achieve their need for instant gratification. A really experienced video poker player could play a hand every three seconds.

To extend the duration of play, casinos introduced a suite of sensory innovations, increasing the number of sound effects from fifteen to more than four hundred. They also included haptic feedback to integrate touch sensations into the experience. The final piece of the environmental design was to streamline the players' access to cash and payouts, developing such services as the PersonalBanker system, so that players would not have to leave the machine to collect their payouts.[13]

The next step in creating a player addict was to embed addictive experience into this manipulative environment. And that was done by engineering a gambling experience that provided the player with an opportunity for large and unpredictable rewards.

The house edge on most slots falls in the range of 6 to 15 percent.[14] A typical payout is 95 cents on the dollar, so if you make 1,000 bets you will lose $50. A slot machine that paid out 95 cents every time the player bet a dollar would produce that result, but not many players would play that game. However, a slot that pays out $500 every 1,000 spins, with occasional intermediate payouts of $10, $50, and $100, will still make the house money while also getting players hooked. Large, highly variable rewards not only create the illusion that you are beating the house but also stimulate what can be addictive levels of dopamine release.[15]

Another step was to give the players an illusion of control and autonomy. Luke Clark, a neuroscientist at the University of Cambridge, has used brain scans to determine that when gamblers feel they can exert control over a game's outcome—for example, by throwing the dice harder, or pulling the lever on a slot machine with more force—their interest in playing increases.

So, the key to extending player engagement is to create appealing, insular environments, to pay out large rewards unpredictably, and to give the player an illusory sense of control over the machine. Needless to say, the designers of video games, social networks, and other virtual experiences have all become attuned to these techniques. They are good for business.

Perhaps the first commercial Internet enterprise to capitalize on all of these concepts was Zynga, which gave the world the innocent-sounding game FarmVille in 2009. In FarmVille, players tended crops and took care of animals. But in fact, its players were being enmeshed in "compulsion loops." *Time* magazine called the game one of the "50 Worst Inventions" in recent decades, "the most addictive of Facebook games" and a "series of mindless chores on a digital farm."[16] But FarmVille was just the tip of the iceberg.

In the early 1990s an aptly named start-up—Silicon & Synapse—became a pioneer in real-time strategy games. In 1996 the company changed its name to Blizzard Entertainment and introduced the highly cinematic, story-driven Diablo, which allowed players to manipulate characters in a way that gave them an unprecedented sense of control and autonomy. In 2004, Blizzard Entertainment released World of Warcraft, which is perhaps the best illustration of the vise grip that video games can exert on their players' minds. As video games go, World of Warcraft is aging; most hardcore gamers consider it yesterday's game. Yet, as its more than 10 million former subscribers can attest, it exercised an unprecedented ability to condition and manipulate their behavior.

What made "Warcrack," as some called it, so immersive and, for many of its players, so powerfully addictive? In the physical world, every day can be a struggle against disappointment—a C on a midterm; unrequited love; the general hardscrabble of real life. But in the richly rendered alternate universe of Azeroth, where World of Warcraft takes place, there are plenty of rewards, self-esteem runs high, and heroism is actually attainable without consequences. For those reasons and more, World of Warcraft became an escape, an obsession, and a home.

The number of minutes it took to become deeply immersed in World of Warcraft could be measured on the fingers of one hand. Its designers perfected a reward technique known as *dynamic difficulty adjustment*, in which ever-more satisfying challenges were customized to a player's abilities and provided at just the right time to keep the player engaged. The "quests" were constant, and so was the promise of rewards. But the sizes of the rewards were varied and unpredictable. And at carefully scheduled intervals there appeared a flash of light, religious in its overtones, to signify a "leveling up," which was a bestowal of higher, more powerful status on the player.

Still more compelling were the game's "guilds." Once you reached your full potential as a solo player, you could join a guild, which had as many as forty players. This meant you were no longer working alone, but for the collective good. Others depended upon you to show up. In the process, relationships developed. "It's like joining a big conference call," says Scott Rigby, a psychologist who studies gaming, specifically online interactive games. "You're playing the game but also talking to each other."[17]

Mike Morhaime, World of Warcraft's chief executive and co-founder, quickly realized that the shared social experience of the game was what made it so compelling. "People log in and they like being part of a community, and meeting people online," Morhaime says.

"They join guilds. They go there to hang out with friends—either friends they know in real life or friends that they met online—in a deeper way they were able to do in any of our previous games."[18]

World of Warcraft's lesson—in Morhaime's words, that "people start playing [it] for the game, and they stay for the community"—is an important one for all information services and consumer companies as they move into virtual space. The useful edge for companies as they market to us is the knowledge that once we're in a dedicated community, we're loath to leave, because that community— be it World of Warcraft, Facebook, Instagram, Twitter, YouTube, or WebMD—has evolved from being merely an activity to being a part of one's identity.

More than anything else, this sense of relatedness accounts for World of Warcraft's astonishing and long-lived success: the pleasure and satisfaction players get from working as a team, supporting other members of their group to accomplish their mission. "There's huge satisfaction in knowing that I matter to you and you matter to me," Rigby says. In his book, *Glued to Games*, Rigby writes that "games are most successful, engaging, and fun when they are satisfying specific intrinsic needs: those of competence, autonomy, and relatedness."[19]

Competence, he found, refers to the innate human desire to gain mastery of new situations. Autonomy reflects the desire to take actions out of personal volition, to exercise control. "Every time I go into a combat scenario in World of Warcraft, there's a very dense field of meaningful choices to make," Rigby says.[20] And, perhaps most important of all, there is relatedness—the powerful human need for connection. This recognition that humans are essentially social animals lies at the heart of games such as World of Warcraft and social networking sites as monolithic as Facebook or as tiny as the new site Pair, which caters to social networks as small as they get: two people.

In Vance Packard's day, psychologists worked hand-in-hand

with advertising companies to help them write their marketing campaigns. Yet among the 160 people at Blizzard Entertainment who worked on World of Warcraft, few really understood psychology—there were no Scott Rigbys, and certainly no Ernest Dichters. This lack is significant, because it suggests those developers had only a limited understanding of the potentially harmful side effects of their product. What they did do, however, was anticipate everything that might get in the way of their program's success—even exhaustion from loving it too much. That's why they added a "rested bonus" feature to World of Warcraft, which rewarded players for taking a hiatus. This was another page that was taken directly from casinos.

In 1997, Harrah's put a loyalty program in place in which customers could earn points for gambling activities and spend them on food, rooms, or more gambling. The program also allowed Harrah's to collect precious data. When customers played the slot machines, for example, they inserted their loyalty cards and every play was recorded.

Harrah's worked hard to learn how much a valued customer could lose and still be counted on to return to the tables. The casino company called this "tolerable bleeding." Lest the bleeding become intolerable, Harrah's learned to give customers who had been gambling heavily for long periods of time (relative to their profile's coupons for meals or shows) breaks in which they could recharge their gambling batteries. Similarly, if the World of Warcraft game program notices that a player is growing fatigued and not advancing, it suggests that they log off for a while. Not only is there no penalty for doing so, the player is rewarded: he or she advances more quickly upon returning.

"The rested bonus is one of the genius designs of WoW," says J. Allen Brack, the game's production director. "The way it's presented to the player is absolutely genius. It feels like a bonus. Let's say I kill a monster and get ten points. If I'm rested, I get twenty points. It's a 100 percent bonus."[21] Like Harrah's, World of Warcraft's resting strategy is designed to keep its customers engaged, not encourage them to leave.

Social networks have much in common with video games and casinos. Rather than being trapped in the casino zone, users become ensnared in the flow. Unlike online games, people come for the community and stay for the experiences.

There is plenty of Rigby's autonomy on social networks: you get to do what you want on your Facebook page. You are in control. But just as the zone has been engineered to keep us playing a casino game, the flow on social networks is constantly being tweaked to keep us engaged. Algorithms determine users' interests and supply them with interesting updates. They get to join all kinds of virtual communities that share those interests and experience the pleasurable reinforcement they get from hanging around with people who feel just like they do. And every time they get an update from a friend or receive a news update that confirms one of their biases, they get a little dopamine kick.

Armored by anonymity and supported by like-thinkers, users can also lash out at progressives, liberals, conservatives, minorities, or racists with few consequences. It is not unlike the thrill of killing monsters, except social networks have created a secure virtual bunker to shoot from.

In 2009, the *engagement supercharger* appeared on the scene when the Facebook team brought the "Like" feature to social networking.[22] It not only created surprising and highly unpredictable rewards but quickly became one of the key elements in creating what Elias Aboujaoude, a professor of psychiatry at Stanford, calls the e-personality.[23] "Like" is a very powerful force for engagement. When a person starts out using Facebook, YouTube, and Pinterest, they are novices. As they get better over time, they get to satisfy what Rigby called the innate human desire to gain mastery. Instead of the kill in a computer game, the proof of mastery is Likes.

The smartphone presented consumers with the final piece of the puzzle. In the physical world, our scope is limited. We can be in only one place at a time. We are either at the shopping mall or at home. If we are in bed, we are not at the dinner table. More to the point, if we are not on our computer, we cannot be in virtual space.

Those limitations were shattered when the smartphone became the principal access mechanism for virtual space. We now carry our phones with us everywhere. The average user touches his phone 2,617 times a day and spends more than two hours doing so. Heavy users touch their phones twice as often, spending close to four hours engaged in the process. The average user engages in 76 sessions per day and the heavy user 132.[24] Seventy-one percent of Americans (and 90 percent of eighteen- to twenty-five-year-olds) now sleep with their smartphones.[25]

Remember—this virtual real estate to which we are addicted was created by commercial interests for commercial purposes. Their goal was to capture our attention so they could make money by selling us advertising and products and services. The tighter their grip on our attention, the more effective they will be. By leveraging our brains' dopamine responses, they create addictive processes that condition us. Those of us who cannot put down their phones, who check alerts while driving, who sleep with their phones, and who allow their most intimate moments with family and friends to be constantly interrupted have ceded control over their lives to commercial enterprise.

In a sense, these observations are already about the past. In 2015 it was estimated that there were fewer than 4 billion IoT devices; today that number is approximately 7 billion—and by 2025, it will be 22 billion.[26] More aggressive forecasts predict a number of 75 billion by 2025.[27] IoT devices will make our clothes smart, listen to our voices, embed in our appliances, control the driving experience in our cars, and be the sensors that let stores negotiate deals with us while we shop. As their prices plummet and their presence increases, their virtual environments will expand their reach. They will no longer seek to dominate our attention only, but will increasingly have the ability to motivate our behavior and control our actions.

And that is just the beginning—because now, with the rise of robots, virtual space is becoming embodied in physical space. As robots become more like humans and gain more control over people, people are likely to become more robot-like as they perform actions motivated by robots. Just as the Dark Web conducts insurgencies on the Light Web, so too will the virtual world raid and capture territory in the age-old natural world.

THE REFLECTED SELF

New tools create new rules, and new rules shape new values and new psychologies. The people who live on one side of a societal phase change can't begin to understand the subjectivity of the people who live on the other side of it. One side effect of the mind-controlling processes that are part of the Autonomous Revolution is that commercial interests are now shaping our personalities.

It will be years before we fully understand all the implications of what is happening, but the evidence is already piling up, and it is not reassuring. More and more of us are exhibiting behaviors associated with addiction and obsessive-compulsive disorder. Our young people are being left poorly equipped to face the challenges of adulthood.

We are living in the midst of a narcissism epidemic. That is the conclusion of a study undertaken by Jean M. Twenge and W. Keith Campbell. After examining data that was gathered from 37,000 college students between the 1980s and the first decade of the 2000s, they noted that narcissistic personality traits had proliferated at the same rate as obesity.[28] In a separate study, Shawn Bergman, an assistant professor of organizational psychology at Appalachian State University in Boone, North Carolina, notes that "narcissism levels among millennials are higher than previous generations."[29]

Facebook, Twitter, Pinterest, and Foursquare have acted as petri dishes for morbid self-centeredness. Researchers at Western Illinois University measured two socially disruptive aspects of narcissistic personalities—grandiose exhibitionism and entitlement/exploitation. Those who had high scores on grandiose exhibitionism, they found, tended to amass more friends on Facebook.[30] In still another study, Buffardi and Campbell found a high correlation between Narcissistic Personality Inventory (NPI) scores and Facebook activity. Conversely, researchers were able to correctly identify individuals with high NPI scores by studying their Facebook pages.

"This shift from e- to i- in prefixing Internet URLs and naming electronic gadgets and 'apps' parallels the rise of the self-absorbed online Narcissus," Elias Aboujaoude notes in his book *Virtually You*.[31] He goes on to state that, "As we get accustomed to having even our most minor needs . . . accommodated . . . we are growing more needy and more entitled. In other words, more narcissistic."[32]

Many of the social and physical restraints on narcissistic behavior are suspended in virtual spaces. Delusions of grandeur, viciousness, impulsivity, and infantile behavior rise to the surface. And, as Aboujaoude observes, "the traits we take on online can become incorporated in our offline personalities."

Beyond the basic social media platforms that narcissists use to display themselves, there is a small but growing support industry that narcissists can turn to for help and advice. Twitter Counter offered a basic $75-per-month program that enabled subscribers to "get approximately 1 Twitter follower on every 100 views." It has been superseded by more than a score of competitive products.[33] Blog posts on how to build networks of friends on Facebook and get books reviewed on Amazon abound.

Disturbingly, those narcissists are setting many of the benchmarks for everyday users, and greater and greater numbers of the latter are becoming depressed because they are being out-twittered and lacking in thumbs ups. Jean Twenge just published her benchmark study of iGen—the cohort of the population that was born in 1995 or later, and who grew up with the iPhone. This group, as every new generation does, thinks differently from its predecessors. They tend to be less religious, more inclusive and concerned about equality issues, less interested in driving, and happy to interact with friends over social networks rather than in person. But that is not the concerning part of the study.[34]

What is of concern is that this generation also is maturing more slowly and experiencing rising levels of insecurity and other mental health issues. There has been a steep rise in the percentage of iGeners who feel that they, somehow, are being left out, Twenge notes.

Depression is on the rise among this group—and the rates are 50 percent higher for women than for men. Fadi Haddad, a psychiatrist at Bellevue Hospital, reports, "Every single week we have a girl who comes to the ER after some social media rumor or incident has upset her."[35]

The popular acronym FOMO—fear of missing out—reflects these deep feelings of anxiety. One study found that this anxiety was higher among those who were most heavily engaged with social media.[36] Also, the number of iGeners reporting that they feel "they can't do anything right" is on the rise. There is some evidence that having online friends who post only their successes exacerbates one's feelings of inadequacy. The percentage of iGeners who report that they are overwhelmed by feelings of anxiety is also increasing. Some speculate that exposure to narcissistic abuse is a trigger.[37] Given all this, it should come as no surprise that suicide rates also are on the rise.

REASSERTING CONTROL

So, what are we to do?

First, we must realize that if we do not manage virtual space, it will manage us. There is much that we can and should do, and much of that involves self-discipline. We can transition from the "push" to the "pull" mode by shutting off all but the most critical alerts and checking for updates no more than once or twice a day at fixed times. We can remove unimportant applications from our phones and shut off GPS tracking unless we need it to navigate or to flag a photo. We can limit the time we spend on social networks or playing online games. We can put our phones away at the dinner table or when visiting friends.

We can set examples for the younger members of our families as to what is acceptable behavior. Just as we teach kids about the dangers of drugs, we should warn them about the deeper agendas of game and website creators.

All good ideas. But ask yourself: how many people will follow them?

Roger McNamee, one of Silicon Valley's most astute investors and the author of *Zucked—Waking Up to the Facebook Catastrophe*, has observed, "Facebook and Google assert with merit that they are giving users what they want. The same can be said about tobacco companies and drug dealers."[38] But we impose punitive sales taxes on cigarettes and require their makers to print warning labels on their packaging. There are no such disincentives in the virtual world.

One reason things have gotten so out of control is that the direct costs of keeping people addicted to the Internet are low. It does not take much computer time or electricity on a per-person basis to keep a social network working. Targeted access to users—and exerting increasing control over their actions—is so valuable that advertisers will cover the costs of services so that they can be given away for free.

Those free services are extremely valuable, and the fact that they are free has created socially undesirable side effects. Services with damaging side effects should come with warning labels, just like cigarettes.

Economists have struggled for years with the problem of how to charge for externalities. For example, individuals who consume large amounts of sugar are more likely to suffer from type 2 diabetes.

The direct cost of treating all types of diabetes in the United States in 2012 was $176 billion. It is estimated that a male between the ages of twenty-five and forty-four who contracts type 2 diabetes will incur $125,000 in treatment costs over his lifetime.[39] Those costs increase the cost of health care and are paid for by higher insurance rates. In this case, the treatment costs for those who consume large amounts of sugar are paid for by others—externalized. If there were a "sin tax" on sugar, it could be used to defray the cost of diabetes treatment. Moreover, it would have the socially beneficial effect of curbing the excessive consumption of sugar and lowering the incidence of type 2 diabetes.

A gambling addiction can make an addict unemployable—putting him or her on the dole, paid for by the rest of us. That's one reason society limits gambling and punishes that behavior when it grows too extreme. We are accumulating more and more evidence to suggest many applications on the Internet are similarly externalizing their costs. The improper use of social networking is associated with increased rates of depression and suicide. Society pays those costs in full. Social networks are the ideal vehicle for spreading fake news, which can generate socially destructive—and costly—behavior. Foreign governments have exploited social networks to undermine our democratic institutions. We are investing large amounts of government resources (paid for by us) to counter those effects.

When applications acquire large amounts of our personal data and sell it for marketing purposes, we are barraged with targeted emails and phone calls that consume hours of our time. Thus, the value of our time has also been externalized. According to one study, dealing with spam emails costs businesses $712 per employee per year.[40] Another study estimates that businesses will spend $257 billion dealing with the problem this year.[41] To put that number in perspective, the combined revenues of Amazon, Google, and Facebook in 2017 were about $328 billion.[42]

In light of those numbers, it doesn't seem far off base to guess that the externalized costs associated with Internet applications are on the same order of the revenues they generate. If the companies had to pay these costs directly, many of them would go broke.

When valuable things are underpriced, they are abused and misused. For example, if cigarettes, drugs, alcohol, and sugary soft drinks were free, consumption would dramatically increase. There would be more smoking and substance abuse. In much the same vein, if using the Internet were more expensive, then both individuals and companies might use it more judiciously. It follows that a good argument could be made that society would be better off if we spent less time on social networks, received less junk email and fewer texts, and spent less time connected. When you think about the problem in that context, a sin tax on sending emails and texts, or on connected time, time spent on social networks, or time spent gaming makes sense.

LEARNING THE NEW NORMS

As we spend more of our time in virtual worlds, we will be confronted with two issues that have not yet been discussed. As noted, in the past societal phase changes have been accompanied by wholesale changes in governance and laws. Some of those issues will be discussed in the next chapter.

But laws can accomplish only so much. Adapting to the Autonomous Revolution will require us to adopt and internalize a whole new set of cultural norms. The Agricultural Revolution drove just such a cultural transformation. Over time, civility and the rule of law replaced localized tribalism. Cities became the centers of invention and the arts. In Babylon, the Code of Hammurabi, one of the first sets of written laws, was inscribed on a seven-foot basalt stele.[43] The city-state of Athens gave birth to the idea of democracy.[44]

Those were the obvious effects. But at the individual level, human behavior also changed. People had to learn to live in one place and in close proximity to one another—and in the process they learned rules of etiquette. They also learned citizenship—they became the *polis*. There were new, and usually less violent and vengeful, gods. Ultimately, the Agricultural Revolution gave birth to civilization.

When much of civilization became stagnant during the Middle Ages, technology again came to the rescue. Printing powered the Reformation, which was followed by the Enlightenment, which brought us the concepts of liberty, constitutional government, the separation of church and state, and the free market. Those important structural transformations positioned society for the epic transformation brought on by the second societal phase change: the Industrial Revolution.

The Industrial Revolution transformed our country from an agrarian republic to an urbanized manufacturing economy. In 1790, 90 percent of Americans worked on farms. By 2000, less than 3 percent did.[45] Just 5 percent of the population lived in urban environments in 1800; that number has grown to more than 80 percent today.[46] Over time, a normative industrial system replaced an agricultural one.

At the individual level, the changes wrought by the Industrial Revolution were just as profound. The extended family became less important and physical and social mobility much more so. Education and literacy were universalized and rose in importance. With greater affluence and the decline of the extended family, we became more dependent on non-family members and ultimately the government.

The automobile changed the way we shopped, where we lived and worked, and how we socialized. In the process, our behaviors changed. We entertained ourselves differently. Church played a less central role in our lives. Instead of entertaining ourselves in our homes, we went to concerts and movies and watched television. We became mass consumers and less frugal.

The Social Security Act of 1935 ensured that retired workers over the age of sixty-five would receive a minimal level of retirement income. The "good job" provided health insurance and pensions. In many respects, government and big business took over the responsibilities of the extended family.

In sum, each great leap in technology sparked changes in values and culture. For better or for worse, it is happening again. So we need to ask ourselves: What constitutes civil behavior in the time of the Autonomous Revolution?

The question breaks down into two parts. First, what constitutes civil and normative behavior in the virtual world? Second, what happens when we attempt to operate at the intersection of virtual and physical space?

Remember that our minds, brains, senses, and bodies evolved and were optimized for survival in the physical world. For example, our tribal instincts were key to our survival in the physical world. The release of the neurotransmitter oxytocin reinforces those instincts. Looking someone in the eye stimulates its release. Affectionately touching someone or giving them a hug has similar effects. Our body language gives others important clues about our feelings. Coauthor Michael Malone, who hosted a public television interview series for a number of years, learned that when his questions struck a chord, a male guest would aggressively lean forward, while a female guest would protectively put her hand to her face.

Conversely, there are things we would never do in physical space that we feel free to do in a virtual environment. In the latter, a small guy feels comfortable anonymously threatening and insulting someone twice his size. He would never do that in a bar in a tough part of town.

In virtual space we leave behind many of our evolved inhibitions and are freed from many of the constraints of physical space. The anonymity that virtual space provides makes it the perfect environment to insult, attack, and threaten others. Thirty-four percent of students report experiencing cyberbullying, and a surprising

15 percent reported bullying others.[47] Then there are the anonymous death threats and cyber-stalking. According to Pew Research, 40 percent of Internet users have been victims of online harassment.[48] In many respects, virtual environments leverage the worst aspects of human nature.

While laws are used to control the most egregious behaviors in physical space, social norms do most of the heavy lifting when it comes to everyday behaviors. We tend not to invite jerks to parties or to join our clubs. Also, the difficulty of doing anything anonymously in physical space exerts a heavy element of control.

What makes all of this challenging is that the things we can do to make it more difficult to be anonymous in virtual environments—for example, getting rid of the use of avatars, making it easier to identify the sources of emails, and eliminating features such as "Like" buttons that encourage narcissistic behavior—are bad for business.

Meanwhile, we should expect little in the way of help from our political leaders. Many benefit from and encourage the irresponsible behavior of Internet trolls. Unfortunately, there are too many bad neighborhoods in virtual space. As discussed earlier, some of them are bad because they exploit users, others because they have adverse affects on our mental health or encourage antisocial behavior. One can only hope that businesses will come to realize that what is bad for their customers will ultimately make their businesses unsustainable. Whether they act out of altruism, out of fear of being overregulated, or simply out of worry that the noxiousness of online environments is driving customers away, business might just take the lead in encouraging socially responsible behavior.

Some evidence of the last possibility is starting to appear. Facebook usage in the United States declined from 67 percent to 62 percent last year—the first decline ever recorded.[49] If trends like that continue, businesses will get the message.

The second issue is what constitutes civil behavior at the intersection between physical and virtual space. Here again evolution plays a significant role. As a society, we have come to believe that we can effectively multitask; moreover, we take it as a given that digital natives, the young members of society who grew up with computers, are excellent at it.

We are wrong.

The word *multitasking* comes from the computer world, and it is used to describe the fact that computers appear to be able to do multiple things simultaneously. In fact, some do. Some systems contain more than one processor, sometimes hundreds, and as a result they are capable of processing and solving numerous problems and dealing with multiple situations all at once—hence, *multitasking*.

But when individual computers appear to multitask, they in fact are switching rapidly between tasks; they don't actually perform them in parallel. Thus, they might devote tens of microseconds to one task, switch to the next task for some number of microseconds, and then go on to another. Because computers switch between these tasks at lightning speed, we simply *perceive* them as doing things simultaneously. But the truth is that single processor computers do one thing at a time.

When it comes to cognitive tasks, humans are in one respect like those single processor computers. We can only do one thing well at any given time. But we are very different from those computers in a second respect: we are very slow at task switching.

In his book *Distracted Minds*, Adam Gazzaley observes that when humans "pursue multiple goals that compete for cognitive resources, our brains switch between tasks—they do not parallel process."[50] This means that if we are focused on one cognitive task, our brains will not be able to respond to a second one until they have essentially stopped working on the first and refocused on the second.

We are just beginning to understand the effects of operating at the intersection of physical and virtual space. In one of the most interesting studies, Ira Hyman had a clown in a purple and yellow costume with bright red buttons pedal around a public square on a unicycle. When asked if they saw anything unusual, only 8 percent of the subjects who were using cell phones reported that they saw the clown, compared to 71 percent of the subjects who were walking in pairs.[51]

More than 2.5 million people were involved in automobile accidents in 2016. Cell phones were a factor in more than 60 percent of the accidents.[52] In 2013, 3,154 people died and another 424,000 were injured in accidents that involved drivers texting or using cell phones.[53]

Even walking has become dangerous. While most of us can chew gum and walk safely, we put ourselves in danger when we engage in tasks that put demands on our cognitive systems. In 2004, one hundred U.S. hospitals reported that 559 people had injured themselves by walking into stationary objects while texting. That number almost tripled by 2010 and was expected to double again in 2016 when the data became available.[54]

Of course, we could do multiple things at once if we could switch between tasks at a fast-enough rate. But "fast" is a relative term. If a person is in a rapidly changing environment, fast means responding in a fraction of the time over which the change is taking place. If the person is driving on a freeway where 10 feet can mean the difference between life and death, fast is hundredths of a second. There is not a lot of data on this subject, but a good guess is that if a driver is looking for a problem, it takes him or her on the order of 0.5 seconds to figure out what to do. If a driver is taken by surprise while driving, that time stretches to 1.2 seconds.[55]

But reaction time is not the whole scenario. You have to know about a problem before you can react to it. In one study of texting while driving, the subjects absorbed in texting only checked for problems every 3.5 to 4 seconds.[56] At that rate, if you are traveling at freeway speeds, you might travel 400 feet before you notice a problem and apply the brakes. If you are texting while walking, like

Cathy Cruz Marrero, who fell headfirst into a fountain at a shopping mall while texting, you might travel as far as 20 feet.[57]

These switching times are relatively fast compared to the ones humans experience when they are involved in deep cognitive tasks. One study done at the University of California, Irvine, found that subjects who switched from one engrossing task to another and then back again to the original task took as long as twenty to thirty minutes to restore their concentration.[58]

Think of the toll the distracted mind takes on social and family relationships. If someone who is texting does not see a clown dressed in a purple and yellow costume with bright red buttons pedaling around a public square on a unicycle, how good will they be at picking up the facial expression of a distressed child?

Of course, technology can help. It can make my iPhone refuse to let me answer a call unless I tell it I am not driving. Maybe one day, parents will be able to buy apps that count how many thousands of words they say to their children each day.

Experience suggests that the proper way to use our new virtual technologies is to employ them primarily to enhance our physical world experiences. The alternative, that we surrender our lives to the virtual world, means that we are not adapting to it, but are becoming enslaved by it. If we surrender, society will incur unbearable social and psychological costs.

It is imperative that we figure out what civilized behavior means in the autonomous world, just as our ancestors did during the two prior Revolutions. Then we will have to teach those norms in schools, act them out in our homes, and have our leaders both advocate them and set good examples.

We can start by shutting off our phones at meals and sharing our beds with our partners rather than with texts and tweets.

CHAPTER NINE

THE BODY POLITIC

Government in
the Autonomous Revolution

IN 1992, FRANCIS FUKUYAMA published his acclaimed book *The End of History and the Last Man,* which proclaimed that, with the fall of the USSR, government had completed its evolution. As he put it, civilization had arrived at "the end of history as such: that is, the end point of mankind's ideological evolution and the universalization of liberal democracy as the final form of human government."[1] In the decades since, the rise of authoritarian regimes (roughly one nominally democratic country has reverted to tyranny every year for the last two decades) and the surge of right- and left-wing populism have cast a pall over Fukuyama's optimistic vision.

While there are many reasons for these trends, societal phase change is behind all of them. The new rules that come with the new tools of the Autonomous Revolution are undermining many of the structures and institutions on which liberal democracies depend. Widespread job insecurity and soaring income inequality are powering much of our political polarization. The middle class, the bulwark of democracy in the United States, is rapidly losing ground.

In the rosiest of scenarios, liberal democracy could evolve into an even fairer, more effective form of government. Yet there is a real possibility that the United States will devolve into greater authoritarianism. If we want to avoid that scenario, we must be prepared to make fundamental changes in our values, norms, and our government itself. Attempting to adapt to the future by holding tightly to the past is a strategy that cannot work.

There are reasons to be hopeful. Our constitutional democracy has already proved itself to be amazingly resilient. Designed at the twilight of the Agricultural Revolution to "establish Justice, insure domestic Tranquility, provide for the common defence, promote the general Welfare, and secure the Blessings of Liberty," it adapted well to the societal phase change of the Industrial Revolution. We can thank the Bill of Rights for that. An extraordinary achievement in itself, it set the precedent for allowing regular changes (albeit with great difficulty, including an all-out Civil War) to be made to the nation's laws.

The Constitution has been amended on more than two dozen occasions since. In addition, the courts have broadly interpreted its original language to make room for new rules. Slowly but surely, America ended slavery, incorporated former slaves as citizens, enfranchised women, and transformed from a loosely aligned collection of colonies to a unified republic that spanned a continent. In the process, the small government of the nineteenth century grew into the big activist government of the New Deal and the postwar years.

When the Constitution was written, the overwhelming majority of Americans worked on farms. Though the nation's industrialization was well under way by the mid-nineteenth century, farming still provided hardworking citizens with a path to prosperity. "Go West, young man," Horace Greeley wrote after the Civil War, and many, especially recent immigrants, listened. Abraham Lincoln's Homestead Act of 1862 allowed citizens, including freed slaves, to purchase 160 acres for $200 in the West. The deal was so good that 1.6 million settlers took advantage of it.[2] But by 1893, the historian Frederick Jackson Turner declared the American frontier closed. By 1930, farming accounted for just 10 percent of GDP, while manufacturing and services each accounted for about 40 percent of GDP.[3]

The structural transformations of the Industrial Revolution included vast demographic changes. Life expectancies leaped twenty years in the United States; many more people now could expect to live into their seventies and eighties.[4] Urban populations grew and income inequality soared. As corporations grew into great monopolies through mergers and acquisitions, industrial workers began to fight for living wages and against the regressive burden of excise taxes.[5] Pressures grew to tax the wealthy.

In response to these changes, the federal government and the Supreme Court began to enact a more progressive agenda. The Sherman Antitrust Act was passed in 1890. A decade later, President Theodore Roosevelt went on an antitrust rampage, suing forty-five companies. In 1913, the Sixteenth Amendment to the Constitution was ratified, making it possible to enact a nationwide income tax.[6]

Then, in the 1930s, as Franklin Roosevelt struggled to pull the country out of the Great Depression, the role of the national government expanded exponentially. In 1933, the National Industrial Recovery Act (NIRA), which established minimum wages and shorter workweeks, and the Agricultural Adjustment Administration Act, which boosted farm prices by paying farmers to grow less, proved a step too far for the Supreme Court, which struck them down as unconstitutional. After winning reelection in 1936, Roosevelt fought back by attempting to "pack" the Supreme Court with more justices. He failed, but by March 1937, the court had surrendered to the country's changing norms. In *West Coast Hotel v. Parrish*, in a 5-to-4 decision, it allowed a minimum-wage law in the state of Washington to stand.[7]

By fits and starts and with many backward steps along the way, the U.S. federal government gradually changed its form. For most of the nineteenth and early twentieth centuries, government spending had hovered at about 4 percent of GDP. Beginning with the New Deal, spending began to rise dramatically, reaching more than 20 percent of GDP by the end of the twentieth century.[8]

In the Agricultural era, citizens mostly looked after themselves,

for better or for worse; as the United States evolved into an industrial society, both governments and corporations took on more and
more of the burdens of the "general Welfare." Social Security ensured a small retirement income for everyone; by the 1950s, health
insurance was an integral part of the "good job."

The past gives us clues to the magnitude of the changes that we
can expect as the societal phase change of the Autonomous Revolution takes hold. The government will have to deal with numerous
issues. It is useful to view these as falling roughly into two groups.
The first comprises issues of *polarization*; the second involves consequences of the *transition* from physical to virtual space. In the
next few pages we will focus on the most pressing of these issues.

LEVIATHAN

For any government to operate effectively, the majority of its citizens must share common goals, values, and beliefs. Throughout history, different forms of government have used different methods to
achieve a unity of purpose.

In 1651, Thomas Hobbes, the first great modern political philosopher, published *Leviathan*, in which he articulated the social
contract between government and the governed, as well as his theories on how to create a common set of goals. Hobbes believed that
for a ruler—specifically, a monarch—to be legitimate, he had to
have and use the fearsome power of a Leviathan, the mythical sea
monster referenced in the Bible's book of Job, waging war on a nation's enemies and ruthlessly controlling what its citizens say and
do at home, lest there be the calamity of a war of "all against all."[9]
Hobbes rejected the idea of separation of powers, maintaining that
the power of the sovereign must be absolute.[10]

In the centuries since, governments and regimes, from Napo-
leonic France to the Soviet Union to Nazi Germany, have been described as embodiments of the Leviathan. Less extreme examples
appear on the left and right today, from Venezuela to China, from
Russia to Iran and Turkey.

Throughout history, governments have used many different techniques to align their citizens around a set of common goals and values. Some leaders highlight their nation's unique culture and shared history. Authoritarian regimes have on numerous occasions used the glue of ethnic hatred and nationalistic wars of aggression. The framers of our Republic committed the country to democratic ideals—freedom of religion and speech, equal opportunity, free markets, and the inalienable rights of life, liberty, and the pursuit of happiness.

For much of our country's history, a white Anglo-Saxon Christian majority has dominated our culture. Not surprisingly, many of the values shared by this group—such as an admiration for English common law, and a conviction that the monarch's prerogatives were limited by those laws—were incorporated into America's norms. In pursuit of what Martin Luther King would eventually articulate as the higher aspirations of the Constitution and the Declaration of Independence—that these documents were a promissory note to the future—idealists fought the Civil War, participated in the civil rights movement, and ultimately enacted the Civil Rights Act in 1964.

But a lot has changed since 1964. In 1960 the United States was 85 percent white, 3.5 percent Hispanic, 11 percent black, and 0.5 percent Asian.[11] America is now multicultural. Non-whites make up approximately 40 percent of the population and are forecast to be more than half of the population by mid-century.[12] Membership in Christian churches is in decline, falling by about 1 percent every year between 2007 and 2014.[13] At that rate, the country will be minority Christian in twenty years. The non-religious have become the country's largest voting bloc.[14]

As we've learned in those intervening years, there is a big difference between being multicultural and being a "melting pot," an expression that dates back to Israel Zangwill's 1908 play, *The Melting Pot*, which celebrated America as a place "where all the races of Europe are melting and re-forming!"[15]

In real America post-1960, this idealized ethnic mixing no longer exists (if it ever did—and it's no accident that Zangwill said nothing about the races from Africa, Asia, and the Levant). Some minorities have worked hard to be assimilated into the white Anglo-Saxon Christian culture. Others have accepted its dominance, remained quiet, and been accepted, tolerated, or discriminated against. Still other groups have made great efforts to maintain their unique cultural identities and establish themselves in opposition to the ruling culture.

What emerged after the Civil Rights Act is what Yale law professor and author Amy Chua refers to as a *super-group*. A super-group, by her definition, is a collection of sub-groups, each with its own identity but bound together by an "overarching collective identity."[16] Chua believes that keeping the super-group intact is key to maintaining democracy as a viable form of government in the United States.

The structural transformations of the Autonomous Revolution come into play here, because they are powering the economic inequality that is undermining the middle class, the group that provided much of the binding energy for the super-group. These transformations are also the motive force behind the rise of virtual social networks. Those networks have made it easy to create powerful factions with unyielding agendas, many of which seem prepared to go their own way. These threats must be dealt with, and soon, if the super-group is going to survive.

That said, while numerous studies and theories discuss how economic inequality undermines democracy, incontrovertible scientific evidence to that effect is missing. The sociologists Kenneth Scheve and David Stasavage have gone so far as to assert that "simple conjectures . . . that wealth inequality leads to democratic failure are not supported by the evidence."[17] What we do know is that, for the last two decades, average annual GDP growth has slowed to a crawl, and wages have stagnated. This lack of expansion has exacerbated competition between groups and heightened resentment of immigrants. Meanwhile, the rise of the global economy and the creation of new financial tools (such as high-frequency trading algorithms) have massively rewarded a fraction of the citizenry, while the rest have fallen behind.

Income inequality has now reached unprecedented extremes in the United States. The top 1 percent of earners capture more than 20 percent of pre-tax income, and the top 10 percent approximately 50 percent.[18] In the past fifty years, the real income of the top 5 percent more than doubled, while that of the bottom 60 percent increased only by approximately 30 percent.[19] The middle class was the big loser in the process. Since 1979, the incomes of the middle 60 percent have grown at about half the rate of the top 20 percent and even more slowly than those in the bottom quintile. That should be good news for the members of that bottom quintile—until you dig more deeply and discover that their average income in 2016 was less than $13,000 per year.[20] The Gini coefficient that measures income inequality now stands at historically high levels of more than 0.4 for the United States.[21]

The decline of the good job has left white Americans especially pessimistic. Just 24 percent of them believe their children will be better off than they are.[22] Economic insecurity is also on the rise. Eighty percent of Americans have experienced at least one year of poverty, welfare, or having an unemployed head of household.[23] The resulting desperation has led nine out of ten adult Americans to express a preference for economic stability over higher pay.[24]

When things are going well, it is easier to be more open to cultural differences. When things are more equal economically, different groups can rub up against one another, become acquainted, and be more accepting of one another's differences. During hard times, it is just the opposite.

In *Our Kids*, the sociologist Robert Putnam describes how his hometown went from being socially integrated to socially segregated as economic inequality grew and its middle class declined.[25] In a prior book, *Making Democracy Work*, Putnam studied the political structure of Italy. Democratic institutions, he found, flourished in northern Italy, where cross-cultural groups shared common interests in such diverse matters as bird-watching and sports. This contrasted with southern Italy, where there were stricter social hierarchies and fewer cross-cultural interactions—and where dem-ocratic institutions were weak and the Mafia powerful. Social capital was higher in the north, where democracy worked, and lower in the south, where it was struggling.[26]

When there is less interaction between groups in different economic strata, social empathy declines. The well-off are less likely to support programs for people who are not like them.[27] And, of course, empathy is a two-way street: if the haves are indifferent to the needs of the have-nots, that opens the door to political populism, class resentment and conflict, and even civil war.

Unfortunately, economic inequality usually translates into political inequality. The wealthy use campaign contributions, their influence, and their power to push legislation and regulations that favor them. As their influence grows, it is used to oppose social programs. Political scientist Jeffrey Winters calls this the "wealth defense."[28]

Moreover, severe economic inequality is closely correlated with a self-reinforcing lack of economic mobility. (Economist Alan Krueger named this the "Great Gatsby Curve."[29]) Children born into families in the top quintile are almost 75 percent more likely to attend college than those at the bottom.[30] The economically disadvantaged are also less likely to have access to the social networks that lead to good job contacts. This becomes a vicious generational cycle, with the rich staying rich and the poor sinking deeper into despair.

When members of the middle class see their jobs evaporating into virtual space, feel the declining value of their work in their wallets, and worry constantly about job stability, it's no wonder that they come to believe that the system is rigged against them. When they see the government lavishing tax breaks on the wealthy while their children struggle to find full-time work, polarization and alienation are inevitable.

The super-group is facing another difficult challenge: the growth of perceived discrimination. Two-thirds of white working-class Americans believe that they are as victimized by discrimination as black Americans are.[31] When you add their numbers to blacks,

Hispanics, Muslims, women, and members of the LGBTQ community, it is safe to say that the vast majority of Americans currently feel some level of aggrievement as victims.

DEATH OF THE SUPER-GROUP

For all these reasons, the cohesive super-group of a half-century ago is facing a perfect storm. Large numbers of its members are worried about their own and their children's future. If they are poor, they feel the system is rigged against them. If they are rich, they are inclined to circle the wagons and engage in "wealth defense." If they are in the middle, they feel squeezed by the poor at the bottom of the economic hierarchy, who are the beneficiaries of government programs, and the rich at the top, who benefit from a host of tax breaks. Rightly or not, many believe they are victims of anti-white and anti-Christian discrimination. Combine that perception with the very real demographic trend in which the dominant white Anglo-Saxon Christian majority is on the verge of becoming another minority. Then provide them with social networks—a breakthrough technology for waging social warfare. It is a deadly equation.

One symptom of this downward cyle has already appeared—a historically unprecedented decline in life expectancy for white American males. The proximate causes are opioid addiction, suicide, and unhealthy lifestyles ... but the underlying causes seem to be depression, despair, and a widespread sense of hopelessness. Given what we've already discussed about growing income inequality and the decline of the good job, these social problems are not going to be easy to repair.

THE REVENGE OF TRIBALISM

Now, consider social networks, which are further tearing apart the bonds of society—and which, ironically, promised to have just the opposite effect.

In their defense, there is nothing fundamentally new about what social networks do, or their use to target and influence populations. They just do it thousands of times better and more cost-effectively than any other medium ever has. For years, political organizations, businesses, governments, and institutions have used crude collections of data and information about people to influence their beliefs and actions. They have convened focus groups and constructed psychological profiles in an effort to learn how to appeal to the public's subconscious feelings, and carried out direct mail campaigns in which they test and hone a variety of messages.

Social networks have essentially weaponized those until-now comparatively weak tools of social manipulation. Social network tools empower a long list of things that undermine our ability to create unity of purpose and make it difficult to hold the super-group together.

For example, governments, including the United States, have used various forms of propaganda to interfere with elections in other countries and stir up social unrest. Russia, for example, has been meddling in foreign elections for decades.[32] What was different about the 2016 U.S. election was that, by using the power of social networking tools to foment confusion and hyper-partisanship (such as organizing both an anti-Muslim demonstration and a leftist counter-demonstration in Texas), Russian interference may have actually changed the election's results.

Beyond organized Russian efforts, social networking tools are powering messaging from groups with narrowly focused agendas, and even individual trolls. As Chua points out,

> The Left believes that right-wing tribalism—bigotry, racism—is tearing the country apart. The Right believes that left-wing tribalism—identity politics, political correctness— is tearing the country apart. They are both right.[33]

Perhaps, the greatest challenge that social networks present to the super-group is that they allow us to spend increasing amounts of our time with people who act like us, think like us, and get information from the same sources that we rely upon. In the process, we end up understanding less about the concerns and issues of those who look, act, or think differently from us. Indeed, it is increasingly difficult to imagine that those people are worthy of our concern. We find ourselves trusting those who are like us and distrusting or ignoring those who are different. In short, the prevalence of social media use makes it more difficult to create trust between groups.

The situation is a mirror version of what Putnam believed made democracy work in northern Italy. For democracy to work, he argued, groups must interact to pursue common goals. Trust is an emergent property of those interactions. As trust spreads throughout the system, democracy thrives. When trust is bled from the system, it weakens.[34]

As daunting as the challenge of income inequality is, the issues presented by social networks may be even more vexing. Recently, there have been a number of calls—and actions by certain social networks, such as Twitter and Facebook—to control the use of bots that spread fake news, block groups that spread hate messages, and set up independent groups to certify the reliability of news sources. In 2018, Facebook announced that it would hire 10,000 new security and content moderation employees.[35] But one criticism of these efforts is that the philosophical and political biases of the content moderators will stifle free speech. As Juvenal famously warned, "*Quis custodiet ipsos custodes?*" Who will guard the guardians?

In the past, the best cure for hate speech, lies, and hyper-partisanship has been free speech. A free press exposes people to objective data—and also invites them, via balanced news coverage and a diverse selection of opinion pieces—to consider other people's points of view. Whether it was exercised on a soapbox in the public square or on national TV, free speech has historically brought us together and reinforced our commitment to our democratic values. But weaponized free speech is a tool that can tear a free society apart.

Of course, the Founders faced some of the same problems we do—if anything, their newspapers were more partisan than Fox News or MSNBC, and the 1800 presidential election had more than its share of fake news. But the Founders didn't have to contend with the weapons of mass civil societal destruction that social networks can be. Social networks have changed the rules in a way that increasingly threatens the basis of our democracy. Because of that, it would seem that the best way to solve the problem is to make the networks less powerful and reduce their use.

In the last chapter, we discussed making social networks more expensive via taxation, much as we use taxes to disincentivize cigarette smoking. If it were more expensive to be constantly connected to a social network, people might spend less time in virtual space hanging around with others who are just like them and more time in the real world interacting with their physical neighbors.

Needless to say, with freeware as pervasive as it is, the very idea of paying fees or subscriptions to be on the Internet seems almost heretical. But as the social costs of freemium Internet services become more obvious, that attitude may change. Indeed, after the recent revelations of the irresponsible sale of personal user information, that shift may have already begun.

Another possible solution is intrinsically more dangerous. Thomas Hobbes was convinced that Leviathan had to have the power to control expression in order to govern effectively. Were he alive today, he would certainly argue for a much narrower interpretation of the rules of free speech. We could make it illegal to knowingly spread fake news—that is, to make statements of supposed fact that are not supported by adequate data.

If, like libel, the definition of fake news was legally circumscribed to include only statements that are known to be falsehoods in light of generally available empirical data, and that are spoken or published with malign intent, and if culpability was treated as a crime and prosecuted in the courts—and if to be a crime, multiple infractions were required, not just one mistake—we might begin to get a handle on the problem. Of course, the potential for governmental misuse of such laws is something that needs to be considered as well—more than one nation has taken such a path to tyranny.

Reducing the networks' power, reach, and levels of interaction with users will not solve the problem, but it will address the basic issue, which is that the powerful tools of mass communication have become too cheap and too easy to misuse. A century ago, Oliver Wendell Holmes Jr. famously declared that "the most stringent protection of free speech would not protect a man in falsely shouting fire in a theatre and causing a panic."[36] Placing more controls on false speech would make it more difficult to do just that. The good news is that we have lived with libel laws for decades and they have not seriously impeded our ability to speak freely.

At best, these solutions are troubling—and a long way from how we like to see ourselves, as free Americans protected by the First Amendment. It is a chilling thought, but if we are to deal effectively with the societal phase change that the Autonomous Revolution has wrought, we may have to place some limits on our democracy in order to preserve it.

Current governance systems were designed to manage physical activities subject to physical limitations within specific geographies. In addition, many of the laws, regulations, and rights granted in the Constitution make assumptions about the economics of certain activities. For example, one-to-many communication was expensive in the past; today it is virtually free. In the past you could not yell "fire" in a theater without being in one; today everyone has easy access to virtual theaters on the Internet. Thus, it is important to realize that the free speech of the past was severely constrained by the technology of the time. What has been proposed above is substituting a form of legal constraint for the technological and economic restraints that existed on free speech in the past.

BEFORE WE'RE READY

While phase changes are still in process, we tend to underestimate their impact and the potential threats they represent. "Technology revolutions arrive more slowly than we predict, but more quickly than we are prepared for them."[37] Then, when we do react to them, we tend to rely on the tried-and-true techniques that worked in the past. History is replete with stories of obsolete societies that tried to apply old solutions to new challenges. Think of the Ethiopian tribesmen who tried to fight Italian tanks with spears. When we are threatened by the future, we tend to react with denial and confusion.

Our reaction to the current threats of cyber war, cyber terror, and cybercrime are perfect cases in point. Once again, we seem to have forgotten the painful lessons of the past.

As pointed out in chapter 5, when the first credit card systems were designed, the companies involved envisioned fraud as a minor problem and decided against incorporating features such as PINs out of fear that they would interfere with market development. The banks made the same mistake again in 2017, almost sixty years after the appearance of the first plastic American Express credit card, when they announced the Zelle payment system.[38] Once again, business urgency trumped security.

The banks had fallen behind PayPal's Venmo in the race to allow consumers to quickly and inexpensively transfer money between accounts. The Zelle payment system put them in the lead, but it also allowed member banks to participate with very low levels of security. Two-factor authentication was not required. Some banks did not even notify customers when transfers were initiated. Many customers only learned about Zelle when money was stolen from their accounts.[39]

Given the size and the importance of the banks that were backing Zelle, the high stakes of the competition, and the increasing levels of credit card theft, you would have thought the banks would have wanted to set an example for safety and security. But they chose the path of least resistance, and users soon found themselves paying to buy items, only to have sellers disappear after they received their cash.

As a country, we should have made cyber-defense a priority, starting in 1982. That was the year that the first cyber-bomb exploded. One might choose to label the explosion an act of cyberwar, but it is probably more accurate to label it a cybercrime gone wrong.

Here's what happened: The United States wanted to disrupt the functioning of a Siberian pipeline to make it harder for the Soviets to export natural gas and earn hard currency. (Remember this was 1982, before the collapse of the Soviet Union.) The CIA found a way to do so after learning that the Soviets were seeking to steal software that would enable them to improve the efficiency of their pipeline operation. The CIA modified the software to reset pump speeds and valve settings, which would create pressures the pipeline could not withstand. Then the agency allowed that bugged software to be "stolen." The resulting explosion, which was visible from outer space, was estimated to have had a 3-kiloton force.[40]

That was back in the Stone Age of the microprocessor revolution, long before the commercial Internet appeared. In 1988, another warning shot was fired when Robert Tappan Morris released the first computer worm into the Internet—an act, he claimed later, that was intended to call attention to the vulnerability of the system and the inadequacy of its security measures.[41] A year later, he earned the dubious distinction of being the first person to be indicted under the 1986 Computer Fraud and Abuse Act.[42] He was sentenced to three years of probation, community service, and a small fine.

Over the subsequent thirty years, the United States has focused a great deal of its energy on building offensive cyber weapons. In 2009, Stuxnet was launched against the Iranian uranium enrichment facility at Natanz. Twenty-seven years after the pipeline explosion in

Siberia, cyber experts nevertheless described Stuxnet as the world's first digital weapon.[43] The virus took control of the Natanz centrifuges and caused a thousand of them to self-destruct.[44]

The NSA has developed tool kits that can be used to engineer cyberattacks. Tragically, some of those tool kits were stolen and sold on the Dark Web. They have been used to engineer the WannaCry, Petya, and NotPetya viruses.

Numerous other even more powerful tools have been developed, and many are in wide use. Phishing software sends out millions of emails designed to trick users into revealing their passwords. Criminals, terrorists, and hostile governments misdirect users to fake websites that install Trojan horse software on their systems and turn them into zombies. Bots can be used to recruit thousands of online devices to flood targeted websites with so many messages that they are overwhelmed and can no longer service customers. Companies from Airbnb and Amazon to Starbucks, Twitter, Visa, and Zillow have been victims of these "denial of service" attacks. Then there are ransomware attacks, in which viruses seize control of computers and encrypt user files unless the user is willing to pay a ransom in a cryptocurrency. In some cases, malware can direct the system to shut down and erase itself, or, as in the case of Stuxnet, speed up until it destroys itself.

Cyber weapons can disrupt or shut down power grids and communication, transportation, and financial networks, and bring commercial operations to a standstill. They can and do cause tremendous physical damage as well. Cybersecurity Ventures estimates the cost of cybercrime at $3 trillion in 2015 and projects that it will rise to $6 trillion by 2021.[45] To put this number in perspective, that represents about 4 percent of the gross domestic product for the world.[46]

To date, most of the damage done by cyber criminals/terrorists/warriors has been economic. But a growing number of high-profile incidents should serve as a warning about what is to come.

In 2007, when authorities in Estonia chose to move a Russian World War II memorial, Russia warned that the action could provoke a response. On April 27 of that year, Estonians became victims of a massive denial of service attack that made bank accounts inaccessible, shut down news services, and tied government websites into knots. Even though Russian involvement has never been proved, Jason Healey, a researcher at Columbia University, believes that "[Russia] put everyone on notice that it was willing to behave badly in cyberspace."[47]

Electric utilities have also become targets. According to Symantec, there have been an estimated one hundred sophisticated intrusions into the SCADA systems that utilities use to control the pumps, motors, valves, and relays that manage power generation and distribution. The hackers behind these attacks are groups called Dragonfly and Energetic Bear, both of which are believed to be linked to Russia.[48] In December of 2015, an operation called Sandworm, also believed to be linked to Russia, turned off power to 225,000 Ukrainians. In 2016, hackers plunged parts of Kiev into darkness.

To date, these attacks have done no physical damage to the electrical networks themselves. But that event almost certainly lies just over the horizon. More than ten years ago, Michael Assante, a security expert at the SANS Institute, demonstrated that a mere twenty-one lines of code could jiggle a circuit breaker on a power generator. Before it died, it shook, blew off parts, and belched a huge cloud of black smoke.[49]

Yet, even now, we—private citizens, businesses, and the government—do not take cyber threats seriously enough. There are many reasons why: countering them is expensive; security measures are inconvenient and tedious to use; the threats are intangible.

Remember the 3-kiloton bomb the Russians dropped on themselves? Figuratively speaking, numerous 3-kiloton bombs are being infiltrated into our vital infrastructure. Some of them are being placed by state actors (such as Chinese government hacker teams), and others by terrorists; there might even be some placed by sick pranksters. The point is, we don't know, and that is a sign of how unprepared we are.

GOING ON THE DEFENSIVE

Go to the U.S. Homeland Security website and you will find quotes such as this:

> DHS coordinates with sector specific agencies, other federal agencies, and private sector partners to share information on and analysis of cyber threats and vulnerabilities and to understand more fully the interdependency of infrastructure systems nationwide.

Or this:

> Because cybersecurity and physical security are increasingly interconnected, DHS has partnered with the critical infrastructure community to establish a voluntary program to encourage use of the Framework for Improving Critical Infrastructure Cybersecurity to strengthen critical infrastructure cybersecurity.[50]

If this strikes you as a totally inadequate, passive, policy response to a very serious threat, you are right. It is spears against tanks. The phase change is under way, the rules have already changed—and governments don't understand what those new rules are. They need to learn . . . and quickly.

In the many cases of cyber war, terror, and crime, the best defense will no longer be an offense. It will be a system of well-planned defensive measures. The U.S. government needs to pass laws and regulate behavior so that businesses, utilities, government institutions, and private individuals will install strong defensive measures and require their use. It will have to force lazy members of the public to use two-factor authentication. It will need to inspect banks, utilities, and businesses to ensure compliance. It will have to mandate that energy companies take steps to harden their networks, so that their pipelines do not become 3-kiloton bombs.

In recent years, many have complained about regulatory overburden. It goes without saying that the regulatory effort required to harden the country against cyber threats will be very large. Cybersecurity brings with it the need for big government to get even bigger and more intrusive.

Another great challenge government will face is how to deal with distributed institutions whose core operations are located in cyberspace. At the extreme end of this spectrum is the phenomenon of cyber currencies, of which Bitcoin is the best example.

Bitcoin is an amalgam of thousands of networked nodes located around the world. Its governance is a free-form network that sets its own rules and direction. It is truly a hydra—it has many heads, and if you cut off one, another will grow in its place. It is also like a ghost that has no form or shape.

For example, bitcoins are mined by computers. Some of those computers are server farms located where they can have access to low-cost electricity. Bitmain Technologies Ltd. has a 25,000 computer server farm in Erdos, Inner Mongolia, where coal power is inexpensive.[51] Iceland's cheap water power has made it a bitcoin miners' paradise—so much so that Iceland is on the brink of using more electricity to mine bitcoins than to power its homes.[52]

Anybody can become a bitcoin miner by purchasing the appropriate hardware, downloading free mining software, and joining a bitcoin mining pool. If you want to save yourself the trouble, you can even sign up with a bitcoin cloud mining service such as Genesis for as little as $30.[53] The current number of bitcoin miners is anyone's guess—though it has been estimated that there may be 5,000 full nodes used by 100,000 miners.

Of course, anything as important as a currency worth billions of dollars cannot survive as pure anarchy. It needs some type of governance. And in that regard, Bitcoin may be a bellwether of the new forms of governance in the Autonomous Revolution. Peer review, consensus building, and acceptance of changes by miners all determine the future of the currency. In the case of Bitcoin, as the number of transactions grew, some felt that changes had to be made to improve its speed. Many of the node operators did not like the proposed solution, so the currency hit a "fork." A new version of the currency, Bitcoin Cash, was created and used by a subset of the node providers. The other node providers continued to support the existing protocol and the old Bitcoin.[54]

It is highly likely in a phase-changed world that some form of virtual currency will be widely used. Now, consider how a government might govern a bitcoin that exists everywhere in an extremely fluid form. It would be nearly impossible. In that scenario, who will protect the public against financial fraud?

In 1976, Friedrich Hayek published *The Denationalization of Money*, in which he proposed the establishment of private currencies subject to the discipline of free markets, not government control. Hayek's vision may well become a reality of the Autonomous Revolution. If some form of virtual currency becomes widely used, governments may lose their ability to issue their own currencies—even the U.S. dollar might lose much of its clout.

Should that scenario develop, many governments may lose their ability to print money and would no longer be able to use inflation to finance their debts. In yet another scenario, one of those free-market currency issuers might find a way to rig the system and abscond with billions.

Virtual currencies will test the limits of our whole system of global finance. With most of their operations virtualized and distributed, their core functions are extremely difficult to regulate. If you regulate it in one place, it migrates to another. In many respects, virtual currencies are like the *Guys and Dolls* song, "The Oldest Established Permanent Floating Crap Game in New York."

SURRENDERING SOVEREIGNTY

Financial institutions are for the most part information proxies, and it is easy to virtualize large portions of their operations. In doing so, many of them fly under the radar of existing regulations.

In 2006, Iceland's banks needed more deposits to improve their disastrously low deposit-to-loan ratios. Landsbanki's had fallen below 0.4:1. To fix the problem, it founded Icesave, an online bank that paid customers high interest rates on savings and provided both security and great 24/7 service. Customers could use their devices to check their balances whenever they liked, see if their checks had cleared, and confirm the status of transactions. They could transfer money easily and watch a transmission happen almost in real time. All of that transparency built trust, but customers also felt safe because they knew their deposits were guaranteed under Iceland's deposit insurance program.

Within five months of its launch, Icesave had acquired more than 60,000 customers, who deposited some £2 billion. By its first birthday, it had more than 110,000 customers and £4.4 billion in deposits, and it had captured more than 40 percent of all new Internet deposits in the UK. Icesave's deposits equaled about one quarter of Iceland's gross domestic product. For a U.S. bank to achieve the same relative size, it would have to have assets of close to $4 trillion, or 50 percent more than the largest American bank has ever held.[55] In one year, Icesave had achieved what no U.S. bank had accomplished in centuries.

Unfortunately, deposit insurance works only if the insurer has enough assets to cover the liabilities. When the 2008 financial crisis hit, many of Icesave's depositors were left holding the bag.[56] Landsbanki wasn't a criminal enterprise. Its executives just took unreasonable risks. That said, two of them are now serving sentences in Kvíabryggja Prison.[57]

As societal phase change takes hold, there will be more Bitcoins and Icesaves. Governments will find themselves increasingly forced to control not just illegal enterprises conducted in the darkest corners of the web, from cyberterrorists to dealers of illegal goods like Silk Road, but legal ones, from online casinos and porn sites to banks and social networks.

This will inevitably lead to the establishment of international agreements and institutions—think cyber-Interpol—to police the borderless virtual world. There will likely also be new international financial regulatory institutions. Governments will be under increasing pressure to surrender some of their sovereignty to these groups, as they now do to the World Court.

To date, the United States, as the self-proclaimed guarantor of freedom in the world, has remained largely aloof from participation in these organizations, and with good reason. For one thing, its special role often requires it to commit to actions from which its fellow nations, protected by the United States, can remain aloof. Also, history has shown a tendency for many of these organizations to be hijacked over time by members, including some of the worst offenders, with their own agendas.

We see no reason for these trends to disappear. Indeed, they may gain impetus in the Autonomous Revolution. How these dilemmas will be resolved is not clear. But what is increasingly obvious is that all governments—the United States included—will be under heavy pressure to surrender ever greater independence to world governance institutions to control virtual organizations that call no country home.

Another reality is that some virtual institutions will flee to countries that will choose not to support those international agreements. That, in turn, will lead to even more agreements, this time to impose various sanctions on nations that harbor irresponsible, rogue, and criminal virtual organizations. Those sanctions—like those placed on Japan in the 1930s, and on Iran and Russia today for their aggressions—could well spur further conflicts, virtual and real.

FASTER TO SCALE

Facebook is a reminder that the ultimate effects of the Autonomous Revolution will be difficult, if not impossible, to predict. Who would have thought that Facematch, a homemade computer program that let Harvard undergraduates play a "hot or not" game about their classmates, would grow into a user application that currently ties 2 billion people together around the world? Who could have predicted that it would be a tool that powered revolutions, brought down governments, and that would reshape our democracy? Or that it would be used as a tool by foreign governments to influence our elections? Who would have guessed that a tool that many thought would empower free speech might force us to pass laws to limit that speech?

About the only thing we can say with assurance about the future of our government is that it will have to design new rules to adapt. We believe that there is a very real risk that it might take a Hobbesian, authoritarian turn. It is essential that this not happen.

Perhaps the words of Ronald Reagan best summarize our responsibilities to the future: "Freedom is never more than one generation away from extinction. We didn't pass it to our children in the bloodstream. It must be fought for, protected, and handed on for them to do the same."[58]

CHAPTER TEN

SACRED VALUES

Novi Coeptus

AS TECHNOLOGY AND THE AUTONOMOUS REVOLUTION race forward, we are being inundated with substitutional equivalences and new institutional forms. In the process, the gap between the culture that was formed in the Industrial Age and the cultural requirements of our new age are widening.

In chapter 2, we briefly discussed William Ogburn and his theory of cultural lag. Just to review, cultural lag occurs "when one of two parts of culture that are correlated changes before . . . the other part does."[1] In the case of the Autonomous Revolution, the parts that have changed are the institutional forms associated with the information, intelligence, and spatial equivalences that define our new age. We are spending more and more of our lives in virtual environments and entrusting more and more of our labor and decision-making to intelligent machines. Yet we still live by the rules, systems of governance, beliefs, habits, cultural norms, values, and economic assumptions that developed during the Agricultural and Industrial Revolutions.

We are truly at a *novi coeptus*—a new beginning. And we are falling victim to cultural lag. How do we begin to close this gap? The first thing we must do is to start calling things what they are and not what we wish them to be.

We can begin by calling the Autonomous Revolution what it is. It is not the "Fourth Industrial Revolution," as many insist on calling it. If we call it that, we will think of it that way. If we believe that we are experiencing the next phase of the Industrial Revolution, we will respond by attempting to rejigger industrial-age processes to deal with the new forms. We will fail to address our new challenges at their roots and we will miss out on great opportunities. Worse still, we will apply obsolete solutions to our most pressing problems.

The three Industrial Revolutions were driven by power equivalences—the First by steam power, the Second by electricity, and the Third by computing. Despite those changes, institutional forms stayed pretty much the same, and they were embedded in a cultural system that was very stable as well. We believed in liberty and democracy, the free market, and the value of hard work in 1787 and we still believe in those things today.

When the steam power of the First Industrial Revolution was replaced by the electric power of the Second, it became possible to put small amounts of distributed power at individual workstations rather than locating workstations in a line that drew their power from leather belts driven by overhead shafts that were powered by steam engines. Factories were still factories—they just became more efficient. When computer power replaced mechanical computation, the factory was still a factory, but the spreadsheets used to control production were no longer produced by clerks with slide rules and accounting pads. Computing power now took over the job.

Throughout the 250 years of the Industrial era(s), our system of governance has remained remarkably stable. While we may debate its size, most of us would not want to return to the minimal national government of the past. Most of us would still want Social Security, Medicare, and some degree of market regulation.

Our habits, beliefs, and cultural norms have been fairly constant as well. Even though we have had a secular government since our founding, Christian values, beliefs, and holidays are still dominant.

The Protestant work ethic has shaped government policies and our perceptions of human worth. We look down on people who cannot hold jobs and are suspicious of those who need government assistance.

The structural transformations that characterize the Autonomous Revolution are changes of kind as well as form. We are moving into a future in which millions, through no fault of their own, will not have jobs, and in which machines will be more valued as workers than humans. We are experiencing a societal phase change, and as such, many of our new forms are fundamentally incompatible with our old rules and norms.

A HARD TURN

The dry words of history books do not do phase changes justice. The hard reality is that these transformations are wrenching. The struggles of workers, children, and families in the early years of the Industrial Age are perhaps best captured in the novels of Charles Dickens, Courbet's painting *The Stone Breakers*, stark black-and-white photographs of industrial slums and cities clouded in smoke, and Charlie Chaplin's classic movie *Modern Times*.

But perhaps the most powerful account of a phase change can be found in allegorical form in humanity's oldest known work of written literature, *The Epic of Gilgamesh*.

Gilgamesh was the king of Uruk, civilization's first major city. Cities represented a major change in societal form, and their growth was driven by the Agricultural Revolution. Like us, Gilgamesh was experiencing a rapid change in forms and norms and he was struggling with cultural lag. To build his army, he forced boys to become disciplined soldiers, whereas in a tribal culture they would have aspired to be freebooting warriors—a change in values.

Gilgamesh himself was a poor excuse for a monarch—self-indulgent, corrupt, and violent, he abused his power. He took the virginity of young girls and slept with his citizens' brides on their wedding nights. The people of Uruk were so oppressed that they prayed to the gods Anu and Aruru to protect them.[2]

The gods, as they must, decided to teach Gilgamesh a lesson. They created a wild man, Enkidu, an emissary from the old, pre-agrarian life, and sent him to Uruk to challenge Gilgamesh to a test of strength. Gilgamesh defeated Enkidu, and they became friends. Together they then journeyed to the dangerous, supernatural Cedar Grove. Driven by their lust for fame, Gilgamesh and Enkidu cut down the virgin stands.[3] Gilgamesh himself toppled the Sacred Cedar. But then they went too far and killed the sacred bull of the goddess Ishtar. Gilgamesh had already gotten on Ishtar's bad side by spurning her advances. Now, furious, she punished him by having Enkidu killed. The old life—the old world—was now gone forever.

Shattered and for the first time truly cognizant—and fearful—of death, a desperate Gilgamesh traveled the earth in search of immortality, his last hope. Of course, his quest was a failure. In the end, the chastened but wiser king returned to Uruk as a mortal.

Early in Gilgamesh's journey, the tavern keeper Siduri gave him some timeless advice:

> Gilgamesh, where are you roaming? You will never find the eternal life that you seek. When the gods created mankind, they also created death, and they held back eternal life for themselves alone. But until the end comes, enjoy your life, spend it in happiness, not despair. Savor your food, make each of your days a delight. . . . Let music and dancing fill your house, love the child who holds you by the hand, and give your wife pleasure in your embrace. That is the best way for a man to live.[4]

Today, as we rush headlong into the Autonomous Revolution, we too are cutting down sacred cedars and killing sacred bulls. Like Gilgamesh and Enkidu, we have gone too far. The victims of our virtual slash-and-burn activities are things like privacy, face-to-face interactions, and thoughtful disagreements with our peers. Porn sites (and soon robots) are replacing sex, and trolls are replacing objective sources of information. Like Gilgamesh, we wander without direction in virtual space, looking for the Plant of Immortality. We Tweet, take selfies, become trolls, join affinity groups, and pride ourselves on our thousands of contentless friendships, all in a fruitless quest for enduring self-esteem.

It is fitting that civilization's first work of literature addresses the dizzyingly disorienting experience of phase change. We too will struggle as we leave the old and familiar behind and begin to try on our new identities. In the process, we will redefine our lives and institutions to mesh with virtual space. But the enduring lesson of *The Epic of Gilgamesh* is that, if we go too far, our wanderings will be futile. Even as we adapt to phase change, we are going to have to pay heed to Siduri's advice and hold on to those things that are too sacred to lose.

ONLY ON THE BRIGHT SIDE

The primary focus of this book has been to examine the changes in form and rules that are already under way. We have identified many of them and speculated about others, from the potential effects of autonomous vehicles to trends under way in the financial services industry. We have identified the types of rule changes that might accompany these new forms and in the process have advanced ideas about the control of free speech, consumer ownership of personal information, how to reduce the power of monopolies that seek to control our behavior, and the potential of building infrastructure to provide new jobs.

In most cases, we can exercise less control over the changes in form than over the rules that govern the behavior of those forms. One reason for that is the pace of change in the virtual world. Think how quickly Facebook, Uber, and Airbnb happened. A second reason is that we see the good in a change first and have a hard time envisioning its bad side effects. Initially many of us thought that Facebook would be a great way to keep families together. Who could have anticipated that it would become a tool for foreign governments to manipulate our elections? We are reluctant, as we should be, to attempt to exercise control over a form that is doing wonderful things, based on an apprehension that something bad— we know not what—might happen.

Finally, these new forms will be extremely efficient and convenient to use. Many will be so appealing that they will win in the free market and rapidly crowd out the old ways of doing things. Think of how quickly WeChat Pay assembled a network of 300,000 stores and 200 million users in China to replace credit cards.[5]

But time is also the reason that we can shape new rules. Once the new forms are locked in, they will be with us for a long time. We will have time to craft our responses to them. But the longer we wait to start, the more difficult it will be to shape them to our liking. Like the freemium business model, once a rule has been established and widely accepted, it becomes extremely difficult to change.

In prior chapters, we have suggested some possible new rules for the Autonomous Revolution. But we also recognize that we are so early in the process that these suggestions are necessarily incomplete—and may ultimately prove misguided. Still, they are a stake in the ground, a beginning from which we can start the critical conversation. There will still be—there must be—considerable debate about what these new rules should be. We are sure that others will come up with different approaches, and many of them will be better than ours.

We expect the changes we have suggested to spark considerable criticism and resistance. As always, some will want to stick with the increasingly unworkable status quo. When the Industrial Revolution came, some people stayed on the farm and in rural villages, even as the jobs went away and the once vibrant local stores vanished from Main Street and ghost towns rose in their stead.

By the same token, many technocrats will want to race ahead

and let the brutal free market set the rules. Allowing its winners untrammeled access to the tools that shape public opinion, giving them unlimited latitude to find out what is going on in our minds, granting them the power to decide what we can read, giving them great power to influence our actions and what we should know is something that would be unacceptable to many.

Of course, making the right rule changes will help to reduce cultural lag. But rule changes will not be enough in and of themselves. The other correlated parts that have to change to reduce cultural lag are our systems of governance, beliefs, habits, cultural norms, and values.

Almost a century ago John Maynard Keynes foresaw many of the economic and cultural challenges we are now facing. Keynes was deeply worried about a new societal dysfunction—technological unemployment (what he called job loss due to automation).[6] He knew then, just as we know now, how difficult it would be for people who were threatened by change to adapt to it, and he accurately foresaw the stresses that rapid increases in productivity would exert on our value system.

In 1930, in his now-classic article, "Economic Possibilities for Our Grandchildren," Keynes postulated the end of the Protestant work ethic—one of our most basic values—and imagined a time when the accumulation of wealth would no longer be of high social importance:

> [T]echnical improvements in manufacture and transport have been proceeding at a greater rate in the last ten years than ever before in history. In the United States factory output per head was 40 per cent greater in 1925 than in 1919. . . . In quite a few years—in our own lifetimes I mean—we may be able to perform all the operations of agriculture, mining, and manufacture with a quarter of the human effort to which we have been accustomed.

For the moment the very rapidity of these changes is hurting us and bringing difficult problems to solve. . . . We are being afflicted with a new disease . . . namely, technological unemployment. . . .

. . . I would predict that the standard of life in progressive countries one hundred years hence will be between four and eight times as high as it is to-day. . . .

. . . This means that the economic problem is not—if we look into the future—the permanent problem of the human race. . . .

The strenuous purposeful money-makers may carry all of us along with them into the lap of economic abundance. But it will be those peoples, who can keep alive, and cultivate into a fuller perfection, the art of life itself and do not sell themselves for the means of life, who will be able to enjoy the abundance when it comes. . . .

For many ages to come the old Adam will be so strong in us that everybody will need to do some work if he is to be contented. We shall do more things for ourselves than is usual with the rich to-day, only too glad to have small duties and tasks and routines. But beyond this, we shall endeavour to spread the bread thin on the butter—to make what work there is still to be done to be as widely shared as possible. Three-hour shifts or a fifteen-hour week may put off the problem for a great while. For three hours a day is quite enough to satisfy the old Adam in most of us!

There are changes in other spheres too which we must expect to come. When the accumulation of wealth is no longer of high social importance, there will be great changes in the code of morals.[7]

An increasingly jobless future isn't such a terrible thing to contemplate if everyone shares in the general prosperity.

The changes that Keynes foresaw in morals and values were

driven by process changes that were taking place during the Second Industrial Revolution. Think of what he might have envisioned if he had anticipated the equivalences that are today changing the nature of space and replacing humans' minds.

Unfortunately, Keynes did not give us much practical advice on how to create those new values and make his fifteen-hour workweek work. As we see it, the key ingredient that will be needed for reducing our cultural lag will be leadership.

To adapt to the Autonomous Revolution—and keep it from going off the rails into nightmare scenarios—our national, local, business, religious, institutional, and educational leaders will have to model a new set of values. The alternative is to continue down the road of extreme political and economic polarization that we are on now.

If we stay on our current path, we will build a new social structure that's based on continual conflict between winners and losers. This will have some very undesirable consequences. Progress will be defined not in terms of problems solved and forward movement, but in undoing whatever solutions the prior group put into place. Because of the constant changes in direction, businesses will become fearful of making long-term investments or taking bold risks. Inevitably, economic growth will suffer.

The consequences of having an economically and politically dominant group of "winners" are also unattractive. When one group stays in power for a long time, it inevitably falls into corruption. And since there will be more losers than winners, social unrest—and ultimately social collapse—are inevitable.

There is another reason why opting for our present, deeply polarized approach will not work. Today's polarized groups are defined by hardline philosophical positions that are based on 250 years and three Industrial Revolutions worth of experiences. They exist to defend those distinct philosophies. Thus, their approaches to the challenges of the Autonomous Revolution will tend to be based on outdated beliefs, thinking, and understandings—and not upon the search for new solutions that will work with new forms.

For these reasons we both hope and believe that Americans will reject polarization.

We hope that Americans will select and follow leaders who will be wise enough to embrace the correct changes while preserving those things that are too sacred to lose. Those values will have to include democracy, freedom and liberty, privacy, and tolerance. They will place a premium on truth and honesty. They will have a healthy skepticism when it comes to extremist positions. They will view technology holistically and attempt to understand not only its operational and economic effects but also its psychological and sociological implications.

They will also realize that, while rules can mitigate cultural lag, they are an imperfect solution. Rules, laws, and technological fixes will not work unless they are supported by values and cultural norms that are thoroughly internalized.

Income taxes are a case in point. The U.S. system depends on voluntary compliance: though it has its auditors, the government essentially trusts its citizens to accurately report their income.[8] That's not naïve. One recent study, based on a sample of two thousand taxpayers, found that only 6 percent of Americans knowingly cheat on their returns.[9]

By comparison, a very large number of taxpayers cheat in Greece. To save on taxes, only 324 residents in one community reported ownership of a private swimming pool—while satellite photos showed that in fact 16,794 existed. Greece has a large underground economy. Because receipts can be used to track unreported income, many professionals choose not to issue them. One customer reported that his auto mechanic charges him quite a bit more if he asks for a receipt.[10]

It is extremely difficult to make a voluntary compliance system work in a culture where large numbers believe it is acceptable to cheat. Tax evasion runs between 6 percent and 9 percent of GDP in Greece. Government revenues would be 20 to 25 percent higher if Greeks were as honest about their taxes as Americans.[11]

Adam Smith understood that moral authority served as the thumb of the invisible hand. If moral authority broke down, the invisible hand would lose its grip.

In Smith's day, business activity was predominantly local. One thing that ensured that market participants remained well-behaved was that most people conducted their business affairs in the communities in which they lived. As a result, control rested with one's neighbors, the people one saw in church, and at meetings of local business organizations.

Smith argued that:

> In the race for wealth and honours and preferments, he may run as hard as he can, and strain every nerve and every muscle, in order to outstrip all his competitors. But if he should jostle or throw down any of them, the indulgence of the spectators is entirely at an end. It is a violation of fair play, which they cannot admit of.[12]

Rules, laws, and cyber controls can help us keep the game fair. But trolls, fake news, cyberbullying, hacking, unethical businesses hiding in virtual space, and groups that encourage tribal cultures and intolerance will continue to exist. Soft solutions may turn out to be the most effective. Charismatic business, government, church, and social leaders are going to have to set and model standards of behavior that turn trolls, cyberbullies, and those who spread fake news into social misfits rather than the heroes that some of them are today.

We must confront two other extremely important issues as part of our adaptation process. The first has to do with the general level of economic insecurity that currently exists. Many have lost well-paid jobs. Some of us have spent years developing valuable skills that will no longer be valuable. If you are fifty and spent twenty-five years as an expert and have just been replaced by a stupid robot and some computer program offers to retrain you for a job at half your prior salary, it is pretty easy to become both cynical and disillusioned. Large numbers of parents are concerned about the economic futures of their children. When people see change as a zero-sum game that they cannot win, they resist it and attempt to preserve the past. If we are going to adapt well to the Autonomous Revolution, we are going to have to confront this issue head on.

The second issue is that things are happening *fast*. Therefore, we need to create new rules to accompany the new forms as quickly as possible.

Hopefully we can find free-market solutions (or private/public solutions), such as investing proactively in the infrastructure of the future and in greater entrepreneurship. If those solutions do not lessen inequality, we are going to have to use other systems for redistributing wealth, such as higher taxes, free universal health care, and universal basic income (UBI). One consequence of all of this is that we may end up with even bigger government. Countries like Sweden spend about 10 to 15 percent more of their GDP on government than we do.[13] Not coincidentally, Sweden's Gini coefficient—the lower the number, the greater the income equality—is 0.259, less than a third of that of the United States.[14]

If the solution to income inequality comes in the form of high tax rates, universal health care, and UBI we will have moved closer to socialism—a very big value change.

To many of us believers in the Protestant work ethic, who sometimes put in fifteen-hour days and think hard work is good not only for business but also for the individual, the economy, and society as a whole, Keynes's fifteen-hour workweek seems almost unthinkable. For those who believe that the best government is the smallest government, moving closer to a socialized system is a suicidal form of heresy. But what seems like heresy on this side of the culture lag may seem like normalcy on the other.

One of the biggest obstacles we have to deal with is our slow reaction to change. In general, there are good reasons for being cautious when we make big changes. When we attempt to solve new problems we do not fully understand, we are sure to make mistakes. Purported solutions can be worse than the problems they are meant to address.

But time is a luxury we no longer have. While the Agricultural Revolution transpired over ten millennia and the Industrial Revolution over 250 years, much of the Autonomous Revolution will be happening in the next decade. We have to react faster.

There are two possible ways to do this. The first is to make our laws less prescriptive and more focused on broad goals and objectives, delegating the details to the regulatory agencies that will enforce them. The less detailed they are, the faster they can be written and put into effect. Of course, if you do this, you are giving the deep state carte blanche to get deeper—another cultural and value issue. There would be more of the agencies that conservatives love to hate, like the Securities and Exchange Commission, the Environmental Protection Agency, and the Consumer Financial Protection Agency.

This, of course, goes to the heart of the biggest value/cultural issue that our leaders will have to grapple with in the near future, which is whether we want to adopt a laissez-faire free-market approach or a big-government approach to the adaptation problem. We suspect—and are not entirely happy about it—that we will end up selecting some form of the big-government solution. But how to do this without devolving into kleptocracy, and authoritarian and totalitarian forms of government? High taxes and onerous regulations can stifle economic growth and shrink the pie they're meant to share. If we must grow government, can we restrain that growth in responsible ways? And what of our liberty? Is this a risk we're prepared to take?

Should we be optimistic or pessimistic? We come down on the side of optimism for five reasons. First, because we believe that we can preserve the things we hold sacred. Second, because we further believe that those things will bring us together and enable us to adjust to phase change in a peaceable way. Third, because we have solved Keynes's "economic problem." That is, because our tools are making us so productive, we have a future of abundance. Fourth, is that our new technologies are making existing products and services better, providing us with new and wonderful services, from virtual travel to having the world's information at our fingertips, making society more efficient, and helping us deal with many environmental issues. Finally, we know there are new rules that will enable us to mitigate the challenging effect of phase change and enable us to enjoy many of its benefits.

We also believe our commitment as a nation to our sacred values, such as democracy, equality, and liberty and freedom for all, will enable our leaders to bring us together in pursuit of common goals. We are hopeful, despite some of the more distressing trends that we read about in the daily headlines, because Americans in increasing numbers are actually rejecting the extremes. Since 2008, the fastest growing group of voters have been Independents—to the point that in sixteen states (where data is available) they make up a quarter of registered voters.[15] We predict this trend will ultimately put pressure on politicians to moderate their positions.

We are also hopeful that in coming years strong leaders will emerge who will ensure both the future of those things we hold sacred and create a shared vision that will enable us to meet our challenges in a constructive way.

What makes us most optimistic is that we have solved the abundance problem. Having done this, we will have the resources to deal with the most challenging issues of phase change.

In a recent article, W. Brian Arthur argues that we have reached what he calls the Keynes Point. Arthur writes, "If total US household income of $8.495 trillion were shared by America's 116 million households, each would earn $73,000, enough for a decent middle-class life."[16]

In other words, there is plenty to go around—something humanity has never seen before. We now have a distribution problem, not a production one—and the former is a lot easier to solve.

Our current technologies are so much more powerful than those of the past. The last two phase changes produced not just incremental, but quantum, improvements in human health, child survival, education, and life expectancy. There is every reason to believe the Autonomous Revolution will do even better.

Humanity has discovered not just a new world, as Columbus did, but a new *universe*—a virtual one. If we learn from Gilgamesh, listen to Keynes, and play the game using phase change rules, humanity will live better in the physical world as a result. At the same time, we can experience the thrill of discovery as we explore this vast new universe, mining its intangible resources and enhancing our lives with its virtual experiences.

If we polarize, argue, fight, call one another names, and stand idly by and watch while phase change destroys all that is sacred, all of us will be the worse for it. Much worse. But if we choose to solve the challenge of the Autonomous Revolution together, we can live better, more meaningful, and abundant lives. It may not be Utopia, but it may be as close as we imperfect humans will ever get.

Notes

Foreword

1. Henry Adams, *The Education of Henry Adams* (Houghton Mifflin, 1918), 382.

Introduction DIGITAL LEVIATHAN

1. "Quotable Quote: Nicholas Murray Butler," Goodreads, https://www
.goodreads.com/quotes/181579-an-expert-is-one-who-knows-more-and-more
-about (accessed June 26, 2019).

Chapter One THE AUTONOMOUS REVOLUTION

1. Clay Chandler, "Tencent and Alibaba Are Engaged in a Massive Battle
in China," Fortune.com, http://fortune.com/2017/05/13/tencent-alibaba-china/,
May 13, 2017.

2. Billy Bambrough, "Facebook Libra Interest Spikes, Pushing the Bitcoin
Price On," Forbes, June 18, 2019, https://www.forbes.com/sites/billybambrough
/2019/06/18/facebook-libra-interest-spikes-pushing-the-bitcoin-price-on
/#2a7c74396e22 (accessed on June 28, 2019).

3. Ruth Sarreal, "History of Online Banking: How Internet Banking
Went Mainstream," GOBankingRates.com, May 21, 2019, https://www
.gobankingrates.com/banking/history-online-banking/.

4. "Urbanization in the United States," Wikipedia, https://en.wikipedia.org
/wiki/Urbanization_in_the_United_States (accessed June 26, 2019).

5. "Ohlone," Wikipedia, https://en.wikipedia.org/wiki/Ohlone#Survival
(accessed June 26, 2019).

Chapter Two A BRIEF HISTORY OF SOCIAL PHASE CHANGES

1. "Desertification Effects, Causes and Examples: Top 10 List," Science
Heathen, January 5, 2015, http://scienceheathen.com/2015/01/05/desertification
-effects-causes-examples-top-10-list/.

2. Na Eun Oh, "Climate Change and the Decline of Mayan Civilization" *Dartmouth Undergraduate Journal of Science*, March 8, 2013, http://dujs.dartmouth .edu/2013/03/climate-change-and-the-decline-of-mayan-civilization/.

3. "The Invention of Woodblock Printing in the Tang (618–906) and Song (960–1279) Dynasties," Asian Art Museum, http://education.asianart.org/ex plore-resources/background-information/invention-woodblock-printing-tang -618%E2%80%93906-and-song-960%E2%80%931279 (accessed June 26, 2019).

4. "Neolithic Revolution," Wikipedia, https://en.wikipedia.org/wiki /Neolithic_Revolution#Social_change (accessed June 26, 2019).

5. "Plough," Wikipedia, https://en.wikipedia.org/wiki/Plough#Hoeing (accessed June 26, 2019).

6. "Urbanization," Ancient History Encyclopedia, http://www.ancient.eu /urbanization/ (June 26, 2019).

7. "Uruk," Wikipedia, https://en.wikipedia.org/wiki/Uruk (accessed June 26, 2019).

8. David Osborn, "The History of Numbers," Vedic Science, http:// vedicsciences.net/articles/history-of-numbers.html (accessed June 26, 2019).

9. "Cuneiform," Wikipedia, https://en.wikipedia.org/wiki/Cuneiform.

10. "The Epic of Gilgamesh," Wikipedia, https://en.wikipedia.org/wiki /Epic_of_Gilgamesh (accessed June 26, 2019).

11. "Trade in the Phoenician World," Ancient History Encyclopedia, https:// www.ancient.eu/article/881/trade-in-the-phoenician-world/ (accessed June 26, 2019).

12. Lynn White, Jr., *Medieval Technology and Social Change* (Oxford: Oxford University Press, 1962), 57.

13. "British Agricultural Revolution," Wikipedia, https://en.wikipedia.org /wiki/British_Agricultural_Revolution (accessed June 26, 2019).

14. "Agriculture," Digital History, http://www.digitalhistory.uh.edu/disp _textbook.cfm?smtID=11&psid=3837 (accessed June 26, 2019).

15. "Percent of Employment in Agriculture in the United States," FRED Economic Research, https://fred.stlouisfed.org/series/USAPEMANA (accessed June 26, 2019); and Nate Berg, "U.S. Urban Population Is Up . . . But What Does 'Urban' Really Mean?," Citylab, March 26, 2012, https://www.citylab.com /equity/2012/03/us-urban-population-what-does-urban-really-mean/1589/ (accessed June 26, 2019).

16. "Neolithic Revolution," History.com, January 12, 2018, https://www .history.com/topics/neolithic-revolution (accessed June 26, 2019).

17. "Orders of Magnitude of the World's Urban Population in History," United Nations Population Commission, October 21, 1976, https://population .un.org/wup/Archive/Files/studies/United%20Nations%20(1977)%20 -%20Orders%20of%20magnitude%20of%20the%20world%27s%20urban%20 population%20in%20history.PDF (accessed June 26, 2019).

18. Saugat Adhikari, "Top 10 Ancient Roman Inventions," Ancient History Lists, April 29, 2019, https://www.ancienthistorylists.com/rome-history/top-10 -ancient-roman-inventions/ (accessed June 26, 2019).

19. "Printing Press," Wikipedia, https://en.wikipedia.org/wiki/Printing _press (accessed June 26, 2019).

20. "FC74: The Invention of the Printing Press and Its Effects," The Flow of History, http://www.flowofhistory.com/units/west/11/FC74 (accessed June 26, 2019).

21. Jeremy M. Norman, ed., *From Gutenberg to the Internet* (Novato, Calif.: historyofscience.com, 2005), 29.

22. Elizabeth L. Eisenstein, *The Printing Revolution in Early Modern Europe* (Cambridge: Cambridge University Press, 2016), 19.

23. "Newspaper," Wikipedia, https://en.wikipedia.org/wiki/Newspaper, accessed June 26, 2019.

24. Eisenstein, *The Printing Revolution in Early Modern Europe*, 104–105.

25. W. Brian Arthur, *The Nature of Technology* (New York: Free Press, 2009), 2.

26. Klaus Schwab, *The Fourth Industrial Revolution* (New York: Crown Business, 2016), 6–7.

27. Joel Mokyr, ed., *The British Industrial Revolution* (Boulder, Colo.: Westview Press, 1993), 186.

28. Sven Beckert, *Empire of Cotton* (New York: Vintage Books, 2014), 141.

29. "Weavers' Cottage," Wikipedia, https://en.wikipedia.org/wiki/Weavers %27_cottage (accessed June 26, 2019).

30. C. N. Trueman, "Life in Industrial Towns," History Learning Site, March 31, 2015, http://www.historylearningsite.co.uk/britain-1700-to-1900/industrial -revolution/life-in-industrial-towns/ (accessed June 26, 2019).

31. Alfred D. Chandler, Jr., *The Visible Hand: The Managerial Revolution in American Business* (Cambridge, Mass.: The Belknap Press of Harvard University Press, 1977).

32. Arun Sundararajan, *The Sharing Economy* (Cambridge, Mass.: The MIT Press, 2016), 5.

33. Timothy Taylor, "What Is a 'Good Job'?," Conversable Economist, April 5, 2016, http://conversableeconomist.blogspot.com/2016/04/what-is-good-job .html (accessed June 26, 2019).

34. "The U.S. Department of Labor Timeline—Alternate Version," U.S. Department of Labor, https://www.dol.gov/general/history/100/timeline (accessed on June 28, 2019); and "Health Insurance in the United States," Wikipedia, https://en.wikipedia.org/wiki/Health_insurance_in_the_United_States (accessed June 26, 2019).

35. "The National Labor Relations Act," National Labor Relations Board, https://www.nlrb.gov/resources/national-labor-relations-act (accessed June 26, 2019).

36. "Labor Unions in the United States," Wikipedia, https://en.wikipedia .org/wiki/Labor_unions_in_the_United_States#/media/File:United_States _union_membership_and_inequality,_top_1%25_income_share,_1910_to _2010.png (accessed June 26, 2019).

37. Ibid., https://en.wikipedia.org/wiki/Labor_unions_in_the_United _States#/media/File:Union_membership_in_us_1930-2010.png (accessed June 26, 2019).

38. "Income Inequality in the United States," Inequality.org, https://inequality.org/facts/income-inequality/ (accessed June 26, 2019).

39. Jennifer 8. Lee, "When Horses Posed a Public Health Hazard," City Room (blog), *New York Times*, June 9, 2008, https://cityroom.blogs.nytimes .com/2008/06/09/when-horses-posed-a-public-health-hazard/?_r=0 (accessed June 26, 2019).

40. Sam Bass Warner, Jr., *Streetcar Suburbs* (Cambridge, Mass.: Harvard University Press, 1978), 1.

41. Alfred D. Chandler, Jr., *The Visible Hand*, 80.

42. Ibid., 98.

43. Ibid., 94.

44. Ibid., 488.

45. Schwab, *The Fourth Industrial Revolution*.

46. Wei Pan, Gourab Ghoshal, Coco Krumme, Manuel Cebrian, and Alex Pentland, "Urban Characteristics Attributable to Density-Driven Tie Formation" *Nature Communications*, June 4, 2013, https://www.nature.com/articles /ncomms2961 (accessed June 26, 2019); Brian Knudsen, Richard Florida, Gary Gates, and Kevin Stolarick, "Urban Density, Creativity, and Innovation," Creative Class, May 2007, http://creativeclass.com/rfcgdb/articles/Urban_Density _Creativity_and_Innovation.pdf (accessed June 26, 2019); Richard Florida, "The Density of Innovation," *The Atlantic*, September 21, 2010, https://www .theatlantic.com/business/archive/2010/09/the-density-of-innovation/62576/ (accessed June 26, 2019); and Gerald Carlino, Satyajit Chatterjee, and Robert Hunt, "Urban Density and the Rate of Invention," Federal Reserve Bank of Philadelphia, August 2006 draft, http://citeseerx.ist.psu.edu/viewdoc /download?doi=10.1.1.233.2108&rep=rep1&type=pdf (accessed June 26, 2019).

47. Geoffrey West, "The Surprising Math of Cities and Corporations," TEDGlobal 2011, https://www.ted.com/talks/geoffrey_west_the_surprising _math_of_cities_and_corporations#t-1033091; and Jonah Lehrer, "A Physicist Solves the City," *New York Times Magazine*, December 17, 2010, http://www .nytimes.com/2010/12/19/magazine/19Urban_West-t.html (accessed June 26, 2019).

48. "Historical Estimates of World Population," United States Census Bureau, https://www.census.gov/data/tables/time-series/demo/international -programs/historical-est-worldpop.html (accessed June 26, 2019).

49. William F. Ogburn, *On Culture and Social Change* (Chicago: University of Chicago Press, 1964), 44–61.

50. "Population Estimates: Year One through 2050 A.D.," Ecology, http://www.ecology.com/population-estimates-year-2050/ (accessed June 26, 2019).

51. Henry Adams, *The Education of Henry Adams*, Library of America (1909), chapter 34.

52. "Land Speed Record for Rail Vehicles," Wikipedia, http://en.wikipedia.org/wiki/Land_speed_record_for_rail_vehicles (accessed June 26, 2019).

53. "Speed of a Commercial Jet Airplane," The Physics Factbook, http://hypertextbook.com/facts/2002/JobyJosekutty.shtml (accessed June 26, 2019).

54. "Cultural Lag," Wikipedia, https://en.wikipedia.org/wiki/Cultural_lag (accessed June 26, 2019).

55. Ogburn, *On Culture and Social Change*, 86.

56. Ibid., 61.

Chapter Three SUBSTITUTIONAL EQUIVALENCES

1. "Willie Sutton," Wikipedia, http://en.wikipedia.org/wiki/Willie_Sutton (accessed June 26, 2019).

2. Ibid.

3. Dancho Danchev, "New ZeuS Source Code Based Rootkit Available for Purchase on the Underground Market," Webroot, March 14, 2013, https://www.webroot.com/blog/2013/03/14/new-zeus-source-code-based-rootkit-available-for-purchase-on-the-underground-market/ (accessed June 26, 2019).

4. "FBI and Microsoft Take Down $500m-Theft Botnet Citadel," BBC, June 6, 2013, https://www.bbc.com/news/technology-22795074 (accessed June 28, 2019).

5. "Russian Developer of the Notorious 'Citadel' Malware Sentenced to Prison," United States Department of Justice, September 29, 2015, https://www.fbi.gov/contact-us/field-offices/atlanta/news/press-releases/russian-developer-of-the-notorious-citadel-malware-sentenced-to-prison (accessed June 26, 2019); and James Vincent, "$500 Million Botnet Citadel Attacked by Microsoft and the FBI," *Independent*, June 6, 2013, http://www.independent.co.uk/life-style/gadgets-and-tech/news/500-million-botnet-citadel-attacked-by-microsoft-and-the-fbi-8647594.html (accessed June 26, 2019).

6. "Leonardo Torres y Quevedo," Wikipedia, https://en.wikipedia.org/wiki/Leonardo_Torres_y_Quevedo (accessed June 26, 2019).

7. "R.U.R.," Wikipedia, https://en.wikipedia.org/wiki/R.U.R. (accessed June 26, 2019).

8. "Turing Test," Wikipedia, https://en.wikipedia.org/wiki/Turing_test (accessed June 26, 2019).

9. Tanya Lewis, "A Brief History of Artificial Intelligence," Live Science, December 4, 2014, http://www.livescience.com/49007-history-of-artificial-intelligence.html (accessed June 26, 2019).

10. "Deep Blue," Wikipedia, https://en.wikipedia.org/wiki/Deep_Blue_(chess_computer) (accessed June 26, 2019).

11. "AlphaGo vs Deep Blue," Reddit, https://www.reddit.com/r/MachineLearning/comments/4a7lc4/alphago_vs_deep_blue/ (accessed June 26, 2019).

12. "Why AI Researchers Like Video Games," *The Economist*, May 13, 2017, https://www.economist.com/news/science-and-technology/21721890-games-help-them-understand-reality-why-ai-researchers-video-games (accessed June 26, 2019).

13. Alex Brokaw, "Nvidia Bets Big on AI with Powerful New Chip," The Verge, April 6, 2016, https://www.theverge.com/2016/4/6/11376616/nvidia-tesla-p100-gpu-worlds-largest-chip-ai (accessed June 26, 2019).

14. "IQ Classification," Wikipedia, http://en.wikipedia.org/wiki/IQ_classification (accessed June 26, 2019).

15. Jennifer Corbett Dooren and Jonathan D. Rockoff, "FDA Approves J&J Sedation Device," *Wall Street Journal*, May 3, 2017, http://online.wsj.com/articles /SB10001424127887323628004578461491259981194 (accessed June 26, 2019).

16. "Computer-aided Diagnosis," Wikipedia, http://en.wikipedia.org/wiki /Computer-aided_diagnosis (accessed June 26, 2019).

17. E. C. Pegg et al., "A Semi-Automated Measurement Technique for the Assessment of Radiolucency," *Journal of the Royal Society Interface* 11, no. 96, (2014), https://royalsocietypublishing.org/doi/full/10.1098/rsif.2014.0303.

18. Steven Millward, "Check Out the Numbers on China's Top 10 Social Media Sites," Techinasia, March 13, 2013, https://www.techinasia.com/2013 -china-top-10-social-sites-infographic (accessed June 26, 2019).

Chapter Four PRODUCTIVITY WITHOUT PROSPERITY

1. "Gunpowder Engine," Wikipedia, https://en.wikipedia.org/wiki/Gunpowder _engine (accessed June 26, 2019).

2. "Henry Ford," Wikipedia, https://en.wikipedia.org/wiki/Henry_Ford #The_five-day_workweek (accessed June 26, 2019).

3. "Designing Smart Vehicles for a Smart World," Ford Motor Company, http://corporate.ford.com/news-center/press-releases-detail/677-5-dollar-a-day (accessed June 26, 2019).

4. Robert J. Gordon, *The Rise and Fall of American Growth* (Princeton, N.J.: Princeton University Press, 2016), 11.

5. "Ford Model T," Wikipedia, https://en.wikipedia.org/wiki/Ford_Model_T (accessed June 26, 2019).

6. Peter Huber, *The Bottomless Well* (New York: Basic Books, 2006).

7. Joel A. Tarr, "Urban Pollution—Many Long Years Ago," *American Heritage* (October 1971), reproduced by Coalition to Ban Horse-Drawn Carriages, http://www.banhdc.org/archives/ch-hist-19711000.html (accessed June 26, 2019).

8. "The Chip That Jack Built," Texas Instruments, http://www.ti.com/corp /docs/kilbyctr/jackbuilt.shtml (accessed June 26, 2019).

9. "Chronological History of IBM: 1960s," IBM, http://www-03.ibm.com /ibm/history/history/year_1960.html (accessed June 26, 2019); and ibid., "1980s," http://www-03.ibm.com/ibm/history/history/decade_1980.html (accessed June 26, 2019).

10. "Global Electronics Market Forecast: $1.74 Trillion in 2017 at a CAGR of 5%," EEHerald, April 12, 2013, http://www.eeherald.com/section/news /onws20131204001.html (accessed June 26, 2019).

11. "Global Revenue from Smartphone Sales from 2013 to 2018," Statista, https://www.statista.com/statistics/237505/global-revenue-from-smartphones -since-2008/ (accessed June 26, 2019).

12. "Worldwide PC Spending Forecast," Statista, https://www.statista .com/statistics/380434/worldwide-pc-spending-forecast/ (accessed June 26, 2019).

13. Louis Columbus, "Roundup of Internet of Things Forecasts and Market Estimates, 2016," Forbes.com, November 27, 2016, https://www.forbes.com/sites/louiscolumbus/2016/11/27/roundup-of-internet-of-things-forecasts-and-market-estimates-2016/#2c6bdf93292d (accessed June 26, 2019).

14. Rachel Courtland, "How Much Did Early Transistors Cost?," IEEE Spectrum, April 16, 2015, https://spectrum.ieee.org/tech-talk/semiconductors/devices/how-much-did-early-transistors-cost (accessed June 26, 2019); and "Handel Jones: Cost per Transistor Flat from 28 to 7nm," AnandTech, June 15, 2016, https://forums.anandtech.com/threads/handel-jones-cost-per-transistor-flat-from-28-to-7nm.2476904/ (accessed June 26, 2019).

15. "M&A Frenzy in the Chip Industry, the Growth of GaN Technology, and Why It Matters," EPC, 2015, http://epc-co.com/epc/EventsandNews/Newsletters/FJGF/Issue16/index.html (accessed June 26, 2019).

16. Gordon, *The Rise and Fall of American Growth*, 16.

17. C. I. Jones, "The Facts of Economic Growth," in *Handbook of Macroeconomics*, vol. 2 (Elsevier, 2016), http://web.stanford.edu/~chadj/facts.pdf (accessed June 26, 2019); "U.S. Population, 1790–2000: Always Growing," United States History.com, https://www.u-s-history.com/pages/h980.html; and "United States GDP Growth Rate," Trading Economics, http://www.tradingeconomics.com/united-states/gdp-growth (accessed June 26, 2019).

18. Jones, "The Facts of Economic Growth.".

19. "Turing Pharmaceuticals," Wikipedia, https://en.wikipedia.org/wiki/Turing_Pharmaceuticals (accessed June 26, 2019).

20. Kathryn A. Francis, "U.S. Postal Service Workforce Size and Employment Categories FY1995–FY2014," Congressional Research Service, October 21, 2015, https://fas.org/sgp/crs/misc/RS22864.pdf (accessed June 26, 2019).

21. Larry Kim, "This Unusual Startup Wants to Disrupt the $7 Billion Greeting Cards Industry," Inc., September 23, 2015, https://www.inc.com/larry-kim/the-unusual-startup-looking-to-disrupt-the-7-billion-greeting-cards-industry.html (accessed on June 26, 2015).

22. Frank Morris, "To Survive, the Greeting Card Industry Will Have to Get Creative," on *All Things Considered*, NPR, July 8, 2015, https://www.npr.org/2015/07/08/420966617/to-survive-the-greeting-card-industry-will-have-to-get-creative (accessed June 26, 2019).

23. Ibid.

24. Amy Mitchell and Katerina Eva Matsa, "The Declining Value of U.S. Newspapers," Pew Research Center, May 22, 2015, https://www.pewresearch.org/fact-tank/2015/05/22/the-declining-value-of-u-s-newspapers/.

25. Don Irvine, "Newspaper Jobs at 50-Year Low," Accuracy in Media, January 1, 2010, https://www.aim.org/don-irvine-blog/newspaper-jobs-at-50-year-low/.

26. Tina Brown, "The Gig Economy," The Daily Beast, January 12, 2009, updated July 14, 2017, http://www.thedailybeast.com/articles/2009/01/12/the-gig-economy.html (accessed June 26, 2019).

27. Stacey Vanek Smith, "An NPR Reporter Raced a Machine to Write a News Story. Who Won?," *Morning Edition*, NPR, May 20, 2015, http://www.npr.org/sections/money/2015/05/20/406484294/an-npr-reporter-raced-a-machine-to-write-a-news-story-who-won (accessed June 26, 2015).

28. Michael Sebastian, "Huffington Post Said to Break Even on $146 Million Revenue Last Year," *Ad Age*, June 30, 2015, http://adage.com/article/media/huffington-post-broke-146-million-revenue/299293/ (accessed June 26, 2019); and Alex Weprin, "Buzzfeed Passes $100M in Revenue for 2014," Politico, https://www.politico.com/media/story/2014/11/buzzfeed-passes-100-m-in-revenue-for-2014-003140/ (accessed June 26, 2019).

29. J. Clement, "Amazon—Statistics & Facts," Statista, February 8, 2019, http://www.statista.com/topics/846/amazon/ (accessed June 26, 2019).

30. J. Clement, "Number of Full-Time Alphabet Employees from 2007 to 2018," Statista, February 7, 2019, http://www.statista.com/statistics/273744/number-of-full-time-google-employees/ (accessed June 26, 2019); and Alphabet Investor Relations, 2019, https://investor.google.com/financial/tables.html (accessed June 26, 2019).

31. Rani Molla, "Facebook Made $188,000 per Employee Last Quarter, Four Times as Much as Google," Vox, August 4, 2017, https://www.vox.com/2017/8/4/16090758/facebook-google-profit-per-employee-comparison-chart.

32. "Netflix," Forbes.com, http://www.forbes.com/companies/netflix/ (accessed June 26, 2019); and "Netflix Inc Sales per Employee," CSIMarket, https://csimarket.com/stocks/NFLX-Revenue-per-Employee.html.

33. "Blockbuster LLC," Wikipedia, https://en.wikipedia.org/wiki/Blockbuster_LLC (accessed June 26, 2019).

34. Carl Bialik, "Netflix's CEO Is Mobilizing for Battle with Amazon," *Wall Street Journal*, October 20, 2004, https://www.wsj.com/articles/SB109786059137346731.

35. Gordon, *The Rise and Fall of American Growth*, 523.

36. "GDP: One of the Great Inventions of the 20th Century," Bureau of Economic Analysis, January 2000, https://www.bea.gov/scb/account_articles/general/0100od/maintext.htm (accessed on June 26, 2019).

37. "GDP as a False Measure of a Country Economic Output," Softpanorama, http://www.softpanorama.org/Skeptics/Financial_skeptic/Casino_capitalism/Number_racket/gdp_is_a_questionable_measure_of_economic_growth.shtml#Kuznets_warning.

38. "2018 Social Progress Index," Social·Progress.org, https://www.socialprogressindex.com/?tab=2&code=DNK (accessed on June 26, 2019).

39. "Quality of Life Rankings by Country 2019," Numbeo, https://www.numbeo.com/quality-of-life/rankings_by_country.jsp (accessed on June 26, 2019).

Chapter Five COMMERCIAL TRANSFORMATION

1. Tom Goodwin, "In the Age of Disintermediation the Battle Is All for the Customer Interface," Techcrunch, March 3, 2015, https://techcrunch.com/2015/03/03/in-the-age-of-disintermediation-the-battle-is-all-for-the-customer-interface/ (accessed on June 26, 2019).

2. "Employment by Major Industry Sector," Bureau of Labor Statistics, https://www.bls.gov/emp/ep_table_201.htm (accessed June 26, 2019).

3. Jordan Weissmann, "How Wall Street Devoured Corporate America," *The Atlantic*, March 5, 2013, https://www.theatlantic.com/business/archive/2013/03/how-wall-street-devoured-corporate-america/273732/ (accessed June 26, 2019); and Erin Duffin, "Corporate Profits in the United States in 2018, by Industry," Statista.com, June 26, 2019, https://www.statista.com/statistics/222122/us-corporate-profits-by-industry/ (accessed June 26, 2019).

4. "Largest U.S. Credit Card Issuers: 2017 Market Share Report," ValuePenguin, https://www.valuepenguin.com/largest-credit-card-issuers (accessed June 26, 2019); and Jamie Gonzales-Garcia, "Credit Card Statistics," Creditcards.com, June 4, 2019, http://creditcardforum.com/blog/credit-card-statistics/ (accessed June 27, 2019).

5. Sienna Kossman, "2015 Credit Card Fee Survey: Average Card Carries 6 Fees," Creditcards.com, July 16, 2015, http://www.creditcards.com/credit-card-news/fee-survey.php (accessed June 27, 2019); and "Average Credit Card Processing Fees," Cardfellow, March 11, 2019, https://www.cardfellow.com/average-fees-for-credit-card-processing/ (accessed June 27, 2019).

6. "Average Credit Card Processing Fees," Cardfellow, March 11, 2019, https://www.cardfellow.com/average-fees-for-credit-card-processing/ (accessed June 27, 2019); and Matthew Frankel, "The Average American's Credit Card Debt May Shock You," *USA Today*, October 12, 2016, http://www.usatoday.com/story/money/personalfinance/2016/10/12/average-credit-card-debt/91431058/ (accessed June 27, 2019).

7. "Donn B. Parker," Wikipedia, https://en.wikipedia.org/wiki/Donn_B._Parker (accessed June 27, 2019).

8. Rick M. Robinson, "The Top 5 Retail Breaches," SecurityIntelligence.com, October 27, 2014, https://securityintelligence.com/the-top-5-retail-breaches/ (accessed June 27, 2019).

9. Elizabeth Weise, "Arby's Probes Possible Data Breach of Credit Cards," *USA Today*, February 10, 2017, http://www.usatoday.com/story/tech/news/2017/02/09/arbys-breach-may-have-hit-355000-credit-cards/97702594/ (accessed June 27, 2019); and "List of the Largest Fast Food Restaurant Chains," Wikipedia, https://en.wikipedia.org/wiki/List_of_the_largest_fast_food_restaurant_chains (accessed June 27, 2019).

10. John S. Kiernan, "Credit Card & Debit Card Fraud Statistics," WalletHub, February 17, 2017, https://wallethub.com/edu/credit-debit-card-fraud-statistics/25725/ (accessed June 27, 2019).

11. "Credit Card Fraud Statistics," Statistic Brain, http://www.statisticbrain.com/credit-card-fraud-statistics/ (accessed June 27, 2019).

12. Lee Mathews, "Equifax Data Breach Impacts 143 Million Americans," Forbes.com, September 7, 2017, https://www.forbes.com/sites/leemathews/2017/09/07/equifax-data-breach-impacts-143-million-americans/#44docf8f356f (accessed June 27, 2019).

13. "Transaction Authorization Process," UniBul's Money Blog, http://blog

.unibulmerchantservices.com/transaction-authorization-process/ (accessed June 27, 2019); "Submission, Clearing and Settlement of Credit Card Transactions," UniBul's Money Blog, http://blog.unibulmerchantservices.com/submission -clearing-and-settlement-of-credit-card-transactions/ (accessed June 27, 2019); Eric Ravenscraft, "This Is Why Your Credit Card Transactions Take So Long to Clear," Lifehacker, September 13, 2016, http://lifehacker.com/this-is-why-your -credit-card-transactions-take-so-long-1786567382 (accessed June 27, 2019); and Brian Martucci, "How Credit Card Payment Processing Systems & Networks Really Work," Money Crashers, http://www.moneycrashers.com/credit-card -payment-processing-systems-networks/ (accessed June 27, 2019).

14. "Credit Card Fraud Impacts Consumer Confidence Worldwide," Security Magazine, August 1, 2014, http://www.securitymagazine.com/articles/85684 -credit-card-fraud-impacts-consumer-confidence-worldwide (accessed June 27, 2019).

15. Newley Purnell, "Alibaba and Tencent Set Fast Pace in Mobile-Payments Race," *Wall Street Journal*, September 22, 2017, https://www.wsj.com/articles /alibaba-and-tencent-set-fast-pace-in-mobile-payments-race-1506072602 ?shareToken=st4499b289902f491a99df8d891ecb83ef&reflink=article_email _-share&mg=prod/accounts-wsj (accessed June 27, 2019).

16. Amber Murakami-Fester, "What Are Peer-to-Peer Payments?," NerdWallet.com, May 31, 2019, https://www.nerdwallet.com/blog/banking /p2p-payment-systems/.

17. Snapchat Support, SnapChat Corporation, https://support.snapchat .com/en-US/a/snapcash-guidelines (accessed June 27, 2019).

18. PopMoney home page, https://www.popmoney.com/ (accessed June 27, 2019).

19. "Ally Bank Review: Everything You Need to Know," The Balance, https://www.thebalance.com/ally-bank-review-315132.

20. "Why Fintech Won't Kill Banks," *The Economist*, June 17, 2015, https://www.economist.com/blogs/economist-explains/2015/06/economist -explains-12 (accessed June 27, 2019).

21. "Understanding the RIA Channel," RIA Channel, http://riachannel .com/wp-content/uploads/2015/03/Understanding-the-RIA-channel-2015.pdf (accessed June 27, 2019).

22. "2016 RIA Industry Study: Average Investment Advisory Fee is 0.99%," RIA in a Box, December 6, 2016, http://www.riainabox.com/blog /2016-ria-industry-study-average-investment-advisory-fee-is-0-99-percent.

23. Jonathan Clements, "It's Time to End Financial Advisors' 1% Fees," *Wall Street Journal*, January 18, 2015, https://www.wsj.com/articles/its-time-to-end -financial-advisers-1-fees-1421545038 (accessed June 27, 2019).

24. "Hedge Fund Industry Assets Under Management," BarklayHedge, 2019, https://www.barclayhedge.com/research/indices/ghs/mum/HF_Money _Under_Management.html (accessed June 27, 2019).

25. "BlackRock," Wikipedia, https://en.wikipedia.org/wiki/BlackRock (accessed June 27, 2019).

26. Jim Pavia, "CNBC Ranks the Top 50 Money-Management Firms of 2015," CNBC, September 15, 2015, https://www.cnbc.com/2015/09/15/cnbc-ranks-the-top-50-money-management-firms-of-2015.html (accessed June 27, 2019).

27. Hal M. Bundrick, "Top 10 Robo Advisors Ranked: Find the Best Automated Online Investing Services," The Street, February 27, 2015, https://www.thestreet.com/story/13060011/2/top-10-robo-advisors-ranked-find-the-best-automated-online-investing-services.html (accessed June 27, 2019).

28. Charles D. Ellis, "The End of Active Investing?," *Financial Times*, January 19, 2017, https://www.ft.com/content/6b2d5490-d9bb-11e6-944b-e7eb37a6aa8e (accessed June 27, 2019).

29. William H. Davidow, *Overconnected: The Promise and Threat of the Internet* (New York: Delphinium Books,2011), 79.

30. Andrew McAfee and Erik Brynjolfsson, *Machine Platform Crowd* (New York: W. W. Norton, 2017), 171–174.

31. Ashlee Vance, "How Two Brothers Turned Seven Lines of Code into a $9.2 Billion Startup," Bloomberg, August 1, 2017, https://www.bloomberg.com/news/features/2017-08-01/how-two-brothers-turned-seven-lines-of-code-into-a-9-2-billion-startup (accessed June 27, 2019).

32. "Elliptic Curve Digital Signature Algorithm," Bitcoin Wiki, https://en.bitcoin.it/wiki/Elliptic_Curve_Digital_Signature_Algorithm (accessed June 27, 2019).

33. Kim Zetter, "That Insane, $81M Bangladesh Bank Heist? Here's What We Know," *Wired*, May 17, 2016, https://www.wired.com/2016/05/insane-81m-bangladesh-bank-heist-heres-know/ (accessed June 27, 2019).

34. Olivier Garret, "The 4 Best P2P Lending Platforms for Investors in 2017—Detailed Analysis," Forbes.com, January 29, 2017, https://www.forbes.com/sites/oliviergarret/2017/01/29/the-4-best-p2p-lending-platforms-for-investors-in-2017-detailed-analysis/#73ed05c252ab (accessed June 27, 2019); and Sonny Singh, "The State of P2P Lending," TechCrunch, January 30, 2016, https://techcrunch.com/2016/01/30/the-state-of-p2p-lending/ (accessed June 27, 2019).

35. Singh, "The State of P2P Lending."

36. Ibid.

37. Shoaib Iqbal, "Global Peer to Peer Market by End-User and Business Model Type," Allied Market Research, March 2017, https://www.alliedmarketresearch.com/peer-to-peer-lending-market (accessed June 27, 2019).

38. "Peer Pressure," PWC, February 2015, https://www.pwc.com/us/en/consumer-finance/publications/assets/peer-to-peer-lending.pdf (accessed June 27, 2019); and Cloud Lending, 2018, https://www.cloudlendinginc.com/about-us/.

39. Jon Henley, "Sweden Leads the Race to Become Cashless Society," *The Guardian*, June 4, 2016, https://www.theguardian.com/business/2016/jun/04/sweden-cashless-society-cards-phone-apps-leading-europe (accessed June 27, 2019).

40. "Sharing Economy," Wikipedia, https://en.wikipedia.org/wiki /Sharing_economy (accessed June 27, 2019).

41. Arun Sundararajan, *The Sharing Economy* (Cambridge, Mass.: The MIT Press, 2016), 27.

42. Paul Barter, "'Cars Are Parked 95% of the Time.' Let's Check!," Reinventing Parking, February 22, 2013, http://www.reinventingparking.org/2013 /02/cars-are-parked-95-of-time-lets-check.html (accessed June 27, 2019).

43. Brian Patrick Eha, "Zipcar Timeline: From Business Idea to IPO to $500 Million Buyout," Entrepreneur, January 2, 2013, https://www.entrepreneur .com/article/225399 (accessed June 27, 2019).

44. Yuan Xia, "What Are the Main Differences Between Getaround and Turo (fka RelayRides)?," Quora, November 2016, https://www.quora.com /What-are-the-main-differences-between-Getaround-and-Turo-fka -RelayRides (accessed June 27, 2019).

45. Turo, company homepage, https://turo.com/.

46. "BlaBlaCar," Wikipedia, https://en.wikipedia.org/wiki/BlaBlaCar (accessed June 27, 2019).

47. Kirsten Korosec, "GM Makes Big Push into a Hot New Business," *Fortune*, January 21, 2016, http://fortune.com/2016/01/21/gm-car-sharing -maven/ (accessed June 27, 2019).

48. Darrell Etherington, "GM's Maven Gig Is a Car Sharing Service Tailor-Made for the Gig Economy," TechCrunch, May 3, 2017, https:// techcrunch.com/2017/05/03/gms-maven-gig-is-a-car-sharing-service -tailor-made-for-the-gig-economy/ (accessed June 27, 2019).

49. Andrew J. Hawkins, "Car2Go Thinks We'd Rather Share Luxury Mercedes-Benz Sedans Than Smart Cars," The Verge, January 30, 2017, https:// www.theverge.com/2017/1/30/14437770/car2go-daimler-mercedes-benz -cla-gla-carsharing (accessed June 27, 2019).

50. "Millennials," special advertising section, *Washington Post*, http://www .washingtonpost.com/sf/brand-connect/millennials/ (accessed June 27, 2019).

51. Ibid.

52. "10 Airbnb Competitors That You Should Know About," Tripping, https://www.tripping.com/industry/rental-companies/9-airbnb-competitors -that-you-should-know-about.

53. "Find Your Next Workspace," ShareDesk, https://www.sharedesk.net/ (accessed June 27, 2019).

54. Connie Loizos, "Uber Just Pissed Off Dozens of Longtime Employees; Now They're Gunning for Management," TechCrunch, June 8, 2017, https:// techcrunch.com/2017/06/08/uber-just-pissed-off-dozens-of-longtime -employees-now-theyre-gunning-for-management/ (accessed June 27, 2019); and Mansoor Iqbal, "Uber Revenue and Usage Statistics (2019)," Business of Apps, May 10, 2019, http://www.businessofapps.com/data/uber-statistics/ (accessed June 27, 2019).

55. "Number of Full-Time Facebook Employees from 2004 to 2018,"

Statista.com, https://www.statista.com/statistics/273563/number-of-facebook
-employees/ (accessed June 27, 2019); and Josh Constine, "Facebook Now Has
2 Billion Monthly Users . . . and Responsibility," TechCrunch, June 27, 2017,
https://techcrunch.com/2017/06/27/facebook-2-billion-users/ (accessed
June 27, 2019).

56. "How to Tame the Tech Titans," *The Economist*, January 18, 2018, https://
www.economist.com/news/leaders/21735021-dominance-google-facebook-and
-amazon-bad-consumers-and-competition-how-tame.

57. "Number of Available Apps in the Apple App Store from July 2008 to
January 2017," Statista, 2019, https://www.statista.com/statistics/263795
/number-of-available-apps-in-the-apple-app-store/ (accessed June 27, 2019).

58. "Amazon Accounts for 43% of US Online Retail Sales," Business Insider,
February 3, 2017, http://www.businessinsider.com/amazon-accounts-for-43-of
-us-online-retail-sales-2017-2 (accessed June 27, 2019).

59. Polly Mosendz, "Amazon Has Basically No Competition Among Online
Booksellers," *The Atlantic*, May 30, 2014, https://www.theatlantic.com/business
/archive/2014/05/amazon-has-basically-no-competition-among-online
-booksellers/371917/ (accessed June 27, 2019).

60. Timothy Stenovec, "Amazon Probably Didn't Get What It Wanted in the
Hachette Deal," *Huffington Post*, November 14, 2014, http://www.huffingtonpost
.com/2014/11/14/amazon-hachette-deal_n_6159414.html (accessed June 27,
2019).

61. David Streitfeld, "Hachette Says Amazon Is Delaying Delivery of Some
Books," *New York Times*, May 9, 2019, https://www.nytimes.com/2014/05/09
/technology/hachette-says-amazon-is-delaying-delivery-of-some-books.html
(accessed June 27, 2019).

62. John Cook, "John Grisham, Stephen King and More Than 900 Other
Authors Press Amazon to Solve Hachette Dispute in NYT Ad," GeekWire,
August 8, 2014, https://www.geekwire.com/2014/john-grisham-stephen-king
-900-authors-press-amazon-solve-hachette-dispute/ (accessed June 27, 2019).

63. Queenie Wong, "Facebook vs. Snapchat: Competition Heats Up Between
Social Media Firms," *San Jose Mercury News*, March 28, 2017, https://www
.mercurynews.com/2017/03/28/facebook-vs-snapchat-competition-heats
-up-between-social-media-firms/ (accessed June 27, 2019).

64. Anita Balakrishnan, "Snap Closes Up 44% After Rollicking IPO," CNBC,
March 2, 2017, https://www.cnbc.com/2017/03/02/snapchat-snap-open-trading
-price-stock-ipo-first-day.html (accessed June 27, 2019).

65. Nicholas Carlson, "Was $1 Billion Too Little to Ask for Instagram?,"
Slate, November 14, 2013, http://www.slate.com/blogs/business_insider/2013
/11/14/facebook_s_1_billion_instagram_buy_did_kevin_systrom_sell_too
_soon.html (accessed June 27, 2019).

66. Adam Lashinsky, "Why Amazon Tolerates Zappos' Extreme Management Experiment," *Fortune*, March 4, 2016, https://fortune.com/2016/03/04
/amazon-zappos-holacracy/; and Andrew Ross Sorkin and Jeremy W. Peters,

"Google to Acquire YouTube for $1.65 Billion," *New York Times*, October 9, 2006, https://www.nytimes.com/2006/10/09/business/09cnd-deal.html.

67. Ben Casselman, "A Start-Up Slump Is a Drag on the Economy. Big Business May Be to Blame," *New York Times*, September 20, 2017, https://www.nytimes.com/2017/09/20/business/economy/startup-business.html?mcubz=1&_r=0 (accessed June 27, 2019).

68. Mark Scott, "Google Fined Record $2.7 Billion in E.U. Antitrust Ruling," *New York Times*, June 27, 2017, https://www.nytimes.com/2017/06/27/technology/eu-google-fine.html (accessed June 27, 2019).

69. Tom Warren, "Google Fined a Record $5 Billion by the EU for Android Antitrust Violations," The Verge, July 18, 2018, https://www.theverge.com/2018/7/18/17580694/google-android-eu-fine-antitrust (accessed June 27, 2019).

Chapter Six **THE DEATH OF THE GOOD JOB**

1. "FBI: US Hate Crimes Rise for Second Straight Year," BBC, November 13, 2017, http://www.bbc.com/news/world-us-canada-41975573 (accessed June 27, 2019).

2. "Income Inequality in the United States," Wikipedia, https://en.wikipedia.org/wiki/Income_inequality_in_the_United_States (accessed on June 27, 2019).

3. Emily Cuddy, Joanna Venator, and Richard V. Reeves, "In a Land of Dollars: Deep Poverty and Its Consequences," Brookings, May 7, 2015, http://www.brookings.edu/blogs/social-mobility-memos/posts/2015/05/07-deep-poverty-income-spending-reeves (accessed June 27, 2019).

4. Aimee Picchi, "Too Bad Wages Aren't Rising as Fast as Home Prices," CBS News, March 26, 2015, http://www.cbsnews.com/news/real-estate-price-increases-are-outpacing-wage-growth/ (accessed June 27, 2019).

5. Laura Lloyd, "U.S.D.A. Says Food Prices to Rise 2.5% to 3.5% in 2014," Food Business News, February 25, 2014, http://www.foodbusinessnews.net/articles/news_home/Purchasing_News/2014/02/USDA_says_food_prices_to_rise.aspx?ID={D30DAA19-8D1C-40A6-AEAF-A53E6CFFDFAD}&cck=1 (accessed June 27, 2019); and "Current US Inflation Rates: 2009–2019," US Inflation Calculator, February 25, 2014, http://www.usinflationcalculator.com/inflation/current-inflation-rates/ (accessed June 27, 2019).

6. Jill Mislinski, "Real Median Household Income Reintroduction, March at $61,227," Advisor Perspectives, May 2, 2018, http://www.advisorperspectives.com/dshort/updates/Median-Household-Income-Update.php (accessed June 27, 2019).

7. "13,320 Series," Federal Reserve Bank of St. Louis, July 17, 2019, https://fred.stlouisfed.org/tags/series?t=wages (accessed June 28, 2019).

8. Kyle Pomerleau and Andrew Lundeen, "Summary of Latest Federal Income Tax Data," Tax Foundation, December 2014, http://taxfoundation.org/sites/taxfoundation.org/files/docs/FF445.pdf (accessed June 27, 2019).

9. Scott A. Hodge, "60 Percent of Households Now Receive More in

Transfer Income Than They Pay in Taxes," Tax Foundation, October 4, 2012, http://taxfoundation.org/blog/60-percent-households-now-receive-more -transfer-income-they-pay-taxes (accessed June 27, 2019); and Alicia Parlapiano, Robert Gebeloff, and Shan Carter, "The Shrinking American Middle Class," *New York Times*, January 26, 2015, http://www.nytimes.com/interactive/2015 /01/25/upshot/shrinking-middle-class.html?_r=0.

10. The Editors, "Will Automation Take Our Jobs?," *Scientific American*, July 15, 2014, http://www.scientificamerican.com/article/will-automation-take -our-jobs/ (accessed June 27, 2019).

11. "Robotics & Automation," McKinsey Digital, 2017, https://www .mckinsey.com/business-functions/digital-mckinsey/how-we-help-clients /robotics-and-automation (accessed June 27, 2019).

12. Shivali Best, "Will a Robot Take Your Job?," *Daily Mail*, November 29, 2017, http://www.dailymail.co.uk/sciencetech/article-5128709/800-MILLION -workers-replaced-robots-2030.html (accessed on June 27, 2019).

13. W. Brian Arthur, "The Second Economy," McKinsey & Company, October 2011, http://www.mckinsey.com/insights/strategy/the_second_economy (accessed on June 27, 2019); and William Davidow, "How Computers Are Creating a Second Economy Without Workers," *The Atlantic*, April 10, 2012, http:// www.theatlantic.com/business/archive/2012/04/how-computers-are-creating-a -second-economy-without-workers/255618/ (accessed on June 27, 2019).

14. Arthur, "The Second Economy"; Davidow, "How Computers Are Creating a Second Economy Without Workers"; and "U.S. Gross Domestic Product GDP History," U.S. Government Spending, http://www.usgovernment spending.com/spending_chart_1950_2010USb_15s2li011lcn__US_Gross _Domestic_Product_GDP_History#view (accessed on June 27, 2019).

15. "GDP per Person Employed," The World Bank, April 2019, http://data .worldbank.org/indicator/SL.GDP.PCAP.EM.KD (accessed on June 27, 2019).

16. "Employment Status of the Civilian Population by Sex and Age," Bureau of Labor Statistics, http://www.bls.gov/news.release/empsit.t01.htm (accessed on June 27, 2019); and "Databases, Tables & Calculators by Subject," Bureau of Labor Statistics, https://data.bls.gov/timeseries/LNS11000000.

17. David Cardinal, "Ten Years After Their Debut, Autonomous Trucks Are Finally Hitting the Roads," ExtremeTech, October 5, 2015, http://www .extremetech.com/extreme/215626-ten-years-after-their-debut-autonomous -trucks-are-finally-hitting-the-roads (accessed June 27, 2019).

18. Dan Fagella, "Self-Driving Car Timeline for 11 Top Automakers," VentureBeat, June 4, 2017, https://venturebeat.com/2017/06/04/self-driving -car-timeline-for-11-top-automakers/ (accessed June 27, 2019).

19. "Number of Motor Vehicles Registered in the United States from 1990 to 2017," Statista, www.statista.com/statistics/183505/number-of-vehicles-in-the -united-states-since-1990/ (accessed June 27, 2019); and Jared Green, "500 Million Reasons to Rethink the Parking Lot," Grist, June 7, 2012, http://grist.org /cities/500-million-reasons-to-rethink-the-parking-lot/ (accessed June 27, 2019).

20. Emily Badger, "Now We Know How Many Drivers Uber Has—and Have a Better Idea of What They're Making," *Washington Post*, January 22, 2015, https://www.washingtonpost.com/news/wonk/wp/2016/01/20/now-we-know-how-many-drivers-uber-has-and-have-a-better-idea-of-what-theyre-making/?noredirect=on; and Kate Rogers, "Who's Your Uber Driver? More of Them Are Women: Survey," CNBC, December 8, 2015, http://www.cnbc.com/2015/12/08/whos-your-uber-driver-more-of-them-are-women-survey.html (accessed June 27, 2019).

21. Independent Cab Co., http://www.taxi4u.com/calculate.html; and Uber Los Angeles, https://www.uber.com/cities/los-angeles (accessed June 27, 2019).

22. "Cost of Owning and Operating Vehicle in U.S. Increases Nearly Two Percent According to AAA's 2013 'Your Driving Costs' Study," AAA Newsroom, April 16, 2013, http://newsroom.aaa.com/2013/04/cost-of-owning-and-operating-vehicle-in-u-s-increases-nearly-two-percent-according-to-aaas-2013-your-driving-costs-study/ (accessed June 27, 2019).

23. "Transforming Personal Mobility," Columbia University/Earth Institute, August 10, 2012, http://sustainablemobility.ei.columbia.edu/files/2012/12/Transforming-Personal-Mobility-Jan-27-20132.pdf (accessed June 27, 2019).

24. Kevin Spieser et al., "Toward a Systematic Approach to the Design and Evaluation of Automated Mobility-on-Demand Systems: A Case Study in Singapore," MIT Libraries, April 2014, http://dspace.mit.edu/handle/1721.1/82904#files-area (accessed June 27, 2019).

25. "Number of Motor Vehicles Registered in the United States from 1990 to 2017," Statista, www.statista.com/statistics/183505/number-of-vehicles-in-the-united-states-since-1990/ (accessed June 27, 2019); and Jared Green, "500 Million Reasons to Rethink the Parking Lot."

26. "Truck Drivers in the USA," All Trucking.com, http://www.alltrucking.com/faq/truck-drivers-in-the-usa/ (accessed June 27, 2019).

27. Alexis C. Madrigal, "Could Self-Driving Trucks Be Good for Truckers?," *The Atlantic*, February 1, 2018, https://www.theatlantic.com/technology/archive/2018/02/uber-says-its-self-driving-trucks-will-be-good-for-truckers/551879/ (accessed on June 27, 2019); and Anika Balakrishman, "Self-Driving Cars Could Cost America's Professional Drivers Up to 25,000 Jobs a Month, Goldman Sachs Says," CNBC, May 22, 2017, https://www.cnbc.com/2017/05/22/goldman-sachs-analysis-of-autonomous-vehicle-job-loss.html (access June 27, 2019).

28. "Truck Drivers in the USA."

29. Nicholas Carlson, "Revenue per Employee Charts Are a Fascinating Way to Judge the Health of Tech Companies," Business Insider, April 9, 2015, http://www.businessinsider.com/revenue-per-employee-charts-are-a-fascinating-way-to-judge-the-health-of-tech-companies-2015-4 (accessed June 27, 2019).

30. "Employees on Nonfarm Payrolls by Industry Sector and Selected Industry Detail," Bureau of Labor Statistics, https://www.bls.gov/news.release/empsit.t17.htm (accessed June 27, 2019).

31. "New Study: For Every New High-Tech Job, Four More Created," Bay Area Council, December 10, 2012, http://www.bayareacouncil.org/community _engagement/new-study-for-every-new-high-tech-job-four-more-created/ (accessed June 27, 2019).

32. Bill Dupor, "Stimulus Spending Had Spillover Effects, Thanks to Commuters," Federal Reserve Bank of St. Louis, October 13, 2015, https:// www.stlouisfed.org/publications/regional-economist/october-2015/stimulus -spending-had-spillover-effects-thanks-to-commuters.

33. "Manufacturing Jobs May 2013," College of Urban Planning and Public Affairs, May 2013, http://www.uic.edu/cuppa/data/CUED_Manufacturing _Jobs_May2013.pdf; Josh Bivens, "Updated Employment Multipliers for the U.S. Economy (2003)," Economic Policy Institute, August 2003, http:// pbadupws.nrc.gov/docs/ML1224/ML12243A398.pdf (accessed June 27, 2019); and "Understanding the Multiplier Effect," Employment in New York State, April 2005, https://www.labor.ny.gov/stats/PDFs/enys0405.pdf (accessed June 27, 2019).

34. "US Employment and Jobs," Department of Numbers, http://www .deptofnumbers.com/employment/us/ (accessed on June 27, 2019).

35. Ken Marshall, "Move to Online Causes Decline of Travel Agency Jobs," Cleveland.com, October 14, 2009, http://www.cleveland.com/pdgraphics/index .ssf/2009/10/move_to_online_causes_decline.html (accessed June 27, 2019).

36. "Occupational Employment and Wages, May 2018," Bureau of Labor Statistics, http://www.bls.gov/oes/current/oes413041.htm (accessed June 27, 2019).

37. Elizabeth Flock, "There Are More Tax Preparers in America Than Firefighters and Police Combined," U.S. News, August 15, 2002, http://www.usnews .com/news/blogs/washington-whispers/2012/08/15/there-are-more-tax-preparers -in-america-than-firefighters-and-police-combined (accessed June 27, 2019).

38. "Occupational Employment and Wages," Bureau of Labor Statistics, May 2018, http://www.bls.gov/oes/current/oes435041.htm (accessed June 27, 2019).

39. "Economic News Release," Bureau of Labor Statistics, http://www.bls.gov /news.release/empsit.a.htm.

40. https://www.statista.com/statistics/208993/us-retail-per-capita-sales -since-2004.

41. "Employent Outlook: 2010–2020," Monthly Labor Review, January 2012, http://www.bls.gov/opub/mlr/2012/01/art4full.pdf.

42. "Economic News Release," Bureau of Labor Statistics, August 2, 2019, https://www.bls.gov/news.release/empsit.t17.htm.

43. "Fifty Years of Federal Deficits as Pct GDP," U.S. Government Debt, https://www.usgovernmentdebt.us/spending_chart_2010_2020USp _19s2lio11lcn_Gof_Fifty_Years_Of_Federal_Deficits_As_Pct_GDP-view (accessed August 15, 2019).

44. Erik Brynjolfsson and Andrew McAfee, *The Second Machine Age* (New York: W. W. Norton, 2014), 221.

45. Bill Snyder, "You'll Never Get Google Fiber—But You Don't Need

It Anyway," InfoWorld, December 6, 2012, https://www.infoworld.com
/article/2616265/you-ll-never-get-google-fiber----but-you-don-t-need-it
-anyway.html.

46. "Hyperloop," Wikipedia, https://en.wikipedia.org/wiki/Hyperloop.

47. "The Rise of Suburbs," Lumen, https://courses.lumenlearning.com
/ushistory2ay/chapter/the-rise-of-suburbs-2/.

48. Brent Nyitray, "Construction Spending Falls as a Percentage of
GDP," Market Realist, August, 2, 2019, https://marketrealist.com/2016/08
/construction-spending-falls-percentage-gdp/.

49. History.com Editors, "The Interstate Highway System," History
Channel, May 27, 2010, updated June 7, 2019, https://www.history.com/topics
/interstate-highway-system.

50. Heather Long, "Where Are All the Startups? U.S. Entrepreneurship
Near 40-Year Low," CNN, September 8, 2016, https://money.cnn.com/2016/09
/08/news/economy/us-startups-near-40-year-low/index.html.

51. Ibid.

52. Charles Murray, *In Our Hands* (Washington, D.C.: The AEI Press, 2016).

53. Jeremy Greenwood and Guillaume Vandenbroucke, "Hours Worked:
Long-Run Trends," National Bureau of Economic Research, September 2005,
http://www.nber.org/papers/w11629.pdf; and Robert Whaples, "Hours of Work
in U.S. History," EH.net, http://eh.net/encyclopedia/hours-of-work-in-u-s
-history/ (accessed August 14, 2019).

54. Jill Mislinski, "The Ratio of Part-Time Employed: July 2019," Advisor
Perspectives, August 5, 2019, http://www.advisorperspectives.com/dshort
/updates/Full-Time-vs-Part-Time-Employment.php/.

Chapter Seven **LIBERTY AND PRIVACY**

1. "Does China's Digital Police State Have Echoes in the West?,"
The Economist, May 31, 2018, https://www.economist.com/leaders/2018/05
/31/does-chinas-digital-police-state-have-echoes-in-the-west.

2. "More Data and Surveillance Are Transforming Justice Systems,"
The Economist, June 2, 2018, https://www.economist.com/technology-quarterly
/2018-05-02/justice.

3. Shoshana Zuboff, *The Age of Surveillance Capitalism* (New York: Public
Affairs, 2019), 282–290.

4. Surveillance-Video, product catalog, https://www.surveillance-video.com
/license-plate-cameras/ (accessed June 27, 2019).

5. Will Oremus, "Forget Security Cameras. Stores Are Using Face Recognition to See If You're a Shoplifter," Slate, November 24, 2015, http://www.slate
.com/blogs/moneybox/2015/11/24/stores_are_using_face_recognition_to
_catch_shoplifters.html (accessed June 27, 2019).

6. JenerationTech, "How Facial Recognition Will Impact the Shopping
Industry," Kairos, November 22, 2016, https://www.kairos.com/blog/how
-facial-recognition-will-impact-the-shopping-industry (accessed June 27, 2019).

7. Stephanie Clipper and Quentin Hardy, "Attention Shopper: Stores are Tracking Your Cell," *New York Times*, July 15, 2013, http://www.nytimes.com /2013/07/15/business/attention-shopper-stores-are-tracking-your-cell.html (accessed June 27, 2019).

8. Cotton Delo, "Industry Group Calls Out Kia for Not Disclosing Behavioral Ads," *Ad Age*, October 1, 2012, http://adage.com/article/digital /industry-group-cites-kia-disclosing-behavioral-ads/237513/ (accessed June 27, 2019).

9. Jarice Hanson, *The Social Media Revolution: An Economic Encyclopedia of Friending, Following, Texting, and Connecting* (Santa Barbara, Calif., and Denver, Colo.: Greenwood, 2016), 294.

10. Dictionary.com, http://www.dictionary.com/ (accessed June 27, 2019); and Bruce Schneier, *Data and Goliath: The Hidden Battles to Collect Your Data and Control Your World* (New York: W. W. Norton, 2015), 57.

11. Schneier, *Data and Goliath*.

12. Natasha Singer, "Mapping, and Sharing, the Consumer Genome," New York Times, June 6, 2012, http://www.nytimes.com/2012/06/17/technology /acxiom-the-quiet-giant-of-consumer-database-marketing.html (accessed June 27, 2019).

13. "LexisNexis Risk Solutions," Wikipedia, https://en.wikipedia.org/wiki /LexisNexis_Risk_Solutions (accessed June 27, 2019).

14. Bruce Schneier, "Do You Want the Government Buying Your Data from Corporations?," *The Atlantic*, April 30, 2013, https://www.theatlantic.com /technology/archive/2013/04/do-you-want-the-government-buying-your -data-from-corporations/275431/ (accessed June 27, 2019); and Zack Whittaker, "Despite Promises to Stop, US Cell Carriers Are Still Selling Your Real-Time Phone Location Data," Techcrunch, January 9, 2019, https://techcrunch .com/2019/01/09/us-cell-carriers-still-selling-your-location-data/ (accessed June 28, 2019).

15. Kevin Murname, "Amazon's Alexa Hacked to Surreptitiously Record Everything It Hears," Forbes.com, April 25, 2018, https://www.forbes.com/sites /kevinmurnane/2018/04/25/amazons-alexa-hacked-to-surreptitiously-record -everything-it-hears/#7c59fff44fe2 (accessed June 27, 2019).

16. Jim Bach, "The Big Shift in Newspaper Revenue," *American Journalism Review*, February 27, 2014, http://ajr.org/2014/02/27/big-shift-reliance-reader -payments-newspapers/ (accessed June 27, 2019).

17. John Wanamaker, quoted in " 'Half the money I spend on advertising is wasted; the trouble is I don't know which half,' " speech by Gerald Chait, B2B Marketing.net, March 18, 2015, https://www.b2bmarketing.net/en/resources/ blog/half-money-i-spend-advertising-wasted-trouble-i-dont-know-which-half.

18. "Targeted Ads Can Improve Click-Through Rates by 67 Percent," American Marketing Association, https://www.ama.org/publications/eNews letters/Marketing-News-Weekly/Pages/targeted-ads-can-improve-click -through-rates-by-670.aspx (accessed September, 2019).

19. Bill Gurley, "Bill Gurley on the 'Free' Business Model," Above the Crowd, July 15, 2009, http://abovethecrowd.com/2009/07/15/bill-gurley-on-the-free -business-model/ (accessed Septmber 2017); and Sujan Patel, "7 Examples of Freemium Products Done Right," Forbes.com, April 29, 2015, https://www .forbes.com/sites/sujanpatel/2015/04/29/7-examples-of-freemium-products -done-right/#64f028a46f15 (accessed June 27, 2019).

20. Stephen Dinan, "FBI No-Fly List Revealed: 81,000 Names, but Fewer Than 1,000 Are Americans," *Washington Times*, June 20, 2016, https://www. washingtontimes.com/news/2016/jun/20/fbi-no-fly-list-revealed-81k-names -fewer-1k-us/ (accessed June 27, 2019); and "U.S. No-Fly List Doubles in One Year," *USA Today*, February 2, 2012, http://usatoday30.usatoday.com/news /washington/story/2012-02-02/no-fly-list/52926968/1 (accessed June 27, 2019).

21. "Muslim-Amercian Group Criticizes TSA Plan and Profiling," CNN, January 4, 2010, http://www.cnn.com/2010/CRIME/01/04/tsa.measures .muslims/ (accessed June 27, 2019); "TSA's New Screening Targets Certain Passengers for 'Enhanced' Checks," DailyTech, October 23, 2013, http://www .dailytech.com/TSAs+New+Screening+Targets+Certain+Passengers+for +Enhanced+Checks/article33597.htm.

22. Eli Pariser, *The Filter Bubble* (New York: Penguin Press, 2011), 125.

23. Don Peck, "They're Watching You at Work," *The Atlantic*, December 2013, http://www.theatlantic.com/magazine/archive/2013/12/theyre-watching -you-at-work/354681/ (accessed June 27, 2019).

24. "Equifax," Wikipedia, http://en.wikipedia.org/wiki/Equifax (accessed June 27, 2019).

25. Ann Carrns, "Consumers Can Check on Data Beyond Their Credit Reports," *New York Times*, January 15, 2014, http://www.nytimes.com/2014/01 /15/your-money/consumers-can-check-on-data-beyond-their-credit-reports .html?_r=0 (accessed June 27, 2019).

26. "Blackstone's Formulation," Wikipedia, https://en.wikipedia.org/wiki /Blackstone%27s_formulation (accessed June 27, 2019).

27. Schneier, *Data and Goliath*.

28. "General Data Protection Regulation," Wikipedia, https://en.wikipedia .org/wiki/General_Data_Protection_Regulation (accessed June 27, 2019).

29. Alex Hern and Jim Waterson, "Sites Block Users, Shut Down Activities and Flood Inboxes as GDPR Rules Loom," *The Guardian*, May 24, 2018, https:// www.theguardian.com/technology/2018/may/24/sites-block-eu-users-before -gdpr-takes-effect (accessed June 27, 2019).

30. "Data Protection Directive," Wikipedia, https://en.wikipedia.org/wiki /Data_Protection_Directive (accessed June 27, 2019).

Chapter Eight WITHIN THE CHIMERA

1. Autumn Sprague, "11 People Who Died Playing Video Games," Ranker, https://www.ranker.com/list/8-people-who-died-playing-video-games/autumn -spragg (accessed June 27, 2019).

2. Ibid.

3. Jean M. Twenge, "Have Smartphones Destroyed a Generation?," *The Atlantic*, September 2017, https://www.theatlantic.com/magazine/archive/2017/09/has -the-smartphone-destroyed-a-generation/534198/ (accessed June 27, 2019).

4. "Early Human Culture," Palomar.edu, https://www2.palomar.edu/anthro /homo/homo_4.htm (accessed June 27, 2019); and Rebecca Morelle, "Oldest Stone Tools Pre-Date Earliest Humans," BBC, May 20, 2015, http://www.bbc .com/news/science-environment-32804177 (accessed June 27, 2019).

5. "Internet Users in the World, by Regions," Internet World Stats, March 2019, http://www.internetworldstats.com/stats.htm (accessed June 27, 2019).

6. Christine Erickson, "A Brief History of Text Messaging," Mashable, September 21, 2012, http://mashable.com/2012/09/21/text-messaging-history /#LZpQOmWb1ZqV (accessed June 27, 2019).

7. "Blackberry," Wikipedia, https://en.wikipedia.org/wiki/BlackBerry (accessed June 27, 2019).

8. "History of Video Slot Machines," VideoSlot, https://www.videoslot.com /video-slot-history/.

9. Natasha Dow Schüll, *Addiction by Design* (Princeton, N.J.: Princeton University Press, 2012), 13.

10. Ibid., 19.

11. Ibid., 36.

12. "Video Game Rooms," Pinterest, https://www.pinterest.com/homebnc /video-game-rooms/ (accessed September 2017).

13. Schüll, *Addiction by Design*, 54–75.

14. "Top Casinos," Odds Shark, http://www.oddsshark.com/casino/slots (accessed June 27, 2019).

15. "Using Variable Rewards to Drive Behavior Change," The Art of Ass Kicking, https://www.jasonshen.com/2013/using-variable-rewards-to-drive -behavior-change/ (accessed September 2017); Wolfram Schultz, "Getting Formal with Dopamine and Reward," ScienceDirect, October 10, 2002, http:// www.sciencedirect.com/science/article/pii/S0896627302009674 (accessed June 27, 2019); and "Operant Conditioning—Schedules of Reinforcement," Psych Exam Review, http://www.psychexamreview.com/schedules-of-reinforcement/ (accessed June 27, 2019).

16. "FarmVille," Wikipedia, https://en.wikipedia.org/wiki/FarmVille (accessed June 27, 2019).

17. Scott Rigby, conversation with William Davidow.

18. Mike Morhaime, conversation with William Davidow.

19. Scott Rigby and Richard M. Ryan, *Glued to Games: How Video Games Draw Us In and Hold Us Spellbound* (Santa Barbara, Calif.: Praeger, 2011).

20. Ibid.

21. J. Allen Brack, conversation with William Davidow.

22. Paul Lewis, "'Our Minds Can Be Hijacked': The Tech Insiders Who Fear a Smartphone Dystopia," *The Guardian*, October 26, 2017, https://www

.theguardian.com/technology/2017/oct/05/smartphone-addiction-silicon
-valley-dystopia (accessed June 27, 2019).

23. Ki Mae Heussner, "Are You Your Avatar? Book Details Dangers of
the 'E-Personality,'" ABC News, January 27, 2011, https://abcnews.go.com
/Technology/online-life-harms-civility-creates-aggressive-personality
-psychiatrist/story?id=12771299.

24. "How Much Are We Really Attached to Our Phones Physically, Cogni-
tively," dScout, 2016, http://blog.dscout.com/hubfs/downloads/dscout_mobile
_touches_study_2016.pdf?hsCtaTracking=9b6ffb9f-3c60-489f-8599-
e6a8d954b7df|6f4e83c4-70ee-4bbb-8e81-cd47f5f376fa (accessed June 27, 2019).

25. Claire Groden, "Here's How Many Americans Sleep with Their Smartphones," *Fortune*, June 29, 2015, http://fortune.com/2015/06/29/sleep-banks
-smartphones/ http://fortune.com/2015/06/29/sleep-banks-smartphones/.

26. Knud Lasse Lueth, "State of the IoT 2018: Number of IoT Devices
Now at 7B—Market Accelerating," IOT Analytics, August 8, 2018, https://
iot-analytics.com/state-of-the-iot-update-q1-q2-2018-number-of-iot-devices
-now-7b/ (accessed June 27, 2019).

27. https://www.newgenapps.com/blog/iot-statistics-internet-of-things
-future-research-data.

28. "Me, me, me! America's 'Narcissism Epidemic,'" *Today Show*, April 20,
2009, https://www.today.com/popculture/me-me-me-americas-narcissism
-epidemic-2D80555351 (accessed June 27, 2019).

29. "Facebook and the Rise of Narcissism," Shrinkrap, April 8, 2011, http://
shrinkrap.co.za/psychotherapy/facebook-and-the-rise-of-narcissism (accessed
June 27, 2019).

30. Damien Pearse, "Facebook's 'Dark Side' Study Finds Link to Socially
Aggressive Narcissism," *The Guardian*, March 17, 2012, http://www.guardian
.co.uk/technology/2012/mar/17/facebook-dark-side-study-aggressive
-narcissism (accessed June 27, 2019).

31. Elias Aboujaoude, "Rise of the Online Narcissist," *Psychology Today*,
February 16, 2011, http://www.psychologytoday.com/blog/compulsive-acts
/201102/rise-the-online-narcissist.

32. Ibid.

33. "Twitter Counter Alternatives and Competitors," G2, https://www
.g2.com/products/twitter-counter/competitors/alternatives.

34. Jean M. Twenge, *iGen: Why Today's Super-Connected Kids Are Growing
Up Less Rebellious, More Tolerant, Less Happy—and Completely Unprepared for
Adulthood* (New York: Atria Books, 2017), 93–118.

35. Ibid., 108–109.

36. Adam Gazzaley and Larry D. Rosen, *The Distracted Mind* (Cambridge,
Mass.: The MIT Press, 2016), 171.

37. Raven Fon, "Anxiety Disorders Could Be Caused by Being Exposed
to Narcissistic Abuse," iHeart Intelligence, March 21, 2017, http://iheartintel
ligence.com/2017/03/31/anxiety-disorders-narcissistic-abuse/ (accessed
June 27, 2019).

38. Lewis, " 'Our Minds Can Be Hijacked' "; and Roger McNamee, *Zucked: Waking Up to the Facebook Catastrophe* (New York: Penguin Press, 2019).

39. Xiaohui Zhuo et al., "Lifetime Direct Medical Costs of Treating Type 2 Diabetes and Diabetic Complications," *American Journal of Preventative Medicine*, 2013, https://www.ajpmonline.org/article/S0749-3797(13)00338-3/pdf (accessed June 27, 2019).

40. "The True Cost of Spam for Your Company," EZ Computer Solutions, https://www.ezcomputersolutions.com/blog/true-cost-of-spam-for-companies/ (accessed June 27, 2019).

41. Emily Bauer, "15 Outrageous Email Spam Statistics That Still Ring True in 2018," Propeller, February 1, 2018, https://www.propellercrm.com/blog /email-spam-statistics (accessed June 27, 2019).

42. "Google's Annual Global Revenue," Statista, https://www.statista.com /statistics/266206/googles-annual-global-revenue/; "Facebook's Annual Revenue and Net Income," Statista, https://www.statista.com/statistics/277229 /facebooks-annual-revenue-and-net-income/; and "Amazon.com Annual Net Revenue," Statista, https://www.statista.com/statistics/266282/annual-net -revenue-of-amazoncom/ (accessed June 27, 2019).

43. Owen Janus, "Code of Hammurabi: Ancient Babylonian Laws," Live Science, September 3, 2013, https://www.livescience.com/39393-code-of -hammurabi.html (accessed June 27, 2019).

44. "Ancient Civilizations: Democracy Is Born," U.S. History, http://www .ushistory.org/civ/5b.asp (accessed June 27, 2019).

45. "Historical Timeline—Farmers and the Land," Growing a Nation, March 21, 2018, https://www.agclassroom.org/gan/timeline/farmers_land.htm (accessed June 27, 2019).

46. "Population: 1790 to 1990," U.S. Census, https://www.census.gov /population/censusdata/table-4.pdf (accessed June 27, 2019); and Nate Berg, "U.S. Urban Population Is Up . . . But What Does 'Urban' Really Mean?," CityLab, March 26, 2012, https://www.citylab.com/equity/2012/03/us-urban -population-what-does-urban-really-mean/1589/ (accessed June 28, 2019).

47. Bahati Russell, "Cyberbullying and Social Media," Hastac, December 2, 2017, https://www.hastac.org/blogs/bahatiakili/2017/12/02/cyber-bullying-and -social-media (accessed June 29, 2019).

48. Maeve Duggan, "On-Line Harassment," Pew Research Center, October 22, 2014, http://www.pewinternet.org/2014/10/22/online-harassment/ (accessed June 27, 2019).

49. Andrew Hutchinson, "New Report Shows Facebook Usage Is in Decline, Which May Be Behind the Latest News Feed Shifts," Social Media Today, February 22, 2018, https://www.socialmediatoday.com/news/new-report-shows -facebook-usage-is-in-decline-which-may-be-behind-the-late/517586/ (accessed June 27, 2019).

50. Gazzaley and Rosen, *The Distracted Mind*, 62.

51. Ibid., 128–129.

52. Kiernan Hopkins, "25 Shocking Distracted Driving Statistics," Distracted

Driver Accidents.com, June 28, 2019, http://distracteddriveraccidents.com
/25-shocking-distracted-driving-statistics/ (accessed June 27, 2019).

53. "Facts & Statistics About Texting & Driving," Personal Injury San Diego,
2019, http://www.personalinjurysandiego.org/topics/facts-about-texting
-driving/ (accessed June 27, 2019).

54. Gazzaley and Rosen, *The Distracted Mind*, 129.

55. Marc Green, "Driver Reaction Time," Visual Expert.com, 2018, http://
www.visualexpert.com/Resources/reactiontime.html (accessed June 27, 2019).

56. Michael Austin, "Texting While Driving: How Dangerous Is It?" *Car
and Driver*, June 24, 2009, http://www.caranddriver.com/features/texting-while
-driving-how-dangerous-is-it-the-results-page-2 (accessed June 27, 2019).

57. Gazzaley and Rosen, *The Distracted Mind*, 129.

58. Gloria Mark et al., "The Task Left Behind? Examining the Nature of
Fragmented Work," University of California, Irvine, April 2005, http://www.ics
.uci.edu/%7Egmark/CHI2005.pdf (accessed June 27, 2019).

Chapter Nine **THE BODY POLITIC**

1. Francis Fukuyama, *The End of History and the Last Man*, reissue ed.
(New York: Free Press, 2006).

2. "Homestead Act," History.com, https://www.history.com/topics
/homestead-act (accessed June 27, 2019).

3. Julian M. Alston, Jennifer S. James, Matthew A. Andersen, Philip G.
Pardey, "A Brief History of US Agriculture," in *Persistence Pays: U.S. Agricul-
tural Productivity Growth and the Benefits from Public R&D Spending*
(New York: Springer, 2008).

4. "Life Expectancy by Age, 1850–2011," Infoplease, https://www.infoplease
.com/us/mortality/life-expectancy-age-1850-2011 (accessed June 27, 2019).

5. Joseph R. Fishkin et al., "Amendment XVI: Income Tax," Constitution
Center, https://constitutioncenter.org/interactive-constitution/amendments
/amendment-xvi (accessed June 27, 2019).

6. Ibid.

7. William E. Leuchtenburg, "When Franklin Roosevelt Clashed with the
Supreme Court—and Lost," *Smithsonian Magazine*, May 2005, https://www
.smithsonianmag.com/history/when-franklin-roosevelt-clashed-with-the
-supreme-court-and-lost-78497994/ (accessed June 27, 2019).

8. "The History of U.S. Government Spending, Revenue, and Debt
(1790–2015)," Metrocosm.com, February 16, 2016, http://metrocosm.com
/history-of-us-taxes/.

9. "Leviathan," Wikipedia, https://en.wikipedia.org/wiki/Leviathan
(accessed June 27, 2019); and Thomas Hobbes, "Leviathan" (1651), Studymore
(UK), http://studymore.org.uk/xhob18.htm (accessed June 27, 2019).

10. "Thomas Hobbes (1588–1679)," Braungardt's Philosophical Explorations,
http://braungardt.trialectics.com/philosophy/early-modern-philosophy-16th
-18th-century-europe/thomas-hobbes/ (accessed June 27, 2019).

11. Lisa Wade, "Sociological Images," The Society Pages, November 14, 2012, https://thesocietypages.org/socimages/2012/11/14/u-s-racialethnic-demographics-1960-today-and-2050/.

12. "Percentage of U.S. Population by Ethnicities 2016 and 2060," Statista, https://www.statista.com/statistics/270272/percentage-of-us-population-by-ethnicities (accessed on June 27, 2019); and Dudley L. Poston Jr. and Rogelio Saenz, "U.S. Whites Will Soon Be the Minority in Number, but Not Power," *Baltimore Sun*, August 8, 2017, http://www.baltimoresun.com/news/opinion/oped/bs-ed-op-0809-minority-majority-20170808-story.html (accessed on June 27, 2019).

13. D'Vera Cohn and Andrea Caumont, "10 Demographic Trends That Are Shaping the U.S. and the World," Pew Research, March 31, 2016, http://www.pewresearch.org/fact-tank/2016/03/31/10-demographic-trends-that-are-shaping-the-u-s-and-the-world/ (accessed on June 27, 2019).

14. Christopher Ingraham, "The Non-Religious Are Now the Country's Largest Religious Voting Bloc," *Washington Post*, July 14, 2016, https://www.washingtonpost.com/news/wonk/wp/2016/07/14/the-non-religious-are-now-the-countrys-largest-religious-voting-bloc/?utm_term=.9f43b2e65d7e (accessed on June 27, 2019).

15. "Melting Pot," Wikipedia, https://en.wikipedia.org/wiki/Melting_pot (accessed June 27, 2019).

16. Amy Chua, *Political Tribes* (New York: Penguin Press, 2016), 12.

17. Kenneth Scheve and David Stasavage, "Wealth Inequality and Democracy," Stanford University Education, 2017, http://web.stanford.edu/group/scheve-research/cgi-bin/wordpress/wp-content/uploads/2017/02/annurev-polisci-061014-101840.pdf (accessed June 27, 2019).

18. Emmanuel Saez, "Income and Wealth Inequality: Evidence and Policy Implications," *Contemporary Economic Policy*, January 2017, https://eml.berkeley.edu/~saez/SaezCEP2017.pdf (accessed June 27, 2019).

19. Jill Mislinski, "U.S. Household Incomes: A 51-Year Perspective," Advisor Perspectives, October 16, 2018, https://www.advisorperspectives.com/dshort/updates/2017/09/19/u-s-household-incomes-a-50-year-perspective (accessed June 27, 2019).

20. Chad Stone et al., "A Guide to Statistics on Historical Trends in Income Inequality," Center on Budget and Policy Priorities, December 11, 2018, https://www.cbpp.org/research/poverty-and-inequality/a-guide-to-statistics-on-historical-trends-in-income-inequality (accessed June 27, 2019).

21. Jeff Guo, "Income Inequality Today May Be Higher Today Than in Any Other Era," *Washington Post*, July 1, 2016, https://www.washingtonpost.com/news/wonk/wp/2016/07/01/income-inequality-today-may-be-the-highest-since-the-nations-founding/?utm_term=.0759a7e38717 (accessed June 27, 2019); and "GINI Index for the United States," Federal Reserve Bank of St. Louis, https://fred.stlouisfed.org/series/SIPOVGINIUSA (accessed June 27, 2019).

22. Chua, *Political Tribes*, 173; Andrew Kohut, "What Will Become of

America's Kids?," Pew Research, May 12, 2014, http://www.pewresearch.org
/fact-tank/2014/05/12/what-will-become-of-americas-kids/ (accessed June 27,
2019); and Damon Linker, "The Troubling Rise of American Pessimism,"
The Week, August 24, 2016, http://theweek.com/articles/644308/troubling
-rise-american-pessimism (accessed June 27, 2019).

23. Claude S. Fischer, "80 Percent of Americans Experience Economic
Insecurity," *Boston Review*, December 18, 2013, http://bostonreview.net/blog
/fischer-american-dream-economic-insecurity (accessed June 27, 2019); and
"80 Percent of U.S. Adults Face Near-Poverty, Unemployment, Survey Finds,"
CBS News, July 28, 2013, https://www.cbsnews.com/news/80-percent-of-us
-adults-face-near-poverty-unemployment-survey-finds/ (accessed June 27, 2019).

24. Aimee Picchi, "The United States of Insecurity," CBS News, April 17,
2017, https://www.cbsnews.com/news/the-united-states-of-insecurity/
(accessed June 27, 2019).

25. Robert Putnam, *Our Kids: The American Dream in Crisis* (New York:
Simon & Schuster, 2016), 20–21.

26. Robert D. Putnam, Robert Leonardi, and Raffaella Y. Nanetti, *Making
Democracy Work: Civic Traditions in Modern Italy* (Princeton, N.J.: Princeton
University Press, 1994).

27. Ganesh Sitaraman, *The Crisis of the Middle-Class Constitution*
(New York: Vintage Books, 2017), 231.

28. Ibid., 234.

29. Alan B. Krueger, "The Great Utility of the Great Gatsby Curve,"
Brookings, May 19, 2015, https://www.brookings.edu/blog/social-mobility
-memos/2015/05/19/the-great-utility-of-the-great-gatsby-curve/ (accessed
June 28, 2019).

30. "Mobility Report Cards for Columbia and SUNY-Stony Brook,"
The Equality of Opportunity Project, http://www.equality-of-opportunity.org
/college/.

31. Chua, *Political Tribes*, 169.

32. Lucan Ahmad Way and Adam Casey, "Russia Has Been Meddling
in Foreign Elections for Decades. Has It Made a Difference?," *Washington
Post*, January 8, 2018, https://www.washingtonpost.com/news/monkey-cage
/wp/2018/01/05/russia-has-been-meddling-in-foreign-elections-for-decades
-has-it-made-a-difference/?noredirect=on&utm_term=.9d7f17f14236
(accessed June 28, 2019).

33. Chua, *Political Tribes*, 166.

34. "Putnam: Making Democracy Work," Wikisum, 1993, http://wikisum
.com/w/Putnam:_Making_Democracy_Work (accessed June 28, 2019);
and Melissa Hudson, "Making Democracies Work: A Comparison of Robert
Putnam and Barry Weingast," Stanford University Education, https://web
.stanford.edu/class/polisci311/mahudson/hudson.week4.doc (accessed
June 28, 2019).

35. Laura Hautala, "Can Facebook's New Hires Take on Troll Farms and

Data Privacy?," CNET, April 11, 2018, https://www.cnet.com/news/can
-facebook-mark-zuckerberg-new-hires-take-on-troll-farms-and-data
-privacy-after-cambridge-analytica/ (accessed June 28, 2019).

36. *Schenck vs. United States*, U.S. Supreme Court, 1919.

37. Michael S. Malone, "Malone's Laws of Technology," ABC News, July 17,
2009, https://preview.abcnews.go.com/Business/Technology/story?i=8103280
&page=1.

38. "Zelle," Wikipedia, https://en.wikipedia.org/wiki/Zelle_(payment
_service) (accessed June 27, 2019); and Jay MacDonald and Taylor Tompkins,
"The History of Credit Cards," CreditCards.com, July 11, 2017, https://www
.creditcards.com/credit-card-news/history-of-credit-cards.php (accessed
June 28, 2019).

39. Stacy Cowley, "Zelle, the Banks' Answer to Venmo, Proves Vulnerable
to Fraud," *New York Times*, April 22, 2018, https://www.nytimes.com/2018
/04/22/business/zelle-banks-fraud.html (accessed June 28, 2019).

40. Alec Russell, "CIA Plot Led to Huge Blast in Siberian Gas Pipeline,"
Telegraph (UK), February 28, 2004, http://www.telegraph.co.uk/news/world
news/northamerica/usa/1455559/CIA-plot-led-to-huge-blast-in-Siberian-gas
-pipeline.html (accessed June 28, 2019); and Wired Staff, "Soviets Burned
by CIA Hackers?," *Wired*, March 26, 2004, https://www.wired.com/2004/03
/soviets-burned-by-cia-hackers/ (accessed June 28, 2019).

41. "Cyber Time Line," NATO Review, https://www.nato.int/docu/review
/2013/Cyber/timeline/EN/index.htm (accessed June 28, 2019).

42. "Robert Tappan Morris," Wikipedia, https://en.wikipedia.org/wiki
/Robert_Tappan_Morris (accessed June 27, 2019); and "Computer Fraud
and Abuse Act," Wikipedia, https://en.wikipedia.org/wiki/Computer
_Fraud_and_Abuse_Act (accessed June 27, 2019).

43. Kim Zetter, "An Unprecedented Look at Stuxnet, the World's First Digital Weapon," *Wired*, November 3, 2014, https://www.wired.com/2014/11
/countdown-to-zero-day-stuxnet/ (accessed June 28, 2019).

44. Gordon Corera, "21st Century Warfare," BBC, http://www.bbc.co.uk
/guides/zq9jmnb#ztq6nbk (accessed June 28, 2019).

45. Steve Morgan, "Cybercrime Damages $6 Trillion by 2021," Cybersecurity
Ventures, October 16, 2017, https://cybersecurityventures.com/hackerpocalypse
-cybercrime-report-2016/ (accessed June 28, 2019).

46. "Gross Domestic Product for World," Federal Reserve Bank of St. Louis,
https://fred.stlouisfed.org/series/MKTGDP1WA646NWDB (accessed June 28,
2019).

47. Emily Tamkin, "10 Years After the Landmark Attack on Estonia, Is the
World Better Prepared for Cyber Threats?," *Foreign Policy*, April 27, 2017, http://
foreignpolicy.com/2017/04/27/10-years-after-the-landmark-attack-on-estonia
-is-the-world-better-prepared-for-cyber-threats/ (accessed June 28, 2019).

48. Kevin Poulsen, "Russia-Linked Hackers Breached 100 Nuclear and
Power Plants Just This Year," The Daily Beast, September 6, 2017, https://www

.thedailybeast.com/breaches-at-us-nuclear-and-power-plants-linked-to
-russian-hackers (accessed June 28, 2019).

49. Fred Kaplan, "Russia's Power Trip," Slate, June 14, 2017, http://www.slate
.com/articles/news_and_politics/war_stories/2017/06/russia_s_power_grid
_cyberweapon_is_scary.html (accessed June 28, 2019).

50. Matthew P. Barrett, "Framework for Improving Critical Infrastructure
Cybersecurity Version 1.1," NIST Cybersecurity Framework, April 16, 2018,
https://www.nist.gov/publications/framework-improving-critical
-infrastructure-cybersecurity-version-11.

51. "Coal Is Fueling Bitcoin's Meteoric Rise," Bloomberg, December 14,
2017, https://www.bloomberg.com/news/articles/2017-12-15/turning-coal
-into-bitcoin-dirty-secret-of-2017-s-hottest-market (accessed June 28, 2019).

52. Alex Hern, "How Iceland Became the Bitcoin Miners' Paradise," The
Guardian, February 13, 2018, https://www.theguardian.com/world/2018/feb/13
/how-iceland-became-the-bitcoin-miners-paradise (accessed June 28, 2019);
and Foreign Staff, "Iceland Set to Use More Energy Mining Bitcoin Than
Powering Homes," Telegraph (UK), February 12, 2018, https://www.telegraph
.co.uk/news/2018/02/12/iceland-set-use-energy-mining-bitcoin-powering
-homes/ (accessed June 28, 2019).

53. "Bitcoin Mining Guide—Getting Started with Bitcoin Mining," Bitcoin
Mining.com, https://www.bitcoinmining.com/getting-started/ (accessed
June 28, 2019); and "Genesis Mining Review," Cryptorival.com, https://
cryptorival.com/miners/genesismining/ (accessed June 28, 2019).

54. Ben Popken, "Why Did Bitcoin 'Fork' Today and What Is 'Bitcoin
Cash?,'" NBC News, August 1, 2017, https://www.nbcnews.com/business
/consumer/why-bitcoin-forking-today-what-bitcoin-cash-n788581 (accessed
June 28, 2019); and Max Gulker, "Bitcoin: Decentralized Governance Put to
the Test," American Institute of Economic Research, May 16, 2017, https://
www.aier.org/research/bitcoin-decentralized-governance-put-test (accessed
June 28, 2019).

55. Amanda Dixon, "America's 15 Largest Banks," Bankrate, May 30, 2019,
https://www.bankrate.com/banking/americas-top-10-biggest-banks/#slide=1
(accessed June 28, 2019).

56. William H. Davidow, Overconnected: The Promise and Threat of the
Internet (New York: Delphinium Books, New York, 2011), 83–97.

57. Edward Robinson and Omar Valdimarsson, "This Is Where Bad Bankers
Go to Prison," Bloomberg, March 30, 2016, https://www.bloomberg.com/news
/features/2016-03-31/welcome-to-iceland-where-bad-bankers-go-to-prison
(accessed June 28, 2019).

58. Bill Murphy, Jr., "27 Awesome Quotes About Freedom for Independence Day (and Every Day)," Inc., https://www.inc.com/bill-murphy-jr/27
-awesome-quotes-about-freedom-for-independence-day.html (accessed
June 28, 2019).

Chapter Ten SACRED VALUES

1. William F. Ogburn, *On Culture and Social Change* (Chicago: University of Chicago Press, 1964), 86.

2. Patrick Taylor, "Why Do the People of Uruk Dislike Gilgamesh?," Quora, https://www.quora.com/Why-do-the-people-of-Uruk-dislike-Gilgamesh (accessed June 28, 2019).

3. "Cedar Forest," Wikipedia, https://en.wikipedia.org/wiki/Cedar_Forest (accessed June 28, 2019).

4. "Gilgamesh and Civilization," Chamelionfire1, December 17, 2013, https://chameleonfire1.wordpress.com/2013/12/17/gilgamesh-and-civilization/ (accessed June 28, 2019).

5. "Fintech, the Incredible Growth of P2P (Peer to Peer) in China," Marketing to China, September 22, 2017, https://www.marketingtochina.com /fintech-incredible-growth-p2p-peer-peer-china/ (accessed June 28, 2019).

6. John Maynard Keynes, "Economic Possibilities for Our Grandchildren," Marxists.org, 1930, https://www.marxists.org/reference/subject/economics /keynes/1930/our-grandchildren.htm (accessed June 28, 2019).

7. Ibid.

8. "What Does Voluntary Compliance Mean, in Regard to Taxes?," Optima Tax Relief, July 29, 2014, https://www.optimataxrelief.com/voluntary -compliance-mean-regards-taxes/ (accessed June 28, 2019).

9. "Study Shows That 6 Percent of Americans Cheat on Their Taxes," Mockensturm Ltd., March 2, 2018, https://www.mockltd.com/blog/2018/03 /study-shows-that-6-percent-of-americans-cheat-on-their-taxes.shtml (accessed June 28, 2019).

10. Suzanne Daley, "Greek Wealth Is Everywhere But Tax Forms," *New York Times*, May 1, 2010, https://www.nytimes.com/2010/05/02/world /europe/02evasion.html (accessed June 28, 2019).

11. Theodoris Georgakopoulos, "Tax Evasion in Greece—A Study," Dianeosis, June 2016, https://www.dianeosis.org/en/2016/06/tax-evasion -in-greece/ (accessed June 28, 2019).

12. Adam Smith, *Theory of Moral Sentiments* (1759), 89.

13. "Country List Government Spending to GDP," Trading Economics, December 2018, https://tradingeconomics.com/country-list/government -spending-to-gdp (accessed June 28, 2019).

14. "List of Countries by Income Equality," Wikipedia, https://en.wikipedia .org/wiki/List_of_countries_by_income_equality (accessed June 27, 2019).

15. Michelle Diggles, "Unaffiliated: The Rise of Independents from 2008 to 2016," Third Way, July 5, 2016, https://www.thirdway.org/memo/unaffiliated -the-rise-of-independents-from-2008-to-2016 (accessed June 28, 2019).

16. W. Brian Arthur, "Where Is Technology Taking the Economy?," McKinsey, October 2017, https://www.mckinsey.com/business-functions /mckinsey-analytics/our-insights/where-is-technology-taking-the-economy (accessed June 28, 2019).

Acknowledgments

This book has benefited from the support of many individuals who made it both possible and better.

W. Brian Arthur has provided many insights and pointed us to the phase change paradigm. Katie Hafner has helped William write articles and blogs and her ideas have greatly contributed to this effort. The editors and people at Berrett-Koehler Publishers have contributed so much to our efforts. We especially want to thank our editor, Neal Maillet, Editorial Director, for his wise advice and support.

Numerous others have provided ideas, read the manuscript, and offered advice. We want to thank the economists at the Stanford Institute for Economic Policy Research for their thoughtful insights and support, especially Ed David and Mark Duggan. As befits his reputation, Mark Fortier has shown a sure hand in guiding us on marketing and promotion.

Also, a special thanks to the legendary Jim Levine, our agent of many years, who not only helped us find a publisher but also, as always, provided many valuable suggestions at every part of the writing process.

Index

Aboujaoude, Elias, 144, 147
abundance, 7, 14, 67, 94, 188, 194–195
accidents, 156
Adams, Henry, x, 37
addiction: gambling, 137, 138–139,
140, 143, 150; gaming, 89, 132,
138–144; income inequality
and, 166; neuroscience behind,
136–138, 140; protections against,
in virtual space, 148–151; smartphone, 133, 138, 145; social media/
networking, 144–145, 148–151;
virtual space/Internet, 132–133,
136–146, 148–151
advertising industry, 62–64, 89, 90,
120–123, 134–135
Agricultural Revolution: Autonomous Revolution contrasted
with, 25–26; cities' origin in, 24,
25–26, 35, 151–152, 183–184; constitutional rights crafted during,
159; cultural norms' creation in,
151–152; governance rules and
systems shift in, 25; population
growth during, 35, 36; Second,
24–25; social phase change of,
6, 11, 13, 14–15, 17, 21, 23–25, 26,

36–37, 134, 183–184; structural
transformations early in, 23–24,
134; substitutional equivalence
in, 14–15; timeline/rates of
change, 13, 17, 21, 25, 36–37, 193
Airbnb model, 44, 70, 86
airline industry, 72, 97–98, 103–104
algorithms and algorithmic prisons,
13, 114, 123–128
Alibaba, 70, 76
AlphaGo, 46–47
Amazon, 64–65, 87–88, 90–91, 119,
150
"Amazon Effect," 105
Anglo-Saxon culture, 162–163, 166
antitrust violations, 93, 160
anxiety, 148, 150
Apple, 10, 88–90
Arthur, W. Brian, 29, 97–98, 103,
194
artificial intelligence: in behavior
prediction and modification,
117; history and evolution of,
45–47; job loss with, 43, 110;
in law enforcement, 115; non-
monetizable productivity of, 60;
substitutional equivalences with,

73, 121–123, 129–130, 169; media industry shift in, 9–10, 72–73; non-monetizable productivity relation to shifting, 60, 65; sharing economy, 83–87; substitutional equivalence and smaller markets in new, 87–88, 103
Butler, Nicholas, 2–3

Campbell, W. Keith, 146
Capek, Karel, 45
cars. *See* automobile industry; autonomous vehicles
cash, 41–42, 82
casinos. *See* gambling addiction
Chandler, Alfred, 33
change: harbingers of radical, 1–4; Hegel on late understanding of, xiii; Heraclitus on constant of, ix–x, xiv. *See also* phase change; social phase change; timeline/rates of change
chess-playing computers, 45, 46
China, 10, 76, 115, 132, 186
ChoicePoint, 118–119, 130
Christensen, Clayton, 87
Christianity, 27, 162–163, 166
Chua, Amy, 163, 167
church authority, 28, 152, 162
CIA, 119, 172
cities/urban environments: Agricultural Revolution's role in origin of, 24, 25–26, 35, 151–152, 183–184; autonomous vehicles' role in population of, 108–109; Industrial Revolution's role in growth of, 30, 160; Transportation Revolution's impact on, 31–32
citizens: democracy dependent on unity of, 163, 166, 168; polarization of, 95, 115–116, 158, 161, 165, 167–168, 189–190, 194, 195; social networking impacts on unity of,

166–170; unity role in government function, 161–166, 168; value system unity and commitment of, 193–195; ZEV, 12, 48–49
Clark, Luke, 140
climate change, 21–22
Collison, Patrick and John, 78
commercial entities: behavior manipulation by, 13, 117, 121, 123; displacement business for, 71, 72–73, 99; Industrial Revolution's rise in power of, 17, 34; virtual, 3–4, 7, 34, 50, 64–65, 89–92
commercial trends, key, 4, 71, 73
communications revolution, 27–28
computer industry: artificial intelligence history in, 45–47; integrated circuitry history of and impact on, 55–56, 58; and microprocessor history, 55–56, 172; monetizable productivity with early, 55–56; non-monetizable productivity in, 18, 58; semiconductor history of and impacts on, 54–55, 56–57; timeline and adoption rate for, 22–23, 55–56; virus/malware history in, 39–40, 172–173
Computer Revolution, 29, 39–40, 99, 111, 182
constitutional rights, 113, 114, 127, 159–160, 162, 168–170
consumers. *See* customers/consumers; retail sector
cookies, Internet, 89, 116, 117–118, 128
corporations. *See* commercial entities
Craigslist, 62, 87
credit cards: cash contrasted with, 41–42; cost of and security risk with, 74–76; cyber/mobile payment systems replacing, 10, 76–77, 81–82, 171, 186; emergence

Industrial Revolution and rise of, 160–161; Italy, study of, 164–165, 168; regulation, social phase change increasing, 160–161, 193; surveillance practices of, 115, 119. *See also* laws and regulations
GPS, 116, 149
Greece, tax fraud in, 190
Greeks, ancient, 26, 78, 151
Greeley, Horace, 159
gross domestic product (GDP), 163; displaced workers and growth of, 105; farming role historically in, 159; monetizable productivity historical impacts on, 52, 55–56, 57; non-monetizable productivity impacts on, 52, 58–59, 66; as quality of life metric, 66–67
Gutenberg, Johannes, 27

Hachette, 90–91
Healey, Jason, 174
health care and insurance, 14, 48, 110, 111, 161
health/illness, 20, 95, 149–150, 166. *See also* addiction; mental health
Hegel, G. F. W., xiii
Henry, Patrick, 113, 116
Heraclitus, ix–x, xiv
Hidden Persuaders, The (Packard), 135
Hobbes, Thomas, 161, 169, 180
Holmes, Oliver Wendell, Jr., 170
Homeland Security, US, 175
Homestead Act of 1862, 159
hospitality industry, 44, 86
housing market, 96
human knowledge, xi, 16, 36
Huygens, Christiaan, 52
Hyman, Ira, 155–156

IBM, 55–56
Iceland, 176, 178–179
iGen, 147–148

illness. *See* health/illness
income: decline in median, 96–97; Depression-era policies on, 160; housing prices increase relative to, 96; retirement, 152–153; total US household, 194; universal basic, 110–111, 192
income inequality: democracy in relation to, 163–164; gig economy's impact on, 7, 34, 63, 84, 85, 94; history of reversing, 96; Industrial Revolution's impact on, 160; non-monetizable productivity increasing, 67; polarization fueled by, 95, 158, 165; political inequality in relation to, 165; present-day levels of, 13, 31, 163–164, 191–192, 194; self-reinforcing generational cycle of, 165; sharing economy's impact on, 86–87; social empathy decline with rise in, 164–165; solutions and action toward, 94, 194–195; tax solutions to, 94; in US compared with Sweden, 192
income tax. *See* taxes
India, 76, 104
Industrial Revolution: automobile's role in, 53–54, 152; change rate and timeline for, 13, 17–18, 21, 29, 37, 193; cities/urban growth in, 30, 160; commercial entities' rise in power during, 17, 34; constitutional rights adapting to, 159; cultural norms created with, 152–153, 182–183; general-purpose technologies driving, 29; governance rules and systems, 33, 34, 182–183; government rise during, 160–161; ideologies birthed during, 31; income inequality with, 160; job market impacts with, 29–31;

About the Authors

WILLIAM H. DAVIDOW has been involved in computer and information technology since the early 1960s. He graduated from Dartmouth College, summa cum laude, in 1957. He received master's degrees in electrical engineering from Dartmouth in 1958 and Caltech in 1959 and a PhD in electrical engineering from Stanford in 1961.

After graduating from Stanford, he ran a computer research lab for General Electric and went on to run marketing for Hewlett-Packard's newly formed computer division. In 1973 he joined Intel to run the Microprocessor Division and then, as a Senior Vice-President, ran Sales and Marketing for the company. In 1985, he started his own venture capital firm with a partner—Mohr, Davidow Ventures.

He is the author of four prior books, *Marketing High Technology*, *Total Customer Service* with Bro Uttal, *The Virtual Corporation* with Michael Malone, and *Overconnected*.

Davidow currently serves on the boards of the California Institute of Technology, University of California, San Francisco, The California Nature Conservancy, and the Stanford Institute for Economic Policy Research. He also serves on the board of Berkeley Lights, a biotechnology company.

Davidow married Sonja Carlson in 1965. They have two daughters and four grandsons. He resides in the San Francisco Bay Area.

MICHAEL S. MALONE has been a journal-
ist, entrepreneur, author, television writer/
host, and educator. He was the world's first
daily technology-business reporter (for
the *San Jose Mercury-News*) and has been a
columnist for the *New York Times* and regular op-ed contributor to the *Wall Street
Journal*. He was editor of *Forbes ASAP*, the
world's largest circulation business-technology magazine. He is the
author of more than twenty books, including the award-winning
Intel Trilogy, *Bill & Dave*, and (co-authored, with William Davidow) the influential best-seller *The Virtual Corporation*. A founding
shareholder of eBay and Siebel Systems, Malone is currently Dean's
Professor of Professional Writing at Santa Clara University. He is
also a Distinguished Friend of Oxford University.

Dear reader,

Thank you for picking up this book and welcome to the worldwide BK community! You're joining a special group of people who have come together to create positive change in their lives, organizations, and communities.

What's BK all about?

Our mission is to connect people and ideas to create a world that works for all.

Why? Our communities, organizations, and lives get bogged down by old paradigms of self-interest, exclusion, hierarchy, and privilege. But we believe that can change. That's why we seek the leading experts on these challenges—and share their actionable ideas with you.

A welcome gift

To help you get started, we'd like to offer you a **free copy** of one of our bestselling ebooks:

www.bkconnection.com/welcome

When you claim your **free ebook**, you'll also be subscribed to our blog.

Our freshest insights

Access the best new tools and ideas for leaders at all levels on our blog at ideas.bkconnection.com.

Sincerely,

Your friends at Berrett-Koehler